AS I WAS SAYING...

The author was born in south London in 1947 and has lived in Surrey since 1971 – so he is well travelled! Despite considering Britain to be a shadow of the well-ordered and structured country it was only a few years ago, there are humorous saving graces to all the dark sides of life. The result is a second book, describing the continuing development of his family's fortune. This has progressed from providing the children with a free taxi service and phone calls, to free oil and water for their cars. Subjects both light and highly controversial are covered and the reader will find views, comments and observations expounded on the world and its partner (hope that is politically correct). As a follow-up to *From Where I Sit*, which received international acclaim – well, someone was rumoured to have read it in Harlow New Town – it explores areas now deleted form public debate in a refreshing, honest manner.

AS I WAS SAYING...

Anthony Mann

TROUSER PRESS

© Anthony Mann 1992
Cover design and colouring in by Tim Harvey

Published by Trouser Press

First published 1992
Reprinted 2017

British Library Cataloguing-in-Publication Data
A catalogue record for this book is available from the British Library

ISBN 97809516501-1-0
09516501-1-4

Printed and bound by CMP(UK) Ltd, Luton, Beds.

Acknowledgements

I am indebted to all the newspapers, both national and local, who have provided inspiration to examine in detail certain stories upon which they have reported.

I am indebted to all those who wrote letters to newspapers, upon which I have commented.

I am indebted to all those who became parents and bestowed upon their children an array of imaginative names.

I am indebted to all those who ingratiated themselves to the point where I felt compelled to mention them in this tome.

I am indebted to all those who wrote to me commenting on my first book, including Mr Pratt. Many thanks.

And I am still in debt to the bloody Midland Bank!!

Contents

Catching up with the news   1

Kate Adie – or how the Gulf was lost   29

Terry Waite and other irritations   52

All I want for Christmas is my sexist doll   74

A New Year, and it's honours time again   103

Recession – what recession?   120

Eau dear, water can the meter be?   144

Crime and a distinct lack of punishment   165

Animal wrongs   184

You haven't seen my keys, have you?   209

They started it, they invaded Poland   229

Come back Rutland, all is forgiven   255

Catching up with the news

I was going to say that bugger-all changes, but there were some milestones, not to mention millstones, during the intervening period. The Poll Tax blew in, Mrs Thatcher bowed out and I discovered that the capital of Lithuania was Vilnius. When I was at school, Lithuania, Latvia and Estonia were always grouped together, spoken about and described as being 'over there' – a stick pointing to the map, in approximation to where the figure 4 is on a dart board. Funny, isn't it, for thirty years I have never needed to know any more.

This democracy business has not actually done anyone any favours. Everybody wants it. A couple of years ago, you knew where you were. The Americans were the goodies, on our side, whilst the Russians were the ones you booed at, the baddies. All of a sudden, the superpowers start to destroy weapons which have cost billions, kept peace, and more importantly, a lot of people in employment. Hey Presto, a lot of little known states and provinces are demanding autonomy. No walls, no secrets, just McDonalds, Madonna, an attendant display of waste polystyrene and a veritable virus of freedom.

These past months have seen me searching for answers to personal in-depth questions. Why is it that irrespective of the make and model of car that I drive, the windscreen wipers will only work on the passenger side? Why is it that having travelled along a traffic-free dual carriageway, I find myself behind the only slow lorry for miles, immediately at the start of a single lane road again? Why is it that I cannot answer questions beginning with an 'R' on Blockbusters? Why is it that when I spray underarm deodorant, most of it goes up my nose? Why is it that I have to wipe my backside, yet my dog can lead an Andrex-free life?

You remember our 'friend' in Spain, the one who took us for a lot of money, well he is still out there, and despite attempts by the CID, no extradition order has been given. I wrote personally to the Chairman of his bank, which is another story that I will relate in this book, or the next, depending on the legal situation.

I received a very courteous reply, stating that they had looked into my case again, but in their view they had acted fairly and disclosed all the information they were legally compelled to do. I am sure they did comply with the law on disclosure, it is what has *not* been forthcoming that concerns me. There seems to be little I can do to retrieve any monies, so there we are, a lesson learned the hard way.

The motor industry is not going through a purple patch either, with the sale of new cars still very low. The knock-on effect is to slow the rate at which used cars filter through the system. There are a lot of nearly-new vehicles available, but it is not the price range which is affordable by the paying public at large. It is the old chestnut, if you have the money, you can pick up a bargain. If you are struggling, there is not a lot to choose from.

Despite the lack of income, we did manage a week's holiday last year, back to Ireland. We stayed at the same cottages in Rosscarbery, Co. Cork, which we had rented twelve months previously, when we went with our friends on that ill-fated trip. This time we went by ourselves! Now, don't tell me you've forgotten; they are the ones who fell out with us, whilst having a discussion on rape, abortion, feminism, adoption, etc. – you know, all the light-hearted stuff!

Because our plane was late in arriving at Cork Airport, the length of time for which we were to hire the car was reduced, so we ended up obtaining a reduction of £17. Unlike the old days, however, you cannot be reimbursed at the end of the hire period. Oh, no. With the aid of modern-day technology, the hirer has to send a letter to the company's rental office, and wait. I received a reply fairly promptly, stating, and I quote, 'The above mentioned documents have been sent to our head office in Dublin Airport for action. They will arrange to refund any monies due. This procedure should take 6-8 weeks.' It did. I particularly liked the use of the word, 'action'. How on earth can it take so long to process? When I worked in car hire, you just deducted any refund due from the total and gave it back to the customer there and then. I suppose every little helps if it is in your account for a longer period. Of course, with inflation, it was worth only £16.25p by the time it did arrive.

On the home front, the tenants who rented our old house stayed until the spring. They left, we re-decorated – have you ever had tenants? The property once more went up for sale. Come August, a deal was struck. In true motor-trade fashion, we took in a part-exchange, a flat in Norbury, South London.

This property also had tenants, but the financial inducement of a flat, plus cash, edged the decision to complete. The bank relaxed their stranglehold slightly. I have to say at this point that our bank manager was the proverbial 'good egg' and did everything within his power to help us. This was an attitude not shared by his employers. A ceiling was placed on our personal overdraft and threats were made by individuals with ego-boosting titles, that if we went over our limit, the interest rate would rise by an extortionate amount.

You don't have an overdraft for fun, do you? It seemed to us that by trying to work ourselves out of trouble was not the right way. More than one person suggested I went 'bust'. That way, they reckoned, the bank would probably freeze the interest owed and with so many in the same position, it would take ages to repossess our house. I remember mentioning the word 'pride' on more than one occasion, but was greeted with their answer, 'pride does not pay the mortgage but the state very often does.' I cannot concur with that philosophy.

We remained uneasily in the new house and decided to see out the winter. The tenants in Norbury subsidised the overdraft to a lesser degree, but the selling of houses and flats throughout the winter was not good. We decided to wait until spring and the end of the tenancy agreement.

About three months ago we heard from the estate agents managing the property. They said that the tenants were moving to fresh fields and that a buyer had been found. It was all very clean, a deal was struck and after a couple of months' paperwork, we finally managed to become a one property family again. The interest on the overdraft and mortgage had accrued to such an extent that the bank sat as heavily on our shoulders as the hump on Quasimodo's back. It was at this time that I was summoned to the inner sanctum of the bank manager's office. Having had his secretary serve tea in neat china cups (how the other half live!) he suggested that I seek a mortgage elsewhere, as better terms could be offered me by other sources. These were investigated and we now only have the current account and the overdraft for the car business left. It is a pity, I have always preferred to be loyal, but this particular loyalty seems to be very one-sided.

Well, there we are, that is the financial position. With regards to the family, Glyn is now 19, Deborah is 17 and William has surprisingly reached 8. Maureen and I are also a little older! What else has happened during the intervening period? We gave Ethiopia another £8.7 million, making £46 million over the last two years, and, oh, yes, we sent some chaps to war. What a farce that was. How on earth anyone could consider the outcome to be a victory for the goodies, is beyond me.

I remember thinking that it would not be long before a spate of Iraqi jokes was doing the rounds. I was shown a mock Iraqi calendar, which was totally blank, except for January, which finished on the 15th, the final day for surrender, apparently. Another wag explained that the Irish had now entered the war, but the Mexicans didn't know what to do with them. (For those of you living on council estates, resident in stone-clad houses, or owners of cars with 'Baby on Board' stickers, there's a Gulf in Mexico as well!) Mind you, the looks of despair on Ministers' faces when war was announced must have been tempered by the thought that here was a legitimate reason for upping direct taxation, VAT, cutting more hospital beds and closing schools. Not far off a prayer being answered really.

From the stagnation of ideas and the suicidal tendencies shown by the Tories over the last couple of years, they must have wondered how on earth they would ever win another election, but lo and behold, a war. Patriotism, yes, the public will like that, after all, wasn't it the Falklands factor that won it before? The lefties and do-gooders will whinge, yes the voters will be upset by that. Let's face it, at the very mention of sending chaps to war, the most positive of socialists are still negative. Add some scare-mongering about what will happen to petrol prices if we do nothing and any remaining floating voters will be gobbled up. They must have been creaming with enthusiasm.

It was, to paraphrase Greavsie, a funny old war. A fair amount has been written about the conflict by now, all right, the subject has been bled dry, so if you are bored, move on! I don't know about you, but I felt there was a very Hollywood feel to the whole proceedings. Whilst every evening news was going through the intro stages with background music, shots of locations with reporters armed with microphones in front of mobile batteries loaded to the gunnels, would zoom onto the screen. I have never been convinced that we needed all of these reporters. I got the impression that being surrounded by chaps filming rockets and bright lights, and noise everywhere, more than a few egos were being boosted. It seems such a long way from the Pathe News days and proper BBC-type pronunciation.

Kate Adie in fatigues is one memory that will always be with me, despite my continuing to take the pills. She always delivers her lines like an unforgiving teacher. How would the war have

been won without her? That, of course, is the 64,000 dollar ques-
-tion. Was it 'won'? I don't know how you feel, but I cannot see
any cause for celebrations when the cove who started it is still in
power, and hundreds of thousands of people are homeless and
living in appalling conditions. Environmentally, smoke and fire
continue to belch out towards the sky, and the wildlife is dying
in horrendous numbers and will be for some time to come, and
to cap it all, the price of petrol still has not gone back down.

There have been many countries invaded by their neighbours
since the last war, but we haven't taken up the cudgels on their
behalf very often. Then again, they didn't have oil. It does seem a
tad naïve of France to sell Iraq millions of pounds worth of arms,
Germany to sell them chemical ingredients – something they have
had a bit of practice at in the past – and the rest of the western
world, including Britain, to continue with the supply of other
weaponry. Mr Hussein has always been treated with more than
a little suspicion. He has never been considered someone who,
although being on the 'wrong' side, could be counted upon to
act in a gentlemanly way and be described as an 'honourable'
chap. Then again, the arms deals *were* profitable.

We have never had a televised war like this before. Interviews
with our brave lads as they climb into their cockpits then interviewed a few hours later on their return. Radar scans showing
rockets coming and going, chats with the womenfolk and kids
left at home, not to mention the tele-messages with hardened,
tattooed-strewn squaddies, holding up banners saying, 'Hello,
Mum.' It was all quite surreal, really.

My over-riding memory of that little fracas was a news item
shortly before we started exchanging unpleasantries. The story
was focusing on the various forces waiting to go into action. The
Americans were being their normal selves – loud. They were
observed squatting, playing that 'crap game' under the shade of a
bomber aircraft's wings. The British, however, were seen marking
out a section of desert sand and planting something – I can't
remember what – but a picket fence had already been 'dug in'
to make the boundaries of this overseas gardener's world. What
a difference.

I remember the BBC telling us that they were going to drop
Allo, Allo, because of the conflict, and thinking, 'every cloud, etc.'
Mind you, isn't it an insult to one's intelligence to monitor, nay,
censor, *Dad's Army*. Mustn't show episodes where bombs are
being dropped. Another victim was Marmite, where ads showed
soldiers running and chanting in true American fashion.

Apparently the viewer could be upset – even traumatised – being reminded of war. I wouldn't mind, but you couldn't get away from it. Every news programme, every bulletin, every special item was ablaze, literally, with weaponry hitting, missing or being launched. Even the credits were cut to show yet another ten feet of land being recaptured, or a radar scan showing nothing that was comprehensible to the viewing public. It was gratifying to know that I am not the only one to feel that trauma and grief have become an industry. A Mr Tom Neale wrote to the letters column of the *Mail on Sunday* regarding the subject. He considered that many people would have smiled at the news that Gulf wives would be receiving counselling. As he says, mothers, wives and children lived in London during the Blitz. They put up with flying bombs, rockets, rationing and often did not know whether their husbands (as opposed to partners – my view, not Mr Neale's), were dead or alive. We were either made of sterner stuff or there were not so many do-gooding busybodies, with misplaced priorities around then.

During the First World War, the Great Western Railway removed the nameplates of locomotives that had a connection with Germany. Interesting really, an engine called the 'Knight of the Black Eagle' became the 'Knight of Liege', because the Flems were on our side, not that you'd really want them.

Another engine, 'Dachshund', lost its plates altogether because it was a German breed of dog. Following on from that, during the Second World War, the nameplates from 'The Belgium Monarch', 'Danish Monarch', 'Italian Monarch' and the 'Japanese Monarch', were all removed at times commensurate with the appropriate country's downfall or their entering the war on the wrong side. Just goes to show how long neurosis has been around.

Of course, while many of our lads were overseas, some people were trying to get to work in the abysmally named County of Avon. I would have given a lot to have been in Bristol when two double-deckers met face to face in a busy street. Parked cars on either side of the road prevented the buses from passing each other. The problem was compounded by the intransigence of the drivers, both women, who don't get on very well. Apparently, they glared at each other through their respective cab windows, in a scene reminiscent of *High Noon*. Despite having walkie-talkies, they steadfastly refused to discuss the matter with each other, or even leave their cabs. The bus company sent a 'trouble shooting' team out, but the women refused to budge. Eventually, an inspector climbed into one of the cabs and reversed the bus out of the way. Female illogic. Perhaps when men obtain equality with women, we will be able to act like that!

Other highlights over the last few months include the Bollinger racket over Christmas, which I enjoyed nearly as much as not seeing the Walton sextuplets, or Eddie Edwards, although there were rumours that he had been seen in Aldershot. Fancy, though, paying over £20 a bottle for champagne, only to find (or not) that you were drinking sparkling Spanish wine, at under £6 per bottle. The hoot was that the connoisseurs could not even tell the difference. The fake was called a Cordon Negro – surprised you can still use that title these days, another case for the Race Relations lot, surely.

Talking of rip-offs, British Telecom adopted a new design with the letters BT and a sort of Pan character in poofy stance, blowing what appears to be a paper aeroplane. The cost of this design change is horrendous, it does not endear the subscriber, who, despite the pleadings, knows full well that he/she (mustn't be sexist) will end up paying for it. They have only had the previous logo for ten years. The reason for this change is to reflect the international standing of the company, so the word 'British' apparently is an embarrassment.

When you think of it, 40,000 vehicles, uniforms for thousands of staff, stationery, kiosks, etc, all have to be altered, renewed, or repainted. Doesn't it appear obscene that so much money should be spent on something so totally unproductive, all at the expense of the marketing man's ego, and more importantly, another forest. It was bad enough witnessing the end of the road for many red telephone boxes, but to consider 'British' a hindrance in one's title, really takes the biscuit. That reminds me, I recently visited Kingston upon Thames and they have obtained a fair number of red boxes leaning up against each other at angles, suggesting that vandals have played havoc overnight. Apparently, this sculpture is considered artistic, – more like autistic! A sad end to an era we knew and cherished.

Obviously the council managed to fund this little farce before we entered a recession – not that we are really in one, anyway. The rest of the population can rest assured now that Mr Lamont, our very own Shetland Pony, has quite categorically stated that what we see around us is only a slightly depressed economy instead.

I am just looking through some notes I have made. This one is rich, a private school for black children was condemned for using up too much time teaching English. The parents of this fee-paying school are happy, the staff are happy, but the government's inspectors decided that there was an over-emphasis on the subject. On one hand we see the government continually arguing for a return to traditional teaching methods (and quite rightly so) and on the other hand, we have the grey bureaucrats working against a sound education. I don't understand it myself. Can you have a private school for white children?

Here's another one. Do you remember the fuss that surrounded Ian McKellen, the actor's knighthood. Whether he deserved it or not is another matter, but why did the homosexual community keep on about it. Those with that inclination have since had a complaint against the *Sunday People* upheld. John Smith, in his column, referred to 'Poofs in the Pulpit' and they took umbrage, pity they didn't take an overdose. The Press Council described the phrase as 'insulting and gratuitous'. Why? Going on from that, the homosexual magazine, *Scene Out*, advocated greater freedom in programmes such as *Coronation Street*, for characters with 'those leanings'. I am sure that most people would prefer C.S. to remain a 'nice' programme with ordinary people. That should upset someone. Let's be honest, you can get no seedier a programme than *EastEnders*. If they haven't been raped, they have love-children. If that's not enough, they are queer, on drugs or have contracted Aids – and that's just Roly! I have come to the conclusion that *EastEnders* is sponsored by a water company. Every time it comes on and I see the low life it portrays, I want to have a shower. I can't be alone in this, surely?

Getting back to *Coronation Street*, though, the way Deirdre behaves, it might warrant Ken Barlow wondering if women are worth it and turning 'Bertie' himself. The cost of all the legislation concerning homosexual and lesbian rights falls on the poor sods who couldn't give a toss – that's a non-sexual toss, of course.

In Labour-controlled Camden, London, a council chief has been under suspension on full pay, because of an allegation that she exposed her deputy as a lesbian. Now, two years later, through lack of evidence, the case, which claimed she had breached the council's heterosexism code, has been dropped and the ex-chief has asked for her job back. The poll-tax payer has had to fork out £200,000 because of certain people's craving for power. Let's be honest, sexism and racism are just headings. They are the vehicle that will transport political subversives to a position of strength. Unfortunately, these positions are generally non-elected ones, where they can hide behind a committee and call a decision democratic. Being surrounded by like-minded trendies who look as if a good wash would do them good, they have access to vast funds, contributed involuntarily by the poor sods who work for a living.

Social workers don't change, either. We had not completed the first week of the new year before another case of a two year-old being beaten to death was in the papers. Again, the husband was not the girl's father. It is always stepfathers and boyfriends, isn't it? What was so sad in this instance was the fact that during the trial, it became apparent that one witness had contacted social services on no less than fifteen different occasions – and no-one did anything. Once again, no-one was specifically to blame, and the tragedy was 'deeply regretted' by the council's social services director. Well, that's all right then. Not that long ago, social services staff were planning legal action against a coroner who forced them to look at the body of a battered child. The little girl in question had been beaten to death with a kettle flex. She had only been removed from the 'At Risk' register six months previously. The staff were cleared after an independent enquiry, but felt the coroner was implying that social workers were still to blame. Personally, if it got home just what hell this child had suffered, then it might inspire a little more thought in future cases, but, no, they wanted to sue. Social workers always seem to channel their aggression towards the wrong people.

Another example where you worry about those in a responsible position was the case in Newcastle-upon-Tyne, where a foster mother of nineteen years' standing had a mentally handicapped three-year-old taken away from her by social workers. An adoption panel decided that a lesbian couple should look after the child. One half of this couple was, in fact, a social worker herself. It took five months for the High Court to rule that it was in the infant's best interest for him to be returned to the foster mother, who, incidentally, had cared for thirty-four children during her period of service. Again, I ask, who are these people who are empowered to make decisions that go against everything normal and decent?

Talking of regrets, I watched the Crufts show on television. One group winner was asked if all her dogs were pets. 'Yes,' she replied, 'they all are.' 'Were you not going to give that one away?' the reporter continued, pointing to the newly selected champion whom the owner was patting and stroking. 'Yes, didn't come up to expectation as a youngster,' came the reply. Up to expectation? So much for the devoted owner of a pet. The part of the show which for me would have been laughable, had it not been so sad, was the way the dogs were paraded around the enclosure on leads held so tight that the animals took on a sort of surreal pose that looks, and probably feels, far from comfortable. Bet the judges were impressed, though. There were 23,000 canine entries with 23,000 human egos. Judging from the appearance of some of the owners, one could be forgiven for thinking that a few scruffy mongrels had by-passed the screening system and entered themselves!

I had to make a phone call the other day and needed to look up the name in the local directory. Having found the number I was searching for, my fingers continued down the listed 'P's'. I bet you didn't know that there are four entries named 'Planterose'; the same number of 'Puddles', fifteen 'Prettys', a brace of 'Puddiphatts' and the same number of 'Puddefoot'. You would have thought that they would have saved paper by placing them as one entry – namely 'Puddefeet'! We then let our fingers do the walking along to the common end of the family – actually, there are three entries. We now have 'Puddifoot' with an 'i'. Here's a thought, as there are three, shouldn't they become a 'Puddiyard'. This lot don't seem to be so much related as in-bred! Further entries include a surprisingly large number of 'Punters', and 'Privetts'. There's a single 'Poke', 'Plodwinkle', 'Pummell', 'Proper' and 'Putty'. There are also one each of my favourites – 'Ponking' and 'Puffitt'.

When I was a little boy, and there are many who would still describe me thus today, the discovery of a nasty smell would be followed by my mother's verbal probing, 'Have you puffed?' I still fart, of course, only I can now enjoy the freedom to 'puff' in the comfort of my own home with pride, and not embarrassment. In the same way that poofs – as opposed to puffs – have come out of the closet, so now, can smelly bottoms.

Talking of Mum, she and Uncle Albert in *Only Fools and Horses* have more in common than sleeping with their mouths open. They also went to the same school in Battersea. What do you mean, you couldn't give a toss?

A quick snippet, Sir John Quinton, head of Barclays Bank, is to receive a 21% pay rise, taking his salary from £332,920 to £404,067 per year. Not bad, is it?

You'll like this. Deborah has recently applied for her driving test. The form is in two halves. One is for answering the questions, the other is full of advice on how to answer them. I have heard about campaigning for plain English, but this must be written for retards. Example: Driver Number – copy this from the top of your

GB Licence... I would never have thought of that, would you? It goes on, 'Type of vehicle'. Tick box, or give details of vehicle in other box. On it goes again. The notes appertaining to motorcycle tests advise you to check that you have chosen the appropriate test centre. 'Those applicable are shown in bold type.' Well, that's fair enough, but what I find worrying is that the last line of the instruction is typed in bold itself, so that those who cannot tell thin from thick are at least given a clue. The 'Notes to help you fill in the form' start to pander to the prospective examinee in a big way. There are phrases like, 'indicate in this box the earliest date you could accept', 'Make sure you are ready for the test', 'Tick the boxes to show mornings and afternoons which are not acceptable to you on a regular basis', 'Please write down individual days or periods (such as holidays) which are not convenient for you.' God Almighty, when I took my tests – yes, I needed two – you turned up on the day and at the time appointed, it wasn't subject to debate or negotiation.

The most disturbing aspect of this form is the section headed, 'Disabilities and special circumstances'. Having informed the reader that they would like to know if you are profoundly deaf why, do they need to bring a megaphone? – you come to the line which reads, 'If you cannot speak English or are deaf, you may bring along an interpreter.' Frankly, if the learner could not speak English, I would not allow them to take a test. We all know who we are talking about though, don't we. Those who have lived here for many years and have never bothered to learn the native language as integration is the very last thing on their minds. I wonder if other countries allow interpreters for citizens who can't be bothered to learn the mother tongue.

No, that is not a racial comment, and just to show how fair I am, speaking English, as opposed to grunting, would also disqualify half the under-25's in council houses. Of course, if the clutch was called a 'Donna', the gearstick a 'Fosters' and the interior mirror a 'Pit-Bull', I suppose it would give them a sporting chance.

On the race tack (as opposed to race track) I shuddered when I read that, according to Mr Hattersley, a future Labour government would impose quotas of black and Asian workers on companies. This sort of imposition would have completely the opposite effect to that envisaged, and would only increase racial tension – often in areas where there wasn't any before. What have they got planned for Tunbridge Wells or Esher? Do they expect black and Asian people to move about the country to balance the books, or what?

Under Labour's scheme, the Commission for Racial Equality, bless 'em, would be able to monitor individual factories to check said numbers. They would really be in their egotistical element, wouldn't they. It would be like reliving a visit from Hitler's henchmen. I can see it now, in deepest white, middle-class Uckfield, Sussex, workers with dark hair, blacking their faces and pretending to be Asian. I just hope that their accent is an improvement over the unconvincing apology uttered by Alec Guinness in *A Passage to India*. There will be blonde chaps and chap-esses hiding in cupboards until the SS – sorry, CRE – have marched out again. These people are only interested in reverse discrimination. Who are they? How did they get the job? You never know, do you.

Hand on heart, can you honestly tell me that the sort of action suggested will help the ethnic population. Of course not, I hear you say. Besides, we are not really talking race here, we are talking colour. Do you think that the Welsh, Scots or Ulster-born have the same 'ear' as the black and Asians within these isles? No, the CRE meddlers have very narrow and somewhat obsessive goals. If I go into an Indian restaurant, I get served by Indians. If I go to a Chinese restaurant, I get served by – that's right – Chinese staff. No-one expects to be waited on by a blue-eyed, blonde headed chap, originating from Burgess Hill. These businesses are, in the main, family businesses. What is wrong with that? I don't get upset because all the staff are black, you wouldn't dream of running to the CRE and crying, 'Please sir', but when it is the other way round...

A writer to the letters column of the *Daily Mail* commented on Mr Hattersley's proposals and also complained about the discrimination in the work place shown to those people in their 40s and 50s. These workers, in his view, have contributed the most to the country's coffers. Is this age-ist?

There was, however, some real initiative used earlier this year. A train had to stop because of a fallen tree across the railway line near Wem, in Shropshire. Usually, no-one would bother to tell you why the train was stationary, but on this occasion, however, the driver, a Mr Richard Mayrick, spotted a public house and having rung his superiors and received the okay, took all eighty passengers for drinks and light refreshments. They stayed in the hostelry until they could get underway again. It didn't cost British Rail a fortune, but the goodwill engendered will bring those travellers back time and time again. Of course, if they find themselves sitting on the platform at Craven Arms Station, when the last train to Shrewsbury has been cancelled and nobody's told them, they might just think again.

I was reading a magazine called *Rail* a little while ago. There was an article on the Channel Tunnel, and one sentence started, 'Frenchman Philippe Cozette and Britain Robert...'. I showed the piece to Deborah and asked her to spot the mistake. She suggested that it was that I'd bothered to read about the Channel tunnel in the first place. 'No,' I said, 'it's the spelling.' The eyebrows furrowed, but, no, she couldn't see it. I pointed to the word, 'Britain', and said, 'The chap comes from *Britain*, therefore, he is a – what?' Pause. 'He's a Briten or a Britan,' she offered. 'He's a Briton,' I said, emphasising the word. 'Oh,' she replied, returning lazily to TV-AM. Still, she is studying English 'A' level and will probably pass with flying colours. I mean, so long as it is near enough. She also informed us that she is going on a college trip to the theatre to see a play, which is in the syllabus of the two-year course she is taking in English. Maureen enquired as to the name of the play. No, Debbie couldn't remember. The writer? The theatre? All questions were met with a shrug of the shoulders and a 'don't know'. Maureen suggested that it would be Shakespeare. I added that it could be worse, it could be Harold Pinter. H.P., as he is probably not known anywhere, and the *South Bank Show* have one thing in common as far as I am concerned, I have never understood any of it.

Deborah does know that if she stands outside the college gates at a time she has already forgotten, the coach will pick her up.

The media works very hard sometimes to come up with yet another sensational discovery about our society. Over recent years many newspapers and magazines have given liberal space to articles about the changing role of men. We apparently help more with babies, cry publicly, create exotic dishes without being asked and it was interesting to read a story by Jane Kelly in the *Daily Mail*, stating that, surprise, surprise, the new man does not actually exist.

A large portion of the article surrounded a survey conducted by *Gentleman's Quarterly*, which is an upmarket businessman's read. One revelation was that while the more mature manager asks his secretary to make coffee, 67% of those under 40 years of age claimed to make the secretary's coffee for her. What they omitted to state was that 66% of them were desperately trying to get into her pants, while the other 1% were homosexual and quite enjoyed the domestics anyway!

Getting back to Crufts, I have since read that the breed of dog which has become 'Supreme Champion', a Clumber, is bred to a standard set by the Kennel Club. Breeders are trying to increase the weight of the dogs to about 100 lbs – far greater than it should be, given the dog's ability to breed naturally. As this unhealthy trend gives rise to hip displacement and other ills, I hope the makers of the pet foods, who wait for the champion breed to be announced, will hold fire when unnatural or genetically engineered specimens are given No. 1 status. It could only be to their credit if they refused to show such a specimen and instead chose the highest placed 'natural' thoroughbred. Perhaps I am being naïve, perhaps money got there first and wiped them all out. I hope not.

One breeder, a Mr James Dorley, who was concerned about the excesses encouraged by the Kennel Club, has reintroduced the working Clumber to the breed. This type of animal weighs in at around 4 stones and is used as a retriever. Of course, it is frowned upon by the so-called aristocrats. Can you understand it? *The People* published an article supported by photographs, showing the breeds which have problems caused by irresponsibility and an over-riding desire to win. How any so-called animal lover can allow hip, back, eye and arthritic problems to be over-shadowed by owning a cup, is beyond me. Perhaps it is the applause, the atmosphere, the money...

Do you remember this milestone? The Transport Minister, Roger Freeman, actually travelled in a commuter train. I have no doubt he needed a briefing as to what exactly a commuter train was. 'Heard of one, but never seen one. Aren't they things secretaries use?' You can write the script, can't you. Anyway, in the wake of the Cannon Street crash, he ventured on this journey of a lifetime. He summarised his little ride by stating that, although the train was crowded, it was up to the individual passenger, sorry, customer, whether they commuted on that train, or waited. Pompous sod! The world and his wife know that the train before and the one after are going to be just as full – and that is if they run, of course. The days of assuming that a scheduled 12 coach train would run with 12 coaches are a very distant memory. As long as the accountant's pen satisfies government's targets, bugger the taxpayer. The saddest aspect of all this is that those elected with the power to effect change never need to be involved with mass transportation. In fact, their only concern is whether or not their suit will clash with that being worn by their chauffeur.

Now what else has happened? Oh, yes. The television licence

fee went up to £77 for colour and a paltry £25.50 for monochrome. I don't suppose you can call it black and white any more. After an absence of 16 years, Noddy was rumoured to be returning, with Big Ears in close pursuit. Not that close, however, as Noddy is to sleep by himself. No golliwogs though, perish the name. In some papers the terms 'golly' or 'gollies' have been used. Mustn't mention the unmentionable. The publishers state that they have cleaned up and updated the cartoons and books. This admittance surely bears testimony to the extent to which this obsession has spread. Those responsible for this unnecessary piece of journalistic vandalism cannot understand that most people accepted these children's stories without suffering any long term mental problems. Not for them a display of neurosis at being exposed to the world of Enid Blyton.

The other alterations, which would be laughable if they weren't so pathetic, were the barring of Mr Plod from spanking anyone, and Martha the Monkey's rise to fronting the feminist cause. With this sort of liberal upheaval and lack of discipline, I look forward to episodes showing golliwogs – there, I have said it – parading and holding banners claiming discrimination. I will surely witness Mr Plod's car being overturned by anarchists, displaying the normal whipped-up fervour, knowing that they will never again be spanked. No doubt Martha the Monkey will be recruited to preside over both the Equal Opportunities and Race Relations Commissions – a certain case of fantasy imitating reality. I do question whether or not it is right to alter someone's work years after the characters were created and without the author's blessing. I suppose the answer is, 'Yes', if you are going to secure the toy and video merchandising angle and wade around in filthy lucre.

You will like this, and I quote... A councillor has revealed in our local paper that, 'We must look at the great future the town has got, we have a premier site here.' This chap was referring to Camberley. If you are reading this in Northallerton or Ripon, stay there. Take my word for it and don't bother to get excited. It's just another case of a councillor requiring a quick savaging by his guide-dog.

Some light relief now. What is 6' x 4' x 4' and takes the piss out of you? Answer: A kidney dialysis machine. Another one? What's the difference between a Rottweiler and a woman with PMT? Answer: You can reason with the Rottweiler! The variation of this last one is, What's the difference between a woman with PMT and a Shi-ite extremist – same answer. Actually, I am not convinced women ever suffered from PMT until they were told about it on Breakfast TV a few years ago. Now it seems to be an ideal excuse for being bloody-minded. Well, they are half-right, I suppose!

One more? Okay. What's the difference between a Rottweiler and a Cleveland social worker. Answer: You have more of a chance of getting your child back from the Rottweiler.

You can plead all you like, but I am going off to eat my din-dins. Will be back soon.

It is not that soon, actually, it is precisely 3.30 pm on a bright, summer's day and I have just come back from Crawley. Yes, I did wear a ring of garlic, just in case I took a wrong turn at a roundabout and ended up in a council estate. I actually got quite a shock. The object of the journey, having stopped off at various points from Guildford, through Dorking and Reigate, was to distribute more copies of *From Where I Sit*. Now the last time I was on the A23, just north of the town, lay the Gatwick Manor Hotel. It was surrounded by countryside. The view now is more reminiscent of Los Angeles. Well, it looks like the intro shots for *LA Law*. High rise, glass-sided buildings have sprung up on both sides of the road to herald one's approach to the great metropolis that calls itself Crawley. Silly me, really, for thinking it would still look relaxed and rural.

Whilst in the area, I noticed a road sign proclaiming (in English), 'Stately Home – Open April to October'. Surely account should be made for those needing interpreters on their tests. These signs should be more 'graphical'. A house with an open door would indicate all year round opening. While seasonal or limited opening times would require a stable door half-open. One must not tax a driver's intellect too much, especially the dice and boxing glove fraternity.

Actually, as I mentioned delivering books, you might like to know a little about self-publishing. It was not a course I took out of choice, but because it was the only way the book would ever see the light of day.

Having received the manuscripts back from the typist, I selected various publishing houses from the (then) latest copy of the *Writers and Artists' Yearbook*. Phone calls prompted samples of the manuscripts to wing their way to London. Some were returned in a matter of days, some weeks and the odd one, months. All the covering letters were of similar vein. 'We thank you for having brought your work to our attention. Unfortunately we do not believe your book would fit in with our existing titles, but we wish you luck...' I actually wrote to seven publishers, which may not sound that many, but the postage is not cheap and time was running on.

At that time, William was in hospital having his tonsils out, when by chance I met a hospital volunteer who visits the children there and reads to them and plays with them. A chat with this lady who, it turned out, had self published over fifteen books, spurred me on to investigate the possibility, not to mention the pissabolity. I rang a friend of mine who is in the magazine business. The conversation was a little embarrassing, to say the least. To tell a mate of long standing that you have written a book is like taking your first girlfriend home to meet your parents. I hasten to add, smarmily, that my wife *was* my first and only girlfriend – that will either impress her or make her stick two fingers down her throat! Anyway, my friend introduced me to his typesetter and designer and estimates were obtained for printing. This was, quite honestly, a very exciting time. I visited my local W.H. Smith, who looked at the cover samples which were supplied before the book was published, to allow me a chance to promote the forthcoming tome. Yes, they said, they would look at it when it arrived. Several weeks later and I was the recipient of 5,000 copies, delivered to a friend's shop. He agreed to store them until I could move them into my garage, or wherever.

I had considered using the services of a distributor and looked at the system in some detail. Unfortunately, you have to know that a lot of books are going to sell before that route is financially viable. I plumped for the personal approach. The long and short of it was that, having secured permission to approach the book buyers at about six branches of W.H. Smiths, the barrier was broken. As time went on, I found the daily round of phoning and visiting book shops a more relaxing activity than at first. It was especially rewarding when I received a call from a store asking for more copies, as they had run out.

Some shop results were encouraging, some were disappointing, but, on the whole, I have not been displeased. As I write, the book is in about 100 branches of W.H. Smiths, plus Hammicks, Martins and Waterstones. Part of the enjoyment is derived from revisiting the shops and building up a rapport with the people at the sharp end. A big boost came a short while ago, when W.H. Smith offered to take a number of copies at their central warehouse in Swindon. Thus, the title has been added to their computerised list – the credibility factor.

Delivery of the first batch of books to their warehouse was an amusing experience. I arrived at the security office and parked behind a pantechnicon, which was just about to unload its cargo of best-sellers. Behind me, another gigantic lorry arrived. The first driver was given his instructions and sallied forth. The security officer was wondering why the second lorry had not pulled up level with the window. He leaned out and saw me, scrabbling about on the passenger seat of my Talbot Samba, searching for the piece of paper I had been so careful to keep, as it housed all my notes that were required on arrival. Seats tipped forward, boxes opened, packets searched, and eventually I found the said note in the driver's door pocket. The 'very nice man' commented that normally a bay was allocated for delivery vehicles, but that I had better go to the ramp at the end of the line and ring the bell. By now, a couple more lorries had arrived and it was with some relief that the Samba started on the button and I made my way towards the indicated ramp. With all of these 30 foot plus long lorries, the Samba did feel somewhat inconsequential, but it was still an exhilarating feeling.

Out of interest, it was while I was receiving all the 'Thanks, but no thanks' letters, one of which accused me of being sexist, racist and homophobic – strange, that, I was informed of a publisher's duty to donate five copies of any new title to various universities. They also have to be sent at your cost. I was also reminded of bar codes. 'Have you got yourself one of those, yet?' said my publishing friend. Now, as it happens, we are a little short of bar code shops in Aldershot. I think they have all been taken over by estate agents. Anyway, to gain acceptance in the majority of booksellers, you have to have one. They come in different shapes and sizes. You also need an ISBN – International Standard Book Number. Again, I was pointed in the right direction for these two items. It certainly keeps you on your feet.

I asked my bank manager why he hadn't wished me luck when I told him I had managed to Publish *From Where I Sit*. He told me that, having the copy I had given him (note, *given*) he did not like the reference to himself, where I described him as having a stammer. Apparently, he has a 'hesitation', so now we know!

Time passes quickly, doesn't it? It seems like only yesterday that I was trying to escape being involved with – or anywhere near, come to that – a soiled nappie. Now, however, both the older children are mobile. Glyn passed his test first time, Deborah at the second attempt. True to the law of sod, the car that is needed is always the one at the bottom of the drive. It reminds me of TV's

Butterflies, every morning. Four cars fire up, if we are lucky, and crunch their way into reverse. Three screech into the lane and wait while the first in becomes the first out. They then return to the places and await the next formation car dance.

Deborah is now at college, studying psychology, so you have got the picture, long skirts, unfashionable shoes and lots of scarves to adorn the ensemble. She looks somewhat reminiscent of Kate Adie on a day trip to Istanbul. Glyn is still in the fast food business. We see little of him once dinner has been devoured. He certainly knows how to give a disco a good time. As for William, well, he is just coming to the end of his 'first' school days and starts in September at what appears to be a very nice middle school in Farnham. We will have to wait and see.

Back to serious, national issues now. St Helens Council in Lancashire, as opposed to Merseyside, has banned pinching, patting, sexual flirtation and lewd comments. Doubtless, all Sun calendars will have to be thrown away as well. The Principal Employee Relations Officer (there's posh) is, of course, female, one Colette Craig. The only surprise is the newspaper's description of her as a 'Mrs'. Surely she should be a 'Ms'. Perhaps's it's a mistake.

A bit big-brother-ish, isn't it, when someone gets chided for wolf-whistling. Does it really matter? Is it a trauma inducing offence? This woman goes on to say that every complaint will be taken seriously – and they will! These people only come to the fore during a confrontation. If there isn't one, they will invent one. Yes, I have serious misgivings about their motives. This action has the support of NALGO, of course, who, according to their spokesman, 'support the rights of women to work free from that kind of harrassment'. The way some women make themselves up, a wolf-whistle would be about the only way they would attract someone to start a pack of their own. Dogs, or what!

St Helens Council must be trying to emulate their cronies in Hackney, London, for the award of 'Sexless Authority of the Year'. It is typical of the left-wingers to denounce a perfectly good word like 'Ladies'. Female Hackney residents are to see their toilet signs replaced with those pronouncing 'Women'. All females over 18 are to be called women, and slapped wrists for anyone overheard calling a woman, 'pet', 'love' or 'darling'. Still, with a 'chair' in control, what would you expect. Do these people not realise just how stupid and childish they appear in the eyes of ordinary people who are too busy doing a 'proper' job to be interested in their classless, sexless actions. I think that any new study on care in the community and mental health could do no better than to look at some of these 'chairs' and their ilk.

Mentioning unions has reminded me of a friend of ours, who works as a secretary for one of those august bodies. She says that the amount of paperwork pushed hither and thither is appalling. There are letters going out to branches enquiring into the number of women, Asians, blacks and handicapped who are employed by the various companies with which this union is involved. However, this flag-waving ivory tower where she works do not employ any ethnic workers at all. There is a blind person who is responsible for the fax machine, but that is the token gesture. This story, which is true (remember I am a used-car salesman) reminds me of the *Yes, Prime Minister* episode when all the heads of departments were asked to employ more women in powerful positions. They all thought it was a good idea for every other ministry, but felt 'for good reasons' that it wouldn't work for them.

Babies next. With figures released showing that one in four babies are born out of wedlock, and that over half the children born were to couples living together, but not married, it comes as a disappointment to learn that virgins and lesbians are to be given help in conceiving a baby. Recently, the British Pregnancy Advisory Service in Birmingham agreed to help three virgins become pregnant. I still maintain, and I am sure the vast majority of the population would as well, that children need *both* parents. What are they trying to prove? Is it because they genuinely hate men or do they require a designer child to add status to their presumably empty lives? Frankly, I see them as nothing better than selfish bitches.

Right, well here's one for all of you who feel there should be no limits to levity. Question: What do paedophiles do at the end of their annual dinner? Answer: They pass round the Under 8s.

Sport now. The highlight of my calendar was a now infrequent trip to a football match. I headed north with some friends to see Woking play away at Everton in the FA Cup. A cracking day was had by all. Yes, Woking lost, but I didn't see any aggression – either on or off the field. It was a friendly day out. Before the match commenced, we parked almost outside the ground and made our way to a local hostelry. There we joined Everton supporters for a bevvy and a sandwich. At the end we walked back to our car and started on the return journey south, stopping off for refreshments at a service station. The place had been invaded by about twenty coaches and numerous cars. Again, no-one was silly. Besides the football, my over-riding memory is the section of journey between St Helens and Liverpool. What a dump the area is. I think that the personnel officer we mentioned earlier and St Helens deserve each other. Liverpool wasn't that wonderful, full of boarded-up shops and shuttered houses – and dog turds. Gaudy terraced houses, some immaculately kept, but, oh, the painted cement between the layers of bricks, themselves subject to cardinal red paint, and gloss to boot! The colours of the doors made no improvement. Yellows, purples, vivid greens and all next to each other. It is also warmer in Guildford.

Mixed fortunes at the end of the football season, though. I was glad that there were no relegations *out* of the league, so Wrexham live to fight another day, but Swansea did not get the promotion they expected. Ah, well.

While I think of it, I got quite a number of letters about the deportation of certain people who I referred to in *From Where I Sit*. No-one actually suggested there should be any reprieves, they all wanted me to add their own pet hates to the list. I was prompted by more than one writer to look at weather forecasters, not something I would do out of choice! I have yet to be convinced that they are necessary at all. Why do the weather presenters tell us what might be about to happen over somewhere nobody's ever heard of. It is not technical, they all read off an autocue. The 'Bill Giles' of the world I can live with, but some of those male presenters foisted upon us look decidedly shifty. One or two look like child molesters to me! It is a bit like the question mark one puts on male nurses. No doubt that will stir up some bastard. Now, women weather presenters generally – and you know I don't generalise – well, not generally, tend to be anorexic. When they turn sideways, they give the impression of being cardboard cut-outs. They are dressed in clothes that can only be described as being totally out of sync with the body they are covering. As for the colours, I spotted Sian Lloyd the other day wearing a little pink number. She looked more like a flat-sided fluorescent pen. In fact, for a moment, I thought I was back in Liverpool with those gaudy doors.

The exception to this is the Swedish lady, and doesn't she just love telling us of her nationality. I once read an article which described Ulrika Jonnsen as 'orribly ambitious'. She is not unattractive and not that badly dressed. She just happens to be the most irritating weather-teller we have on TV. I just hope she is not moving across to one of these new channels.

The irritation manifests itself in the way she always tries to muscle in on the conversation that preceded the weather report. You are just not interested in her opinion any more than you are in mine, but I paid for this to be published, so yah boo and socks, and you can't get much more emphatic than that!

So, come the glorious day of the forecasters' overthrow, there will be a fair number to line up against the wall or be deported to Canvey Island. Whilst on the subject of weather, I have long accepted that the days when 'the news' referred to this country have long gone. It has been increasingly noticeable that the weather is following the same route. We commence by learning about what is happening over Spain and then continue over the rest of Europe, especially during our summer. I don't want to know. Barnsley's weather is scarcely going to interest me, let alone what is going on in some left-hand driving, donkey torturing state, which I have no wish ever to visit. And so it goes on. That 'low pressure' over the Med, that 'high pressure' over the Atlantic. It is all so remote. We never have any of those things over the Cotswolds. Just sit back and look out of the window, if it's sunny, it's sunny, and if it's raining, it's raining.

Doesn't it make you feel proud to be British when you read a report that members of a pop group visiting Disneyland pushed and shoved a worker dressed as Goofy? The reason for this act of unprovoked aggression was due to a ride being closed for maintenance, the timing of which was not convenient to these louts. The last thing you need at a leisure park are spoilt, overpaid primadonnas, like those who think the world exists solely for their benefit. I would have them deported – to Japan. This country is always on the look-out for animals upon which to conduct scientific research. I would have thought they would have been ideal subjects and of course, it would keep them out of Surrey.

I haven't seen anything about it since, but earlier this year, some well known celebrities, including actresses Judi Dench and Susan Hampshire, signed a public letter accusing the charity 'Oxfam' of 'flagrant dishonesty' over its policy to fund birth control programmes. The charity hit back by saying that the signatories were misinformed. They may have been, but Oxfam stated that 11% of their budget went on health programmes, of which family planning formed a significant part. Now the word, 'significant' is very open to interpretation. Even allowing for family planning accounting for half the health programme allocation, it does not seem to be nearly enough. What is the point of all this aid if the control of population is not to be the number-one priority. Mark my words, the problems facing the world are not that of religion or politics, but water. I remain convinced that Mother Nature is trying to give us the broadest hint while there is still time. Not just in parts of Africa where the drought is severe, but in the western world as well. Every time we build a new estate, more pressure is put to bear on the water services. With the low rain fall, natural and man-made reserves are drying up. We should be encouraging a lower birthrate throughout the world, and Britain could do its bit by phasing out child benefit. I suggested this in *From Where I Sit* and I am even more convinced than ever that this burden on the country should be stopped. If you want children, you should pay for them yourselves. I would also like to see introduced – and there could be those who would deem this proposal controversial – legislation forcing irresponsible males and females to have vasectomies and sterilisations. It is just all too easy bringing a child into the world. There are parents who you continue to read about in the papers, with hordes of kids, ranging from 'pregnant again' to 15 years of age. These people are totally selfish and socially unacceptable. They might think twice about contraception if the state, i.e. you and I, were not paying for the up-keep of the little bastards – and they generally fit this description.

It is not as if the responsible British family are having it easy in other ways. The poor sod who works for a living to support his wife and family is constantly hammered by ill-conceived government action, and there is little debate, let alone an opposition who can offer any choice. If there had been some genuine opposition to the Tories, instead of the lightweight and politically suicidal labour 'shadows', the Daddy of all follies, the poll tax, may never have seen the light of day. I remember going along to a meeting only a couple of months before its implementation. A capacity crowd turned up at the Ash Recreation Centre. That is the building architecturally more akin to a giant stable, but I digress. There we were, being addressed on the said subject by local councillors and our MP, Mr Cranley Onslow. Even at this late stage there were many questions that could not be answered. I forget the exact figure, but it was working out at about £330 per person. So the poor sod who previously paid rates of £250 per annum on his little terraced house, would soon be presented with a bill for himself, his non-working wife and their son who had just turned 18 years of age. There were indeed several housewives who asked, 'How were they expected to pay, when they didn't work.' There will be a rebate scheme for those on low incomes. Never, ever, has there been introduced such an unfair tax – well not since VAT anyway.

To compound this obscenity, for that is what it is, the government expected the populus to accept without murmur, a system that allows one borough to charge £600 per person, while its neighbour asks for £200 each. Months, years of planning by so-called experts, millions of pounds thrown at schemes and ideas, think-tanks, committees, sub-committees – and at the end of it all, they come up with this.

At the meeting a friend of mine asked about the £60 that had been built-in to the total due and had been designated as a 'safety net'. The idea of this little piece of direct taxation was that it acted as a subsidy for deprived areas. Councillors emphasised that this was a 'one off' inclusion and would not be repeated. So, despite all the talk of paying only for the services you received, this actually wasn't the case. Further questioning, however, from a member of the audience failed to produce a guarantee that next year's demand would be less £60, plus a small rise to take inflation into account.

Interestingly enough, this year's poll tax has been lowered by £6 – due, apparently, to the £60 saving. As everybody knew, we wouldn't actually see the full amount restored. So the real increase was £54 per person. Was inflation really that high, or are we to twin with every capital in the world? Once again, all the waffle spouted in defence of this tax turned out to be what everyone knew it to be, a cartload of bollocks – weighed in imperial measurements, of course!

There are a lot of proud people out there who have never had to lower themselves to a means test, but this is what has happened. Students are expected to pay 20% of the total. How? Was it assumed that every parent would pay up and say nothing? If there had been a universal personal tax of £200 per person, across the board, lodged on all workers over the age of 18, there would have been little disquiet.

I became deeply concerned at just how out of touch these people are with ordinary life and everyday events. This country has never witnessed such unwillingness to pay a tax. In Scotland, those who have not paid the poll tax face being placed on a computer blacklist. This could mean people not being able to buy any furnishings on credit, or being authorised a loan for the purchase of a car, or a holiday. Credit card applications could be refused, as might be application for a mortgage. Overall, a total of £1 billion was uncollected at the end of March. We never had this trouble with the rates.

The real answer, surely, lies in abolishing all forms of local taxation and raising the income tax to 30p in the pound. It must be cheaper to administer. After all, it is not as if any local authority has any real say in its finances. The rate support grant is controlled by central government and constraints are activated by them. The introduction of the unified business rate allowed many small businesses to fall by the wayside. I just cannot see the logic. The result is a loss in income to the Treasury, not a gain. To pay increased council charges – call it what you will – you have to increase the cost of your service or product. Price increases, fuel and wage demands, which, in turn, fuel inflation. This is not new, so how can we remain competitive? Every time the gas and electricity tariffs go up, so do the factory gate prices, resulting in even less goods being exported. What happens when businesses fail? People are out of work and the state pays out again. Out of work can mean out of your home and into bed and breakfast. Who pays? The state again. I am not suggesting it shouldn't, I am merely concerned with getting the best value for the money available – and we do seem to be throwing good after bad. Still, could you imagine what the situation would be like if we were in a real recession! Oh, well.

It is funny, isn't it, but very often people say things that you remember for years. I have just said cheerio to a friend of mine, Horace, who has been in the car business all his life. He is one of the real 'salt of the earth' types, always willing to lend a hand, and like me, has had it bitten off on more than one occasion. Anyway, I offered him a car, which I thought he might like to buy. Instead of saying, 'No, I don't have any luck with those,' or, 'It's not my cup of tea,' he said, 'I ain't going to buy another one of those as long as I've got an 'ole in my arse,' so he is obviously not going to buy one for quite some time, then! Another 'gem' he offered was when he was describing someone he disliked. 'I wouldn't cross the road to piss on him if he was on fire.' Lovely, isn't it. I was once in a car with him, the radio was switched on and Pavarotti started to sing the World Cup theme. 'Yeh,' said Horace, turning up the sound, 'I like this one about the Japanese mini-bus.' I looked at him, thinking I had misheard. 'This one,' he repeated, pointing to the radio, 'Nissan Dorma, isn't it?' I half laughed, and to this day I am not convinced he wasn't being serious!

There was a knock at our door earlier this morning. Everybody was out, and, no, it wasn't some big-busted blonde wanting to show me a good time. It was two beefy chaps in military police uniforms, wearing peaked caps that covered most of their eyes and nose. They enquired as to whether a certain person lived at the house. 'Yes,' I replied, 'he's my son.' 'Does he own an Austin Mini, registration number..., as it has been abandoned at the side of the road on an army estate?' I explained the possibilities, either he has run out of petrol, out of oil, or out of luck generally. I offered a fourth possibility. 'He could be giving a squaddie's wife a "seeing to".' Brave, I thought, really. I added, 'Neither of you live on that estate, do you?' They both smiled (I think). Anyway, they asked where he worked and said they would go and see him to find out when it would be removed. They added that their normal little jape was to inform the unfortunate soul whose car it was, that the vehicle had been blown up as a precaution before saying, 'only joking'. Glyn did survive the visit and the mini lived to see another day also. It was out of petrol, and so was the spare can.

A planned visit to the outlaws was timed to coincide with the Putney Fair. Maureen had taken William a couple of years ago and recommended it. Two years can make a world of difference. Talk about pond life. The place was heaving with NQOCD's – Not Quite Our Class, Dear. There was one of those macho types in denim, with black rimmed sunglasses, sporting a ponytail and just about holding his own with a pit-bull terrier. Now the dog's harness was studded with star shaped, silver coloured baubles, surrounding – wait for it – a medallion. This sat at the junction where the straps met on the dog's chest. The female accompanying this low life was dressed, as all good hippies are, complete with oversized floppy hat – magic mushrooms, or what! She fairly wafted around the site, vaguely overseeing the antics of a little boy about four years of age, who was dressed in similar fashion – or lack of it. It did cross my mind that this child was a suitable case for the social workers. Then again, those guardians may well have been social workers. The dog was probably being re-acclimatised to the world at large, having suffered depression caused by a bad press. The whole ensemble were, I assumed, on a day trip from Brent.

From being a family-type affair, the event has obviously degenerated into the usual rides, amusements and take-away do, aimed at the 6-20 year olds. In this case, a large number of the machines were not working and the rides unbelievably short. It was a hot day, with a lot of visitors, so I imagine the view was taken to 'make hay while the sun shines'. My sister-in-law was accused of not paying for a ride and I considered a few of the operators to be rather menacing and intimidating. I wasn't in a position to defend my sister-in-law as I suffer from a stomach complaint – no guts.

Now that reminds me of a time, several – all right, many – years ago when I was young and ambitious. I was called to the area office of the car hire firm I worked for in Southampton, for a Sunday meeting. Dressed like the 'dude' I was, and sporting my newly purchased maroon suit with flared bottoms, a psychedelic tie and 'shades', I made my way onto the Farnham Bypass. For those of you in Accrington, this bypass decides 'not to be one' for a short stretch, while it ferrets its way under a bridge, before blossoming out once again. I was overtaking – remember, I was wearing shades and travelling at no more than 60 mph in my company Morris Marina, but all the same, I felt I had arrived in the big time. Behind me, as we approached what is effectively a chiccane, was a large Vauxhall, driven by a chap who, viewed through the rear view mirror, looked as if he came from the lower orders. He was so close to the boot of my steed, I couldn't see the bonnet of his car. So as to prove that he couldn't toy with the egotistical tendencies of a would-be executive, in his de-luxe saloon, I applied the brakes momentarily. Through my mirror I could see him skidding merrily behind me. Ho, Ho, I thought, that will teach you to ride on my tail. The bridge was passed and we reverted to dual carriageway. In an instant, he was behind me again. Without indicating, he pulled out and overtook me. Unfortunately, he didn't proceed down the road but instead, continued across the nearside lane, cutting me up and forcing me off the road and onto the grass verge. He stopped several yards in front. I opened the door of the Marina, being 'pretty damned annoyed', as they say in upmarket dramas. When I looked up, he was blocking out the sunlight and looking down at me. I started to speak, 'Now look here'... I didn't manage to complete the sentence. He grabbed me by the collar and uttered the immortal words, 'If you don't fucking apologise, I'm gonna stuff your head (it could have been 'ed) up your arse.' I will never forget the charismatic way he described my impending surgery. I started again, 'Now look'... He raised his fist. 'Sorry,' I said, feebly. 'What,' he barked. 'Sorry,' I proffered again. He lowered his arm, released my neck and walked slowly back to his car, muttering expletives.

All the way to Southampton two little voices sat on either shoulder. One kept telling me that I had done the right thing by not retaliating, as once aroused, my natural masculine aggression would have shown no bounds, and this common chap would have needed hospital treatment. I also had, of course, the self satisfaction of knowing that one's own restraint had shone through as an example of one's better breeding. The other voice said, 'Bollocks, you were scared shitless.' I listened to these two voices all the way to the Hampshire city. Having parked my car in the hotel car park, I adjusted my clothing and ran my fingers through my hair, not in an effeminate way, you understand, but with an air of 'devil may care'. Unfortunately, much as I wanted to believe the voice congratulating me on showing true British phlegm, I think – I know – that the other voice was right, I was still shaking like a leaf.

Kate Adie – or how the Gulf was lost

Earlier this year the council which administers the Yorkshire town of Ripon tried to dispense with the services of the town crier. This chap is paid £2,400 per annum for preserving a slice of English tradition – not ethnic – but English. Apparently a trumpet has sounded at the four corners of Ripon Market Square for many years, and only after much protesting by the good people of the city, did sense prevail. Let's face it, the amount saved by his demise would barely have been enough for drinks at a town twinning meeting or the ribbons for the mayoral car.

At about the same time as the above piece was making headlines all over, well, Ripon at least, a court case was being instigated by lawyers in America, claiming 'slander and intentional and negligent infliction of emotional distress'. This action was being pursued on behalf of a traffic policeman who was slapped by Zsa-Zsa Gabor. The amount being claimed was £20 million. I suppose they work on the theory that you only get one bite of the cherry. I bet he settled for 3s. 8d. and a signed photo.

I was interested in a short story concerning a product of Sainsburys called 'Flintstones'. To quote, they are 'Five oatflake biscuits covered in thick milk chocolate'. The wrapper depicts a dinosaur carrying a child, hotly pursued by the four main characters – mums and dads, not guardians. Fred is leading the chase, followed by Wilma. Right behind, legs at 20 to 5, are Betty and Barney. Being just in front, Betty's rear leg is shown jutting down from Barney's groin, between his outstretched leg. You could, if you were of that inclination, assume that the foot was in fact a willy. Now you and I would recognise the protrusion as a foot, but then you wouldn't have a story!

The article contains statements from horrified mums, who complained to Sainsburys about the packet. These mums have been made aware of this awful gaff by their children. In each of the two quoted complaints, the mothers describe the 'terrible embarrassment' caused when trying to explain the reality of it all to their four year old offspring. What embarrassment? Couldn't they explain that it was, in fact, a foot, not a willy. If they had problems with this form of logical answer, they could have pointed to the children's lower extremities, showing them that they possess feet as well, proving conclusively that feet are not the sole (sorry) preserve of cartoon characters. At the end of the day, however, we are not talking about real complaints or trauma, only a mother's desire to get her, and her child's, fizzog in the papers. As she isn't likely to win a million pounds on the pools, this looks like a safe bet, and you will be the talk of the neighbourhood for about three days. All this time spent 'milking' the story would, of course, have been better spent washing up or dusting. Bet the children go to dance classes.

Two letters have recently appeared in the *Daily Mail* with regard to articles I have commented on previously. The first was from a writer who wondered why it was necessary to alter the storylines, nay, characters, in the Noddy books, and I particularly liked the point made, that if parents thought Noddy books as they were printed originally to be unsuitable, what on earth were they putting in their place. Whilst nodding – or noddying – in agreement, my attention was drawn to the second letter, written by a 'Ms' with concern to the 'new man' story. Well, I don't know what page it was on, flick back and find it, you weren't doing anything else. Anyway, this 'lady' suggests that the 'new man' is here and that today's female intelligentsia would not welcome working in a power-house all day and then coming home to, quote, 'wash socks for a wimp'.

In her case the home is shared by a 'partner', who as well as being a freelance modelmaker working from home, 'cooks, irons, cleans and does the gardening without any fuss.' This 'gem', as she goes on to describe him, also looks after their 18-month-old daughter by feeding and entertaining her, changing nappies and getting up in the night, if need be. And all because the lady is on an ego trip. She continues by adding that 'he manages to complete his own commissions and still be a wonderful lover.'

I just wonder if in time to come the daughter does not wonder or ask why this perfect partnership did not get married. There is a social stigma about unmarried parents and I have no doubts that children prefer the security of knowing that their mums and dads have actually taken the vows, instead of the baloney spewed out by half of these modern couples. As far as I am concerned, the time she sat letter-writing would have been better spent if she had washed the socks. Another thing, what was she trying to prove by commenting that her 'gem' is still a wonderful lover. She must be terribly lacking to have written that.

Whilst I have always sympathised with the view that men and women should be paid an equal amount for doing the same job, I never cease to be amazed by the off-hand, and in some cases, downright cocky attitude shown by a number of women promoted to positions of power. They seem to think an awful lot of themselves and I feel this has something to do with their not quite coming to terms with equality. Have you noticed how many female newsreaders have deep voices. It is either that they feel they have to compete with men, or they are using Carole Barnes as a role model. Now I would not be surprised if there were a few women who might contest that view.

Here's a case in point. There is a woman, single, with two sons, already expecting a third child. She is a company director in London, and French by origin. I am already biased as I have yet to discover one redeeming feature. Anyway, having had the usual tests, she is none too pleased when the doctors won't tell her the baby's sex. You will like this. She wants to know if it is a girl, so that she can prepare herself for a new experience. Pregnancies go on day in, day out, without any of this fuss, but this female is prepared to take her case to the European courts, which is hardly surprising. I have no doubt that if the argument is settled before a journey to the continent is necessary, she will actually be quite sorry. People like her live for confrontation. Why does she need to know? Parents should love their children regardless of their sex. The only worry should be that they are all right, with five of everything, and two of everything and... As the doctor said, we live in times where litigation is rife and you cannot always be 100% certain. What are they to do? Tell her what they think and risk being sued for trauma, neurosis, loss of sleep, loss of earnings... The hospital cannot win. Our nasally friend from across the English Channel is, you will not be surprised to learn, backed in her campaign by the 'Association of Improvements in Maternity Services' – whatever that is, when it's at home!

One important and serious point about this is the fear that if all women know the sex before birth, there will be a number of would-be mothers who will have an abortion if they find that they are expecting a girl. Designer children for designer parents – usually single. What time is the next ferry to France!

'Virgin mothers three children', was a heading that greeted

readers of *The People* on Sunday. It seems, to cut a long story short, that this deeply religious schoolteacher decided at the age of 21 to become pregnant. As she wanted children, but hadn't found Mr Right, the idea of being a single parent took hold and she approached the Pregnancy Advice Clinic. She is now the mother of two daughters, who share the same father, and a two year old boy, who has a different dad. I find it all rather sinister that staff at this clinic matched the woman's eyes and hair colourings to the characteristics of a sperm donor. Having given birth – I suppose they still call it that – in 1983, she decided to have another go after 18 months had elapsed and went back for a second dose of the same sperm – which was still available. What a prolific donor! Hey, presto, another instant offspring. Another three years go by, and guess what, it's a boy. Different father this time, as I said earlier, because the sperm from the previous subscriber had to be destroyed, along with that of its peers, due to Aids screening.

Reading this story made me angry, but getting to the point where she says that being told that the donor father was a medical student, 'so at least they will be bright' made me bloody livid. This woman, whom I can only think of as self-centred and irresponsible, is living on £140 DSS money – sorry, our taxes. It is possibly some compensation to note that they are well cared for and apparently speak nicely – is that through education or inheritance from the donor dad? She acknowledges that it will not be easy having to reply when she is asked about 'daddy'. Unlike adopted children, they won't be able to trace their fathers. I would not allow donated sperm to be used, unless the woman was married. As Kath Davies of the anti-abortion group, 'Life', said, 'It reduces human procreation to the level of farmyard husbandry.' If anything goes wrong with those children because of a one-sided upbringing, I hope that woman considers the choice she made and accepts responsibility. Other than disgust, words fail me.

Notwithstanding the pressure which is forced upon children by families – or the lack of them – they grow up at the mercy of advertising, desperate not to possess an unfashionable figure. For unfashionable, read thin. The companies who extol the virtues of size 8 figures have been responsible for so much misery and in some cases, death. Then again, we are talking about greed, so anything goes. It has come to a pretty pass when you have young girls worrying about their being slightly overweight. As the producers aim at a wider market, the neurosis affects younger children. I have just read of a nine-year-old going on diets because of her 'need' to look like a model depicted in a magazine. A leading psychologist explained that mothers who constantly diet put a lot of pressure on their daughters and added that the media image is of slim equalling success, whilst fat is undesirable. I liked his observation that there is a merging of childhood and adulthood, and it is making childhood as a safe haven disappear. They all grow up earlier now, but it won't help them in the long run. It comes to something when doctors are treating eight-year-olds for anorexia.

The parting shot comes from a nine year old girl, who says, 'I don't like any of my body, I am sure I'd have a boyfriend if I was thinner.' Another girl of the same age commented that 'fat people aren't popular.' It is that sort of attitude being displayed which shows just how powerful TV and magazines are. Sad, isn't it?

The naïvety of some people never ceases to amaze me. Do you remember the 'lovely Aimee McDonald' from films and sketches in the sixties? Well, she was caught drink-driving. As her new business had cost so much to set up, she did the driving side of it herself. Knowing the rules, and knowing the penalties, would you not think that she would abstain from drinking when on business? Poor Miss McDonald wept in court as a result of her disqualification, adding that she had not drunk in four hours and thought she would be all right to drive. The tears and sorrow shown by her and others I have read about always seem to be for their own concern and inconvenience. They never appear to consider their good fortune not to be in court because of a tragedy they might have caused. It could be your child, or mine. As I have said before, there should be a lifetime ban for the first offence, it might have some effect, then again...

Locally, a few noteworthy events took place. First, yet another act of vandalism. Historians and local conservationists lost another battle to save a slice of heritage. This time it was a 16th century mill in Fleet, Hampshire. The site was owned by a company with the terribly impersonal and cold title of 'First Technology PLC', so you have got some idea already. The really good news is that the mill is going to be replaced by 2,500 sq yds of office space – we really need that, don't we? The first plans were thrown out because of the height and size but a subsequent application with reduced bulk has been given the okay. Some councillors said the new plans were still ugly and out of keeping, some said the mill should be saved, but we all know that in the real world where only money talks, it has about as much chance of being saved as Anneka Rice has of winning the TV personality of the year award!

Another local council is to donate £12,500 towards the installation of a commercial satellite TV system on one of its estates. Why? If the tenants want one of these obnoxious add-ons, they should chip in together and pay for it. A preferable alternative would be for them all to move to Canvey Island. I hear the whelks are lovely there.

An area of heathland has been earmarked for a new mini-town. This latest plan for a brick and concrete maze is on the outskirts of Fleet, at a place called 'Railroad Heath'. Not one of the more idyllic names, but there we are. One thousand, five hundred and fifty homes and the obligatory office development are in the pipeline.

Talking of destruction, do you remember my mentioning the arcade in Aldershot, which was a lovely Victorian covered area, which had been allowed to become dilapidated by the owners? Well, it was demolished earlier this year, the tenants were turfed out in October and the place was boarded up. They could have carried on trading until Christmas, but no, it wasn't to be. When the new mock-Victorian arcade comes to fruition, will the same family-run independents manage to afford the rent? I think not.

On a lighter note, Rushmoor's councillors have been arguing over the system used to determine their mayor. The Tories don't like it as the opposition parties have a majority in the voting. The opposition still consider that their views are not taken seriously, so *they* don't like the system – and all for the post that promotes sycophants. Frankly, I can't take any of it seriously.

On to another pet hate now. It was reported that youngsters from all over the borough are forging friendships with the youth of Rushmoor's German twin town – Oberursal. I think it is pronounced Over-Arsehole! I can imagine all these youngsters hearing the emotive cry, 'Germany calling, Germany calling', and heading full steam for the adventure of a lifetime, well, four days anyway. It is all so ingratiating. The Town Twinning Committee heard plans from two schools to entertain the Krauts and 'agreed to fund both ventures'. I can see them now, bowing and scraping and patting each other's backs – which is less obscene than patting each other's fronts! Money never seems to be an object. There is another school which is to play host to over 20 boys who will be on a return visit. During this little episode of Euro tit-for-tat, or 'dump-your-sprog-here-and-hope-he's-adopted', as surely would be the wishes of many parents, a six-a-side football competition will be held. The committee has been very busy, it has also given away more taxpayers' money by approving grants for group visits to Germany. This time it is for students and scouts. Someone on the committee has described all this money as 'investment in the future for all of us'. I really don't know who is included in that last statement, because I have yet to meet anyone who does not think it is a complete waste of time and money. The town-twinning budget this year is £17,800, just think of all the good causes that money could go towards.

When I was writing *From Where I Sit*, developers had been given permission (when aren't they?) to build on railway land around Farnborough Station. A little while ago this complex was officially opened, with not an office let. 'Spectrum Point' is the name allotted – do you remember it now? No? Well, it just shows how little you take in! I bet if it had been called 'Tina Turner's Points' you would have remembered it – or them, oh well, never mind. Anyway, this sprawling block, actually 86,000 sq feet of it, is built in brick, but it is so overbearing – listen to this, or in your case, read on. The Mayor (him again) one Councillor Ferrier, thanked the developers for choosing Farnborough. I can't imagine anyone being pleased with the result at all. He went on to thank them again for 'tidying up' this part of the borough. Another councillor presented the Director of the developers, Crest Estates, with a photo of the railway station at the turn of the century, and then the Director handed over a cheque for £250 towards the mayor's annual charity appeal. How nice, it is like a masonic ladies' night.

That well-known local M.P., Mr Julian Critchley, was in attendance and commented that Rushmoor was the biggest growth area after Milton Keynes. To be the second biggest growth area is nothing to shout about, to be mentioned in the same breath as Milton Keynes is positively distressing. Think I am going to have one of my 'heads'!

A few years ago now, we used to go for a meal to a local public house, the Kings Head, in Ash. Yes, those were in the days when we could afford that kind of luxury. It had not previously been noted for its class of clientele over the years, but the new management had put a lot of money and effort into the project and they deserved success. For whatever reasons, they moved on after a couple of years and the pub ran downhill and was eventually closed. Now this building is 150 years old and was originally a private house called 'The Elms'. The car park outside is currently used as a public dumping area. The site is quite large with outbuildings, some nice walling and a goodly amount of shrubbery. As in all too many cases, a planning application has gone in for 23 flats to be built. Guildford Council are currently considering the application. Attempts have been made by individuals to buy the building and turn it back into a private residence, but the owners, typically named 'Premier Properties PLC' are not interested. It is such a shame when yet another landmark is destroyed. Still, while it is standing, there is hope, although we all know what the outcome will be. Guildford Borough Council will only see it as extra income through the poll tax.

I went to the annual general meeting of the Citizens Advice Bureau, held in the local school. The actual meeting was of little interest to those unconnected with its work. However, they traditionally have a speaker for public consumption afterwards. This year it was the turn of Guildford Council's Planning Officer. He was very interesting and the talk enlightening, but what did come across was that local councils have little power at the end of the day over building within any given area of its land. All decisions governing large-scale housing and office development are taken by central government.

This view was reinforced when the council who controls Railroad Heath (Hart Council) apparently did not object to the draft plan for North East Hampshire. A few councillors mumbled protestations, but no-one actually did anything. They probably see the futility of any objection. The local MP, Mr Michael Mates, was asked by a local anti-development group if he could do something. Alas, he said, he couldn't help. Somebody must be able to. You never get to reach the people who actually decide the 'where and how many'.

The local elections in May prompted me to do nothing for the first time. I have always voted Tory, but the poll tax killed that for me. I obviously wouldn't vote Labour, but the slight chance of my putting crosses against the Lib/Dem candidates was cancelled by the following. They started a vigorous campaign some time ago and instigated a local 'Focus' news-sheet, even when the elections were some way off. Did the Lib/Dems really care about the area? The Tories only send out their news sheets when there is an election, so far so good. The problems started with the L/D screed, which was so ingratiating. When I read the candidates' profiles, any thought of an automatic vote was put on hold. One female candidate was already a county councillor and she is involved with so many committees that I am concerned whether she should not be quite so deeply into local politics and perhaps spend a little more time with her children. The next candidate was a founder and director of a third-world agency, so he should be out there getting a proper job. The third nominee listed his interests as amateur radio, computers and the organ, so he has been dismissed, on grounds of being in possession of rose-coloured glasses and wearing them! He comments that 'further development of the village must be carefully planned'. Village? What village. We live in an urban sprawl. The fourth name on the list was concerned about traffic management. Well, at least none of them lived with partners! Okay, so I have got the vote, I might still use it – or so I thought. Two incidents put paid to any crosses being placed on the form. On one occasion, I stood behind one of the candidates in a local supermarket and they part paid for their goods with '10p off' tokens. I am always suspicious of people who meticulously save up their wrappers for this purpose. Shortly afterwards, I passed one of the other candidates' house and noticed stone cladding and a satellite aerial – so I will say no more!

As it happened, they didn't need me. Elected en bloc and now busy changing the face of the universe, well, as long as they are happy.

One of the best titters I have had recently concerned a court case where the accused, a young barrister, was fined £75 for kerb crawling. He was also ordered to pay £250 costs. Now I am certainly not going to denigrate the poor chap for what he did, it was his defence that slayed me. He said he was in the Chapeltown area of Leeds, checking some side streets in connection with a reckless driving case he had previously dealt with. He added that this prostitute then opened the conveniently unlocked passenger door, and got in, just like that. You have to say the last bit wearing a fez and gently shaking your hands. It won't make the story any funnier, but if you are on a train and you see someone else doing it, you will know that they are reading the same story! Anyway, our young barrister chappie was, quote, 'shocked and apprehensive' and had 'no idea what a red light area would be like'. Apparently he did not expect to see groups of young women parading about and standing on street corners. I don't suppose he helped his case when he stated that he drove off with this woman, because he was 'afraid that other people would get into his car'. He drove to a quiet car park on an industrial estate because she seemed 'upset and frightened'. Apparently, when asked by the prosecutor, the 'previously convicted prostitute', as the paper defined her, said he asked if she was in business, and she replied, 'Yes, it is £15.' Frankly, I have never known it as cheap as £15 myself, so I am just off to Sheffield!

The papers love it though, don't they. It is all the little unsubtle bits like the 'previously convicted prostitute', 'Chapeltown, home of the Yorkshire Ripper.' Oh, yes, and they added after the barrister's age and height that he was a 'Church of England official and a devoted voluntary worker' - says it all, really.

Did you know that it was on 15th February 1991 that the Bank of England pronounced the recession to be shorter and less severe than the one we suffered a decade ago. It added that lower pay rises would help avoid further large rises in unemployment, ease the recession and speed up interest rate cuts. All we got was an increase in VAT, more unemployed, higher inflation and vastly disproportionate rises in chairmen's salaries – funny that.

A sign of the times. The other day I went to deliver some books to Hammicks Bookshop in Epsom. I am talking about *From Where I Sit*, not this one. I am still writing this, aren't I. Where was I, oh, yes, having completed the transaction with the very charming manager, I returned across the concourse of the Ashley Shopping Centre and started walking up the stairs to the overpriced concrete tub they call a car park. About three steps up, an elderly lady was pulling up one of those shopping trolleys on wheels. I offered to carry it upstairs for her. 'Thank you,' she said, 'but I will do it myself. If you hurt your back on my behalf, you will sue me!' I thought she was joking, but no. I felt a little miffed at first, and then just sad. The influence, not to mention the effluence, of American legal practice bites deeper.

One of the good points so far this year, and there have not been many, was seeing the dolphin named Rocky, late of Morecombe Marineland, now happily swimming off the Turks and Caicos Islands. For 26 hours and 10 minutes, the animal was out of water, but having arrived safe and sound, he was the first of his species released into a retirement home covering 80 acres. Hopefully, there will be more dolphins to follow from other British, European and American zoos. What lovely pictures they were.

Riding on the back of the news concerning Rocky was the announcement a little later that the two dolphins from Brighton Aquarium will join him. It has taken a long time for public opinion to shift against the acceptance of performing seals, dolphins and whales, but perhaps we are not too far away from all animals being freed from the subjection of a caged environment.

On the other hand, of course, what chance do dolphins, turtles, seals, etc. have out in the oceans at the hands of the drift net fishermen. Two years ago there was an outcry about the decimation of whole species because of this greed, but we are still witnessing countries employing these 'walls of death' as they have quite rightly been described. In the meantime, back home in dear old blighty, there is a publican living near Hull, who keeps a sea-lion and two seals in tanks nearby. These tanks are barely twice the size of the animals. The RSPCA and other environmental bodies know of the situation, but are powerless to do anything because this cove has a licence to keep them. Okay, so somebody made a mistake, issuing him with a licence in the first place, but surely there is some legislation governing the size of tanks in which sea-lions and seals are expected to swim? Obviously not. Well that is a pub I won't be visiting. A mass boycott wouldn't be a bad idea.

I have found a friend for the publican though. A letter was printed in the *Mail on Sunday* recently and I assume it wasn't a wind-up. Our writer, hailing as he does from London SE12, so he is not from a very nice area, starts off by telling us he is an ordinary working class chap, well his address told us that, who has worked 'hard and long' to buy his wife a real fur coat. She, in turn, wears it with pride because he 'wanted her to have it'. He goes on to say that it looks better on her than on some nasty, vicious rodent and that the anti-fur gang should, along with anti-smokers, live on a desert island. I think that SE12 and our smoking, fur wearing friend deserve each other.

Going on from that, there has been an increase in the sale of fur coats. The article I read on this matter prompted letters to various dailies. One odd letter was from a Mrs (not Ms) who described the anti-fur coat campaign as another way for men to put down women. Is she really married? She goes on to say that she hasn't noticed any fuss being made about the ritual slaughter of animals by Muslims. Well, you wouldn't, what was it I said about politicians liking a quiet life when it comes to racial issues. Although it shouldn't be one, a lot of people would make it a debating point. Let's be honest, when has animal cruelty ever superseded the priorities of a religion, especially one not practised by the indigenous population of this country. This female concludes her letter by stating that in her experience, nothing keeps her as warm as a fur jacket. I hope it takes on a life of its own and bites her. All right, so I am being bitchy, but they get you like that.

I warmed more to the letter from a lady who suggested that not every animal lover is a member of ALF – Animal Liberation Front or 'butch', and that fur definitely looks better on an animal in Africa, instead of people in the city.

It was sad to see that the RSPCA had found a large number of sheep, deer and rabbits either dead or dying on a recent visit to an island off the Welsh coast. What infuriated me was that when the paper reporting the story tried to interview the owner, they 'declined to comment'. This get-out-of-jail-free card is used far too often. You see a report of major accusations against Windscale – sorry, Sellafield – nuclear establishment, or some other national company, and all you get is, 'they declined to take part in a debate', or 'no-one is available'. I wouldn't allow these gutless bastards to get away with it. A problem arises that affects a town, a county, the whole nation, it matters not, but 'they' aren't going to discuss it with anyone. Recently, a manufacturer of health foods, described as 'animal friendly' has been accused of cruelty to animals, stating that rabbits, baboons, calves and rats have died in toxicity tests. The manufacturers are brief with their comments, saying that 'testing caused no pain or distress'. Well, I am satisfied with that, aren't you?

I am always surprised as to the people Sunday supplements seek out in their quest to find someone interesting. The *Wales on Sunday* magazine have recently chosen to focus on a chap called Donald Humphries, known to all and sundry as 'Curly' Humphries. I must confess, he did look as if he was sporting a perm. Having built up a used car and hire purchase business, not to mention a 32-site service station group, the man has become Wales' third richest man. His petrol outlets, trading as Action Stations, have just been sold to Gulf Oil for £17 million. The first part of the story goes on to tell how he came from a poor family, working his way up by trading motors, until he opened his first garage. So far so good. I am all in favour of someone making something of themselves. Now, however, we start to find the question marks appearing. This chap has been married three times, although the paper does state that his first wife died 'tragically young'. He has two children and a brother, to whom he no longer speaks, and lives alone in a house with the largest extension in Wales – lucky Curly, I say! His business has an annual turnover of £108 million and he says that money does everything for you, you buy power and feel it'. Now, I would have thought that the interviewer would have wanted to comment on that statement. Instead, she adds that he is ruthless, bad tempered and demanding, and has enough money to buy and sell *whoever* he pleases. Again, what a peculiar thing to write and not make comment upon. Working on the theory that whoever it is that doesn't satisfy goes, he dismissed both sons from the business and states that, 'you have to put your business first'. The sale to Gulf Oil will be bringing him in more than £15,000 in interest a week.

It is funny the different priorities people have. If I were a millionaire, I would give up work as we know it, but I would not sit around. I would buy lots of 'prime building land' which developers would kill for and retain it as open space. Whereas some people flaunt their money by being seen in Rolls Royces or at the 'right' clubs, I would flaunt mine by refusing to develop land so that the public at large, and more importantly the wild-life, could enjoy the existence of areas which would otherwise be swallowed up and turned into the next Bracknell, Telford or Milton Keynes.

Our man in Wales, however, brought a new plaything, a Bentley, with add-on bits that upped the price by £28,000. That's right, £28,000 for the bits, isn't it obscene? He appears proud to have stayed at the Savoy – at £1,700 per night. Surprising, and somewhat disappointing in many respects, is the fact that, according to the photographs accompanying the article, his house does not look like the Ponderosa or some over-dressed Spanish villa. The building is very ordinary, painted in cream or beige. However, an indoor swimming pool, snooker room and bar give some indication to the fellow's priorities. I find it more than a little sad when someone his age has to say that, despite being 69 – my favourite number – he feels 40 and is a self-confessed playboy, whatever that means. I assume it means making a prat of yourself trying to get into clothes that won't fit you, sporting a hairstyle that doesn't suit you and going to places you were too old to visit years ago.

He says some funny things, too. I put it down to insecurity. To say he feels 40 is one thing, to say that he has to produce money and hang around with youngsters in order to stay young, is something else. We then read another example of his defensive reactions. He states that he has got a few years left and can go anywhere he wants because he has the power to do that. It is the constant reference to power which I find worrying. Cop this though, his three alsatians – well, they would be – are called Sultan, Sheba and Nero. What is wrong with Ben, Bella and Sam? Living in Wales, they could have been Aled, Nerys and Geraint. Anything would be better than the macho names these dogs answer to.

Among the pictures accompanying the article is one of him standing proudly beside his Rolls-Royce, one foot resting on the front bumper. The car obviously possesses the all important personalised number plates – VPM 1. The article does not enlighten one as to the significance of these letters, but I don't suppose they stand for 'very prattish mollusc'. Other insights gleaned from the photos include a look at the bar, a must for every lacking-in-taste millionaire. Seven lightly stained wooden bar stools stand in front of what appears to be a stone-clad facia. Beer taps – couldn't see any real ale – optics and mirror retreats nestle between walls of – you've guessed it – stone-cladding. The pelmet is also of wooden construction, plywood probably, with a glass tray encased in similar woodwork running the length of the bar. Coloured lights trail along the base, green, red, yellow, blue, red, orange – and on it goes.

To be fair, the snooker area looked acceptable, but the swimming pool – well! One wall seems to have been painted by somebody who was presumably paid for the job. I think the stonework surround is also painted, but the main theme is of nymphs bathing on the shoreline of a sea or lake. Greenery and shrubs are in profusion, with oriental or phoenician boats completing the scene – or is it obscene. It really is horrendous. I don't know if it's trying to depict an exact location, but it is certainly not Bognor or Hyde Park. This wall is complemented by an orange-coloured carpet, with oversized black footprint offcuts upon it, giving you the impression that you are following a Yeti around the place. The whole ensemble is set off by a lifebuoy fastened to the side of some ornamental concrete walling, while the aforementioned carpet plays host to poolside furniture, some cane and some MFI, white patio style. The writer finishes her article by asking Mr Humphries about his happiness. He concludes that owning a Rolls-Royce for 25 years and having the largest extension in Wales, some one third of an acre, *is* happiness. He signs off his interview by saying, 'I do what I want to do, I am Mr Humphries, no fool.'

I would not dream of calling myself Mr Mann in an interview. It is up to other people to bestow that title on me. I always say, 'It's Anthony Mann here', or, 'The name's Anthony Mann' – even if it is not, but you know what I mean. I don't know about you, but I have occasionally picked up the phone to be greeted by someone saying, 'Good evening, my name is Mr Whatever.' It is not up to them, it is as bad as the tele-sales girl who comes on the phone to sell you double-glazing, or some other home improvement, and says, 'Hi, I'm Tracy', or some other C.H. name. It bloody annoys me.

You remember what I was saying earlier about PMT. OF COURSE YOU DO! There, that's better. I've got rid of 5 days' aggression in four words. If equality is good for women, then men should be irrational as well. Where was I? Oh, yes. A woman in her thirties who hatched a plan to steal clothes from a store, pleaded that she suffered from PMT. The judge fined her £350 and £150 costs. If she had not had the benefit of mitigating circumstances, she would have been jailed. Perhaps men of my age can claim to be suffering from the male menopause – another unreal condition paraded by those who should know better. Then again, how are those authorities on PMT, Claire Rayner, etc. going to keep themselves on breakfast TV.

There was an amusing article not so long ago, which claimed that husbands are being threatened with knives and saucepans and are subjected to abuse and violence from their wives, all because they are the victims of PMT. Maryon Stewart, founder of the Women's Nutritional Advisory Services, says that they get a lot of chaps asking for help for their other halves. She said she had even spoken to men who sleep in the garden shed for a few nights every month. In a 'WNAS' survey, over half of the GPs quizzed said they had difficulty treating sufferers. Apparently it is all down to nutrition and the majority of doctors are not nutritionally trained. This lack of training is, according to WNAS, a scandal, and doctors are not 'well educated' about PMT or the scientific ways of treating it. Women are being left to fend for themselves when there is a perfectly natural and effective solution at hand. I think an effective solution would be for bosses to tell their female staff who used this 'women's problem' as a catch-all for 'hangovers', 'lazyitis', etc. that they won't get paid if they don't come in. Seems simple enough to me. To WNAS, however, it is the doctor's fault. It had to be somebody else. Frankly, you can forget all the scientific claptrap, it is all in the mind, in most cases. They have been conditioned for years by people who know, Claire Rayner again, telling the how awful it is and now they believe them. It begs the question, who are these men who go to the garden shed? They obviously have not gone for the subtle, understanding approach and called the wife a selfish bitch, who should have thought more about serving up an imaginative variation on fish fingers and chips and less about their own peccadillos. (No, you can't go and buy one in a sex shop.)

I must tell you, a strange thing happened this morning. I got out of bed feeling a little 'uneasy'. I walked downstairs, into the kitchen, and opened the door under the sink. I looked out the shoe black, removed the lid and started to smear the contents all over my face. I then went into my office, took hold of the Tippex which was lying on the desk, and brushed it around my eyes and lips. I was sweating like a pig when I had finished. I rushed back upstairs and stood by the bed. 'Maureen,' I cried, 'what's wrong with me, what has happened to me?' 'It's all right,' she said, 'you're suffering from pre-minstrel tension!' Okay, close the book, put it away, see if I care!

I know it is corny, but it gets worse. Some while ago I passed a friend in the street, whose wife I knew to be pregnant. 'Hello,' I said, 'has the missus had the baby yet?' 'Yes,' he said, and stood there. 'Well, go on,' I said, 'what did she have?' 'Eh,' he paused, 'she had a tram.' 'What,' I exclaimed. He thought again. 'No,' he said, 'it was a Routemaster.' A Routemaster? 'Are you sure?' I asked. He scratched his head and then said, 'Got it, it were trolleybus.' (He is a Lancashire lad and they say 'were' instead of 'was'). 'She can't have given birth to a trolleybus,' I shouted, in desperation. There was a silence before he lifted his head, smiled, and announced with conviction, 'Now I remember, she had a miscarriage!'

We went away for a long weekend to Guernsey last week. The weather couldn't have been better. The hotel was superb and the hire car brand new. We packed a lot into the four days and thoroughly enjoyed ourselves. It didn't start off quite so well, though.

Down the M3 we drove, joining the Winchester-by-pass and occasionally venturing into the middle lane – when we came across a Reliant Robin – in our quest to reach Southampton Airport. Our mode of vehicle being our trusty Talbot Samba 1118cc LS, with black vinyl roof and twin go-faster stripes. We arrived in good time to check in. Southampton Airport is, at the present time, still a small, friendly, well, fairly friendly, set up, where you go to meet someone and actually strike up a conversation with an employee. It is that sort of place, soon to change, I hear, according to a Television South report. Another injection of cash and hey presto, you could be in Edinburgh, Ringway or any other modern airport with on-site facilities, intrinsic to today's operations and customer needs. Here, the buildings go back yonks. The newspapers and magazines are sold from what appears to be a gap in the corner and when we were there, the toilets were closed for cleaning. It is either that, or they had heard I was coming and considered me a health hazard! During the time that we had the house up for sale last year, I was banned by Maureen from going 'poos' at any time from an hour prior to the prospective punters' arrival, till after their departure. It is not as if I have curry every night either, but Maureen said she would find it hard trying to convince these would-be purchasers that we were not living next to a cess-pit, or that my hobby really wasn't walking around with a dead rat up my arse! I have found, however, that the best time to weigh yourself is just after a trip to the loo for 'number two's'.

Back to Southampton Airport. It has been some time since we have needed suitcases, and I have had a clearout since then, no, not the loo again, I mean the suitcases. We have, sorry, had three cases which sat one inside t'other when stored. One of the larger ones had broken straps, so this was the one which should have been thrown away. I got it wrong and discarded the perfectly good example. Only 20 minutes before the start of our epic journey south did we finally come to strap the case and found they were broken. Not only that, but the framework of the case had bowed considerably. There was nothing to do but take this near-useless container and hope. In the queue at the check-in Maureen noticed a pair of pants and a bra lying on the floor. No, they weren't mine, but they were Maureen's. I was as surprised as everyone else in the slow moving line of would-be passengers. I didn't know the other half had an example of the crotchless variety! We scrabbled around, picking them up and stuffing them back into one of the bowed sides and remained in our place. The lady in front, who was 'emigrating' to Sark, commented that if she had known earlier, she would have brought some tape with her. Quips like that really make you feel second-class, don't they?

Eventually we reached the desk. 'Have you got anything electrical or containing batteries,' the operative enquired. No, we hadn't. This was going to be a 'clean living' weekend. After all, I was taking the wife, not a bit on the side! Security was where we encountered the most miserable woman in Hampshire. 'You, here,' she pointed impatiently. 'Handbags and hand luggage on there.' She stood, legs together, in her uniform, looking for all the world like an SS officer. I mean, you pay a lot of money for this sort of service in the West End. We collected our wares on the other side of the barrier, having successfully passed the screening and walked into the departure lounge. There are two 'gates'. One either end of the lounge. A stewardess entered, picked up a microphone situated on the wall next to Gate 1 and announced the impending departure of the Paris flight. 'Would all passengers for flight so-and-so to Paris please have their boarding cards ready at Gate 1.' They duly queued and with the formalities over, walked all of thirty feet to the steed which would transport them to that most obnoxious of cities. They appear to have more beggars there than we do at Kings Cross Underground Station.

I digress. The obligatory late arrivals dashed up to Gate 1 and were ushered through quickly. A small, fragile looking chap (sorry, that should be foreign, not fragile, but I can't read my own writing) with a woman who was not the worst-looking thing in the world, made their way to the steps, and stopped. Out came a camera from the man's shoulder bag. He gave it to the girl, who stepped backwards and took several snaps of said chap who stood with arms outstretched for one shot, and down by his side for another. Well, they were foreigners – probably French, as it was a Paris flight. So long as they were going home, I was happy. To the right of this scene, a small plane had arrived. Neither of us had seen it move into position. It probably crept in and tried to remain hidden, judging by the size of it. Apparently it was a Fokker something. Our resident-uniformed stewardess, having made several calls on an internal phone, now rushed from Gate 1 on the left, across the lounge area to the other set of doors (Gate 2). She picked up the microphone. 'Would all passengers for Guernsey, etc. etc.'

Another stewardess entered, a whispered conversation ensued. It turned out that the Paris flight was overbooked by one person and a volunteer was being sought, who wouldn't mind being whisked away, at the airline's expense, to another airport, to catch a later flight. We never saw anyone descend the steps, so I assume the lure of further travel on our soil didn't find many takers. As we were going through the glass doors, all right, the orifice made available by the opening of the said doors, I enquired as to whether an airline waits a pre-determined length of time for a volunteer, and if one is not forthcoming, shoots someone. I received a half-hearted smile, actually, it was more like a grimace, from the stewardess, so I suppose I was right. You can imagine the captain, can't you, gun in hand, announcing, 'Right, there were no takers for the nice way out, so one of you will have to go. Come on, out with your passports, whoever has the least stamps, will be "it".' Frankly, I would have shot the swarthy looking cove with the camera, regardless!

Walking out onto the runway area is so far removed from the telescopic connections of main airports. It gives you the feeling of being among the first, that pioneering spirit. Having said that, it was Guernsey, not Guatamala, but still, it was a break. No wonder the plane had been embarrassed to come too close to the lounge, I have never seen such a small aircraft. The aisles were wider on an inter-city train. I suppose it is the cutbacks. You could see out of the windows on both sides without moving an inch. I was a bit concerned while the pilot conducted his taxi-ing (please stop me if I am getting too technical). Part of the runway was in process of being dug up, I think it must have been a Roman site or something, anyway, with an internationally experienced chap like this pilot, we managed to miss the holes. To be fair, it did take off and stay up. The view of Southampton as we circled around gaining height gave a really good indication as to the state of our nation. New factories spreading out into previously wooded areas, deserted railway lines and the obligatory gypsy camp. Quite a neat package, all told. The factories are no doubt unoccupied, saving 'Greedy Bastard Property Developments PLC' a fortune in tax, the railway lines will be the next starting point for 'GBPD PLC' to site their next tax fiddle and where better for poll-tax money to be spent than on prestige land to house those who contribute least? A fair analysis, I feel. After all, I am not given to sweeping statements!

I am stunned, cut to the quick, gob-smacked, etc. It seems that the good and wise Mr Lamont has been labouring under a false premise. It now appears as if we may still be in a bit of a recession. Not a full one, you understand, more a recession-ette. I had so much faith in that man telling me the truth, after all, he is a politician.

The recent case of the young ladies who were spanked by their driving instructor amused me. It was no doubt the talking point of many a chap over a pint in his local, basically out of jealousy. The driving instructor was fined £400 and ordered to pay a further £200 to one damsel and £100 to the other. I suppose the compensation differential was based on the severity of the spanking. What I found a hoot was that one of the young girls 'endured' the treatment for ten lessons. She has been seeing a psychiatrist every week since it happened. Ten times? Ten times before she complains? It is a toss up as to whether you would pay £700 up the West End for the same service, but it probably wasn't bad value. Mind you, he did lose his job. I haven't got time for a cold shower, so could you pass me that sheep, please?

The *Mail on Sunday* published a story today on the plight of '60s star, P.J. Proby. The photograph of him sitting in a dishevelled state on a sofa, holding a tin of Special Brew, summed up his life, really. I remember saying in my youth that when he matured, he would become one of the best 'standard' singers around. How wrong can you get? When I think about it, I have been wrong about all the singers who I predicted would become legends in their own death-throes. Long John Baldry, Scott Walker and Joe Cocker are another three I tipped for immortality. So there it is, a nod from me is the kiss of death.

So, Dr David Owen is to retire as an MP – another one I was wrong about. Be interesting to see what happens to Rosie Barnes and John Cartwright.

'Best equation of the month' award goes to the *Mail on Sunday* for its comment that 'Kate Adie is the BBC's answer to Indiana Jones, dodging bullets and running around with someone else's blood on her shirt.' Wonderful stuff. Still, we've seen little enough of her since the Gulf War, which is surprising, considering she won it for us.

Aren't the Americans pathetic. We have them to thank for greedy solicitors, trauma experts and marriage contracts – and, no doubt, PMT – and they still have no balls. The new Robbie Coltrane film, *The Pope Must Die* has had to be renamed, *The Pope Must Diet*. Americans would be shocked and upset by the original title, we are led to believe, so a change of title was necessary. If it were about the Royal Family, a similar sort of wording to the original would be perfectly acceptable, but religion! No sense of humour, some people.

As one of the millions of poor sods who has to buy his gas from the same outfit as everybody else, i.e. we none of us have any choice of supplier, isn't it reassuring to learn that Larry Hagman and Burt Reynolds are being paid £1 million to appear in their advertisements. It is no good complaining, either. You have got all their regulating quangos such as Ofgas, Ofwat, Oftel and F-off, etc. but besides exchanging pleasantries and answering questions in 'round terms about their brief' what else do they do. I cannot see for the life of me, what justification these ex-nationalised monopolies can have for paying out such obscene and excessive sums. It is not as if they are chairmen! We have still got Maureen Lipman earning a nice crust. Again, there is no competition, and who pays?

Sit back in despair, Yogi Bear is to be revived, but... he could never come back as we know him, could he. The new look Yogi is a street-wise bear, working in a shopping mall, with Boo-Boo racing around on a skateboard. They can't leave anything alone, can they.

What never ceases to amaze me is the hypocrisy shown by successive British governments on the subject of race. An article in a Sunday national referred to the plight of Polish people, now naturalised Britons, who are not allowed a visit from relatives still living in their homeland. There were many cases cited throughout the article. One prime example related to the case of a lady living in Britain for 33 years, her father fought with the British army. She has been working in local government, but has been told she cannot invite a cousin to stay for two weeks on holiday. Now, I fully accept that not everyone will play the white man and go back at the appointed time, but if this is the reason, how do so many Asians get in on short-stay passes, only to go AWOL.

The main problem confronting the Poles is not the parlous state of their economy, or their craving for freedom in the west, but the fact that they are white.

Somebody I know works for a county council, a Conservative-run administration, no less, and has been told that they must go on a 'Gender Awareness Programme'. This scheme involves everybody in a clerical position who works for the council. Can you imagine the cost of this non-productive claptrap, that at best is nauseating and at worst, insulting and extreme. I await a verdict with interest.

Deborah has reached the age where she is no longer my little girl – although she will always be six years of age in my eyes. The first boyfriend has arrived on the scene and we await a meeting.

Have you noticed how everything that suffers a cutback in the educational field is 'native knowledge' based. A campaign has been started in that great seat of learning – Oxford – to drop Anglo-Saxon from the English syllabus. If English comprised words of African origin it wouldn't be dropped. In the same way, geography teaches youngsters nothing of their own country. I am continually astounded by their complete lack of bearing when faced with a map of our own islands. Some teenagers do not even know where the home counties are in relation to the midlands or the north. Even worse, there appears to be no real interest in learning. Africa, however, is a different proposition. We devalue our country continually throughout education. I am just waiting for history to be re-written, in order to placate ethnic minorities who might be embarrassed by our colonial past.

Do you remember when beggars who failed to extract money from the first passer-by would switch their attention to the next, and so on. Some oik of no fixed abode has been jailed for two months for punching a lady in the face because she refused to hand over money. He has got what he wanted, eight weeks' board and lodgings, paid for by you and me. The report makes no mention of compensation. I am aware he hasn't got any money. I am also aware of that fact that there was no mention of his being disabled, to wit, he was minus two arms. So while he is inside, he should be made to work bloody hard so that he can repay the victim in some small way. If, of course, he is unable to work for any reason, then I would take the money out of his benefit, because, let's face it, this man will be receiving every freebie going. Have you noticed how the 'system' for acquiring money from the state appears to be quite a growth industry in itself. There are now leaflets telling you about 'rights' which most normal people who work would consider a 'cheek', but they are freely available in many Labour-run boroughs in London. It is all about bucking the system, there is no incentive to work for some.

Well, here we are, another bastion of 'life as we know it' being killed off. A temporary stay of execution has been welcomed by campaigners attempting to stop Camden Council from closing Belsize Library. It is due to a lack of money, says the council. The crack is, it is middle-class and unacceptable. Doubtless, the one-armed, legless, black lesbian sub-committee won't lose a penny. Every day in all walks of life, measures are being taken which are eating away at the very fabric of our society. These authorities are hell-bent on sacrificing institutes and bodies who uphold learning, law and order, decency and respect. The very buildings that ooze strength, solidity and calm are in direct conflict to the powers that be, elected or otherwise. It is as if they see white, middle class well-being as a threat.

The happy family face that EC ministers continue to foist upon us doesn't seem to extend to French farmers, or the French in general, come to that. Okay, so you don't agree with this or that, but regardless of the rights or wrongs, to set fire to British lorries carrying sheep defies belief. At the end of the day, you can force changes to one's nationality, one's customs, currency, liberties, etc., but France will only look after the French – particularly those engaged in agriculture. Germany will likewise look after blonde, blue-eyed nationals, whilst tolerating Slavs, Romanians and other second-class citizens. Britain, however, will continue to play it the fairest, because that's the way we are. Ironically, we are probably more European than the rest – if for no other reason than our tolerance and inexplicable toadying to foreigners.

Talking of arseholes, I have just read an article in *Wales on*

Sunday newspaper concerning some character who has shooting rights on around 1500 acres of land in North Wales. Now this 'person' organises shoots – goat shoots. He passes off this activity as culling. He operates this presumably profitable exercise from a public house, which says it all, really. He defends his actions by stating that the 'large' population of wild goats in the area, 'damage stone walls and saplings', but so do humans with bulldozers! He adds that sometimes the animals are injured, so he is helping by putting them out of their misery. This comment is, I suppose, designed to justify a blood sport. Having admitted that some people have complained, he said he 'treats them with the contempt they deserve'. I wish he was injured. I would have him shot.

Here we go again. Rushmoor Council are to increase car parking charges. The revenue increase is calculated at being around £100,000 over the next six months, not bad, is it? The increases have been blamed on budget problems. What they mean is that the poll-tax payer is having to subsidise the council again, because they were so greedy with the amount they expected everybody to cough up in the beginning. You can't get blood out of a stone. One car park mentioned in the report is to raise its charges from 20p to 40p per hour – 100% increase, probably in line with inflation. I always love the 'throwaway lines' councils use when trying to justify another rip-off. It states that no written objections have been received. Well, of course, they won't have been received. Most people wouldn't have been aware of the increase until the time came to insert their euro-size coins or they picked up the paper and read about it. If they did know, it wouldn't make a ha'porth of difference. Have you ever known a council to listen to its electorate? The best you can expect is for your baby to be the recipient of an extremely wet kiss at election time. The baby should not suffer any lasting damage, unless the cove up for election is homosexual or has just returned from Africa!

Just looking through the *Mail on Sunday* letters column, and noticed one from the BBC regarding the paper's article on Kate Adie. The Beeb consider the comments, 'a damaging attack' and they list her achievements, sorry assignments, since the Gulf war. She has apparently been to Northern Iraq, Belgrade, Slovenia, East Croatia and the Baltics. As if their people haven't got enough problems.

Terry Waite and other irritations

It is a different world for some, isn't it. Our local paper has reported on a case of non-identification concerning Farnham's mayoress. This post is currently played by one Zora Bransby-Williams, whose name is right out of a '40s black and white British film, where everyone speaks with clipped diction and looks away from the person they are talking to. Mayoresses never have names like Hilda Micklewhite or Daisy Shufflebotham, do they. Still, Zora Bransby-Williams epitomises all that is decent and stoic about Farnham, a veritable gem in a land swamped with gerry-built squats. The problem currently confronting this lady concerns her apparently ordinary car and its not being recognised when on official business. As she said, some town mayors have Rolls-Royces, where there is no trouble, but, 'you find yourself in a queue of many cars trying to squeeze in somewhere'. Just reading this, you can see it is a major problem. The solution has been provided by the town's Finance Committee, who have agreed to provide a pennant for the mayoral car. The good lady mayor has also suggested car stickers worded, 'Farnham Town Councillor', which could be used when on official visits or, and I quote, 'as we move about so people know who we are and perhaps have a word with us'. I would have thought that the last thing some poor sod wants after negotiating the absurd one-way system in Farnham and queueing for one of the over-priced car parks, is to have a tête-à-tête with a double-barrel.

Now this one is more serious. An advertisement has appeared in a local paper on behalf of Guildford Borough Council. The ad is positioned next to four smaller ones offering Durex at reduced prices, a bureau for friendship, model escorts (credit cards accepted) and the last, advice and help on abortion! Guildford's entry is seeking the services of someone to become 'mayor's secretary'. Unusual, really, the advert starts off by stating that a successor is required for the current secretary who will be retiring in the spring. They name the present incumbent, which is a little odd, and add that the successful candidate will work with her 'to ensure the continuity of this important role'. Apparently it is a challenging and interesting post, supporting the mayor's civic role and related activities. It goes on to inform us that the mayor undertakes some 800 engagements during a year – there's busy, isn't it! As well as possessing first-class secretarial skills, the person appointed must have the personality and maturity to deal with visitors and contacts 'in a manner which reflects the importance of the mayoralty'. This little number is up for grabs at £17,500 per annum. What a disgusting waste of money. All that for helping someone whose ego is boosted by being surrounded by sycophants on freebies. Still, I am sure the good taxpayers of Guildford will be impressed and pleased that their hard-earned money is being so well spent.

I have just been reading this last item again and it is just sinking in. £17,500 a year for some clerical bod to arrange visits from town twinning oiks and potential investors to the locality, on the one hand, and visits to junkets providing the largest alcoholic content on the other.

It was a costly visit to a local church for about half a dozen motorists last week. The church concerned is close to a public house and despite being prominently displayed, drivers ignored the 'You Will Be Clamped' notices and parked in the public house car park. When they returned, clamps had been fitted and it cost them £50 each to be able to drive away. I suppose it is God's way of telling you not to go to Christenings!

We received a letter from the bank today. It was concerning their 'periodic' review of mandates. I won't bore you with the details, although I don't know, I have bored you with everything else. Anyway, after the PP Manager, there was a P.S., and I quote...

'On the mandate you are required to indicate whether you require "either" or "both" to sign. In the past this has caused confusion and we hope the comments below will assist you in this connection.

Either: Either one of the signatories required to sign all cheques, etc. independently.

Both: Both parties required to sign on cheques, etc., together at all times.'

They are right, aren't they? Isn't it all so dreadfully confusing? The quicker all these words are replaced by symbols, the better.

We have yet to meet Deborah's boyfriend but I have spoken to him several times on the telephone. Nice diction, please and thank you's – sounds promising.

It seems such a far cry from the days when you could meet friends at a local pub for a social drink, doesn't it. Of course, there are many places where one can still go, but the writing is on the wall when a paper prints the 'latest results' in disturbances at local public houses. There is a list of those suffering problems with gypsies. Others have managerial difficulties, where those in charge cannot cope, encourage after-hour drinking or allow the premises to be used for illegal bookmaking. I am convinced that the breweries themselves are to blame for a lot of the latter situation. The old way of tied houses with tenants, brought continuity to the industry and allowed the development of relationships between landlord and customer. The greed of the big monopolies over recent years has seen more and more traditional, family houses turned over to managed establishments. These are often fronted by inexperienced couples pushed in as cheaply as possible to maximise profits. The newly ensconced couple usually have little knowledge of the area, the people or the trade. Within a short while they are gone, disillusioned and on to pastures new, probably out of the trade altogether, only to be replaced by more of the same.

Sad to read in our local paper that far from reducing crime, the locality seems riddled with it. The area is no different from anywhere else in the country, so why is there such a lack of respect for other persons and property these days? Earlier this year, we learned about a gang of four 'teeny terrors' who vandalised a children's playground – not once, but on numerous occasions. One councillor comments, 'We are always going to have vandalism in Tongham.' That resigned attitude will get us nowhere.

Earlier this year, our worthy *Aldershot News* reported on vandalism in the locality. This ranged from graffiti to the pulling up or breaking of trees. The taxpayer pays for it all, be it through local taxation or income tax. In Hampshire, a reasonably pleasant county on the whole, the cost of these crimes has reached £26 million. The police apparently no longer record statistics where the value of the damage is lower than £20. Why not? Let the public know exactly what the cost is. Everything that has to replace that which is damaged or destroyed costs more than the original. Street furniture has to be stronger and wall coatings have to include anti-graffiti chemicals, which put up the cost again. What I find frustrating is the financial imbalance between the cost of replacement and the compensation paid by the aggressor. I don't care whether the criminal committed an act of vandalism through drink or not, he is still guilty and should be made to pay. I cannot see why there is such resistance to making it hard for these bastards. In August, parents and staff at a local school helped workmen repair areas that had been set on fire by arsonists – aged between four and six years. Molotov cocktails were used by someone the same month to destroy some poor chap's car. This incident took place in Farnborough. I tell you now, the more housing estates that are erected, the greater the spread of crime. The only real answer is to have a cull. I would get rid of so much pond life, the inside lane of the M25 would be dedicated to picknicking!

Talking of wishful thinking, Aldershot Football Club are proposing to turn the council-owned 'Recreation Ground' where they play – or attempt to, anyway – into a 'Super Stadium'. Every club in the league appears to want one. What concerns me is the number of clubs announcing such developments, when daily you hear of their financial plight. Only last year Aldershot narrowly avoided being wound up. A 10,000 all-seater stadium with bowling alley, sports centre, health club, swimming pool, restaurant, shops and a 350 space underground car park are all on the drawing board. Nearly forgot, a crèche is included in the design, got to have one of those. The cost? A cool £9 million, or so. Their fortune on and off the field this season has not been in marked contrast to their display over recent years, so where is the money to come from? Hang on, I have just read on a little. The club tell of 'unnamed sources'. So we now know it is all an ego trip, it will never happen.

Clear your mind of reality, however, and visualise the proverbial flying pig coming into land. I dread to think of the type of structure this planned stadium would look like. The present corrugated series of sheds are very homely. They remind me of an oversize Southern Railway station canopy, so I am bound to be in favour of their retention. The problem is that development plans are a bit like Topsy, they never finish at the end of the area which needed rebuilding, it always extends to roadworks, tree-cutting and landscaping. I cannot see the greenswards and the trees which border the High Street being retained. You can also bet your bottom dollar that the name 'Recreation Ground' would have to go. That pleasure will probably go to a 'partner' they have found to fund the venture. There will have to be some mini-roundabouts, if for no other reason than (1) they are in vogue and (2) their very being indicates that something has happened. I wouldn't be surprised if current statistics read that for every two mini-roundabouts being built there was one new superstore being erected not more than ten feet away. To travel from one roundabout to another, you will need an approach road. These tarmac-ed extensions are often named after somebody who had something to do with the development. The Chairman of the club? No, they never seem to be very permanent. The manager? No, any success he has on the field or in the transfer market would be inherited by the Board of Directors to show how clever they had been in their choice of manager. Think I am getting closer now! What about one of the names of the towns we twin with? No, they have both been used. Can you imagine being a resident of Farnborough and feeling a sense of empathy with the French and Germans as you drive along Meuden Way or Oberusal Way? No, neither does anybody else.

Of course, if we do twin with Poland, we could have Pole Way, Prague Avenue or Lech Walensa Street. Mind you, it could be called Yeltsin Street and the majority of prolls who make their way to a football match wouldn't have heard of either, anyway. They will probably think it is the name of a lager that is sponsoring the match ball. Why don't they come clean and call it Sycophant Way or Brown Nose Job Way, although that isn't quite so clean. As far as I am aware, there are no detailed plans, well, there won't be, because, as I said earlier, it won't happen.

Here's a classic case of 'bandwaggoning'. People of all ages are, apparently, being treated for, yes, trauma, after seeing a plane crash happen. Not that it is a pleasant sight for anyone to witness, but I stand by my view, that an awful lot of people enjoy being comforted. I suggest that many of them are probably such miserable bastards that it is the only way they can acquire sympathy. Now here's a cracking name, Lennox Cumberbatch, from Powys Social Services – there's lovely – has stated that advertisements are to appear in local papers, offering help on coping with traumas. That is asking for trouble. They will get all the hangers-on and all the nosey parkers. They are even taking referrals from those they have counselled previously. Talk about justifying yourself, still it might get somebody onto TV-AM. You can imagine the social work department of any council you care to name. The scene is set. A phone rings in the SW Department and Ms I.M. Gay, senior social worker for the over-privileged, picks up the receiver. She listens, then answers. 'What's that, there's a child we have just removed from the "At Risk" Register, who is just being beaten senseless by his 18-year-old single mother's boyfriend and you want us to do something? Sorry, I am involved in much more important work, I am counselling a woman in a case related to the recent train crash. No, she wasn't injured, no, she wasn't actually on the train itself, or in fact anywhere near the incident, but 30 years ago her brother had a model railway and the trains kept derailing on the points and now she suffers near apoplexy at the very mention of Hornby-Dublo.'

My friend has now completed the two day gender awareness course. The result was, and is, best described by the friendly chanting of Aldershot football fans. In time with scarves and arms waving from side to side, one sings, 'What-a-load-of-bollocks.' Not for nothing are they known as Aldershit! The course was taken by two people, one male, one female. So far, it is unbiased. One was from the north-east and the other wore dangly earrings, but I am not sure which was which. The first day's programme included such illuminating headings as 'Equal Opportunity Police, Facts and Fantasies'. The second day's listings were sexist language, sexual harassment, etc. Under these headings were more general descriptions of the programme. You get the idea of the context by looking at the following. 'The day will begin with introductions (including some sharing of work and non-work aspects of our lives). Expectations and agreeing ways of working together and an introduction of the Kolb learning cycle' – as opposed to a Raleigh or Peugeot cycle, I suppose.

Having waded through equal opportunity policy and statistics, you break for lunch. The afternoon session starts with 'an exercise to explore our pathways to adulthood as women and men, looking at the significance of gender in our lives'. After tea, which seems to be the most sensible heading, there is, 'Some time and space for work in single sex gropes – sorry, groups – an opportunity to raise issues of concern to us as men and women, in different contexts and roles in or out of work. Exploring concepts of "gender"; "sexist"; "sexism"; "anti-sexist"; "feminist" etc: Small groups can choose whether or not to give feedback to the full group.'

This is followed by 'review learning from the day'. You can smell the left-wing, disruptive ambitions of this mischievous couple, can't you. Apparently, the first thing the female presenter said, by way of introduction, was that she objected to junk mail being sent to her address if it was marked 'Mr'. She also stated that she detested the terminology of the Masters Degree which she had achieved. It should, according to her, be called a 'Persons' degree. Oh yes, she wasn't wearing a wedding ring, either.

The second day kicked off with a session 'in which we look at some of the issues around sexism and language, spoken and written, and consider strategies for change'. In this everyone had to write down sexist words that should be altered to bring about the kind of neurotic, bland world which people would like us to inhabit, while they take control. Terms like 'mankind', 'manhunt', 'manhole' are all allegedly sexist. According to my friend, the general feeling by this time from both the female and male participants, was that the course was very wearing and clutched at tedious, narrow-minded and idealistic straws. As someone in the group asked, 'Would you like to see Manchester renamed Personchester, or Mansfield become Personfield. How far do these people want to go in their quest? No doubt the "son" in person is sexist, anyway, so those two offerings would doubtless be open to debate.'

After coffee it was time to 'explore some of the issues in sexual harassment and strategies for dealing with it'. Lunch was followed by 'identifying the values that underpin a commitment to gender equality'. No-one could understand it, let alone discuss it. The highlight of the afternoon – tea – was followed by 'action planning time in which staff have time to review (or nod off) their own progress and learning needs in respect of gender awareness and anti-sexist action. Planning for some meantime work between now and the follow-up day.' The only good thing to come out of this is that the council concerned have asked all participants to report their views. That should make interesting reading.

I recently attended, as an exhibitor, the Small Press Fair at the Horticultural Hall, Victoria, London. I was ably assisted by my very good friend, Mark. Yes, you know him, he fitted our kitchen. Actually, he popped in for a chat and a cup of tea the other day and I mentioned to him the fact that our dishwasher had stopped working. He gave a cursory glance across the kitchen in the direction of the offending machine and said, 'Well, it was a heap of crap anyway.' I responded by reminding him that at the time of its purchase, along with the rest of the equipment, he described the model *he* guided us into buying as the 'best on the market', adding that it was the 'all-singing, all-dancing, most reliable you can get, etc. etc.'. 'Yes,' he said, quite unperturbed, 'but I was selling it to you then.' There's nothing like honesty and that was *nothing* like honesty!

Back to the Horticultural Hall, the exhibition was very enjoyable, very well attended and very friendly. What I did notice, however, was the number of publishers who were purveying books advocating anarchy and dissension, or over sympathy to minority causes. If I mention that the fair was supported by

Time Out magazine, you will get the drift. There were a number of fringe publications, some very specialised and others almost mainstream. In jacket, shirt and tie, I could have felt overdressed, immersed as I was in a sea of denim, ageing flower power skirts and the token transvestite in a blue sequin dress and red wig. I didn't, of course, I just felt superior! How many of them would be driving home to Surrey!

I stacked out the stand I had hired with copies of *From Where I Sit* and worked on the 'mud at the wall' theory. I also borrowed the book rack from a club to which I belong and filled that with advertising material, copies of letters I had received from readers and reviews from newspapers. It all helped, I think, as we covered the cost of the stand. One chap, a cultured, moustached type, with a soft, slightly effeminate voice, said to me, having scanned through my 'display' copy, 'Your book is not radical enough, the words are understandable and form meaningful sentences.' I wanted to reply in the same meaningful way, so I told him to sod off. Well, he wasn't going to buy one anyway. He reminded me of the timewasters one gets when selling cars. Bearing in mind that half the 'I'll be over in 20 minutes' brigade don't actually arrive, the number of punters who are genuine is minimal. Most are Sunday shoppers. The ones I really love are those who kick tyres and keep peering under the bonnet, trying to look intelligent, pulling this, poking that and sound like John Major. The 'poking that' bit is all right, providing the recipient is blonde and under 25, but anyway. These would-never-be buyers cannot be honest, either. If it is not what they want, or up to the required standard, they can never tell you straight. No, they would rather think up an excuse. Having stood by the car going through the motions for twenty minutes, the arse then announces, 'I thought the Fiesta had five doors.' One answers in a resigned fashion that five door Fiestas have only been in production since (I am just looking in my Glass's Guide) 1989. The car in question is a 1979 model, marked up at £295. Why doesn't the time-waster say, 'It is the heap of crap, we both know it to be.' If it wasn't, it wouldn't be £295.

Remember what I was saying about vandalism and theft. We awoke to find that Glyn's car had been broken into and that his stereo cassette (a present from his grandparents), some clothing and other personal goods had been taken. We called the police, who offered sympathy and a notebook, but commented with total resignation that this sort of thing went on nightly, so that's that.

According to the papers, there is a good chance that Terry

Waite will soon be released. I wonder how over-the-top the authorities and the media will get when that day arrives. I think I'll stay in bed, it's the best place when you are feeling queasy. Seeing all the hangers-on toadying and all the friends doing the 'hail fellow, well met' hero bit is definitely going to turn my stomach.

Well, Freddie Mercury's got Aids. He has been boasting for years about his sexcesses. It was bound to end in tears. Still, if it helps the sale of records...

The more I discuss religion, the more confused I become. A friend of mine has just gone 'all religious'. We agreed on many things in the past, and still do, it is just the emphasis that has changed. According to him, everything has a religious basis and can be found in the book of Whatever. This fall-back allows him to have a bloody answer to everything, you have just got to look it up. This chap is a business man whose trade has plummeted. He has gone – in his own words – pear-shaped, or bust. A decline in the number of sales, coupled with increased costs like the unified business rate, had a lot to do with his downfall. He is married with children, has a business loan, a mortgage and all the usual responsibilities that go hand in hand with modern day self-employment. The bank want their money, the house is up for sale and the future is bleak. So instead of getting out there and fighting for his corner, he has turned to God. As far as I can make out, he is looking for a comfort blanket. I can understand some people taking this course when the chips are down, but he seemed so level-headed, so cynical of life, so disbelieving. He says he feels much better, far more calm, able to cope. I would be panicking like mad, but that's the rub. According to him, God or one of his earthly disciples, will take care of things. We will have to wait and see whether this is a love affair or a one-prayer stand.

The above happened at about the same time I was reading of a church minister's objection to the Labour Party, due to Mrs Kinnock 'giving up God'. Off the subject, and while I think of it, come election time, Glenys K. will make herself very prominent around the constituencies. It will be like an American presidential show with Mr and Mrs K. waving to the masses. I bet she will get her fizzogg on the box a lot more than Norma 'Peas' Minor.

Anyway, back in the pew. The Rev. Huw Pritchard, there's nice, says that he finds Glenys K.'s comment that 'the commitment to religion that I had in my youth has largely gone' to be 'disturbing'. He adds that she is saying she has principles without faith and that you can't have that. Why not? *He* can't, so no-one else can.

I find that all rather typical. The good reverend goes on to say that he finds it strange she feels this way when she was brought up in Holyhead. Frankly, coming from Holyhead, I think she's done very well to get out of the hole. Having escaped from that north-west frontier, she marries Neil, someone who many people see as promoted above his level of competence. I suppose it is indicative of the competition, really. With regard to the Labour leader, the Rev. H.P. is now left wondering how he can ask his flock to vote for someone who 'lost his Christian belief'. I didn't know he had to. I assumed they thought for themselves and voted accordingly. I never cease to be amazed at the importance religious buffs place on their contribution to life. I can honestly say that by being a non-believer, I feel totally cleansed of all religious burdens, for that is what they are.

Back to politics, a poll just published shows the Labour party seven per cent above the Tories (46% against 39%), with the Lib/Dems at 12%. I maintain that when the election does take place, there will be no overall winner and the Lib/Dems will take about 22% of the share. There will be another election within a few months when the Tories will retain the balance of power with a small majority. The Labour party will ditch Mr Kinnock and John Smith will be elected as leader. If I am wrong and the Labour party win, then Mr K. will remain at the helm and the Tory knives will be out in force. I think the Lib/Dem vote will be strong because of the lack of real authority shown by the respective Tory and Labour leaders. I actually believe that if John Smith was leading his party now, they would win, assuming John Major is still Prime Minister at election time. Conversely, if Michael Heseltine was leading the Tories, with Mr K. still at the forefront come an election, then the Tories would win.

A couple of months ago, we decided to go to the pictures, a rare outing for us. In fact, the last time Maureen and I went, we watched Dirk Bogarde and Charlotte Rampling in a film about post-war Vienna. I can't remember the title, but it was very good. We saw the film in Farnham. Shows you how long ago it was, the cinema was pulled down several years ago and the site has been sporting weeds ever since. It was with some relish that we made our way to beautiful downtown Basingstoke. The two elder children had recommended the Warner Bros offering – 5000 screens or something. We got there, parked, and it is easier to find a space in Piccadilly Circus, and entered this most awful of buildings. We were the only ones over 20 years of age, from what we could see. We searched the various adverts for 'Silence of the Lambs'; noted the screen number and walked over to the cash desk. There was no queue, not surprising really. The cinema was already full to capacity. We looked at the options, all full except for Robin Hood, Prince of Whatsit, and we didn't fancy that. It is basically a meeting place for youngsters with nothing to do. The added attraction from standing on a street corner is the warmth, the noise and the junk food readily available at many outlets in the foyer. This is all a far cry from the Granada, Clapham Junction, where the floor would move and up would pop Reginald Dixon at the organ. I have just remembered what the Dirk Bogarde film was called, it was *The Night Porter*.

My parents very kindly paid for Maureen and I to go away for the weekend to Corfe Castle in Dorset. To show that their sense of romance wasn't dead, they even booked the room with the four-poster bed. Manacles were not included, however! On the Saturday, we ventured into Swanage and noticed that the local cinema-cum-theatre was currently showing *The Silence of the Lambs*. We will try again, we thought. The evening beckoned and not wanting to get caught out and miss the blockbuster again, we ate fairly early and made our way to what can only be described as an oversized coal bunker. This '60s memorial to all that is cheap calls itself the John Mowlem Centre, or something like that. It is the sort of building where, should it be demolished, the sight of rubble would be preferable. It contains large windows on the first floor which would definitely benefit from a good clean, and inside, stacked against the dirty glass are boards and ladders, so the impression created is not good, to say the least. Anyway, into the theatre, up to the kiosk; 'Two tickets, please.' Where was the queue? We looked around, but there was no-one else. I half expected the cashier to inform me that I had mis-read the advertisement or that somebody had sent the wrong reel. With a very pleasant smile, she handed me the tickets and my change. We turned to walk into the auditorium when we were confronted by Anthony Hopkins. There, in front of us was Hannibal himself in the uniform he wore in prison. Hair swept back, eyes staring through me, he didn't blink once. 'Good evening,' he said, 'I hope you enjoy the film.' 'Thank you,' I croaked. We were genuinely taken aback. We walked through the door, into the theatre proper and sat down – we were the only two there! When the usherette said, 'Sit, anywhere,' she wasn't understating our choice. About five minutes later the lady with the lamp showed another couple to their choice of seats. The usherette then came and sat next to us. Anthony Hopkins, by this time, had also entered the auditorium and stood by the doors. 'He is a good likeness,' said our guide, nodding towards him. 'Yes,' we said in unison – showing how easy it is to give away 22 years of marriage (not partnership). Maureen asked if he had been hired. 'No,' said the usherette, 'he works for the local paper, he entered a look-alike competition and won it.' I wasn't surprised. Most 'lookalikes' need tags around their necks so that everyone knows who they are, but this chap was the proverbial 'dead-ringer'. As the attendance grew, I couldn't help thinking that we had chanced upon a social club. 'Hello, Geoff, hello, Kate,' the friendly employee would say to the new arrivals. They likewise would respond in first-name terms. Nice that. By the time the film had started, the attendance had risen to 42. That included the tall man who came in by himself and sat at the back, eating crisps, loudly, out of a bag. The screen was one of the smallest I had seen. I think the tripod-mounted example my father had for his 8 mm films was larger than this offering. All of it made for an entertaining evening and the film was well worth waiting for. As it happened, the Swanage Railway was running a special steam-hauled evening service to the terminus at Harmons Cross. We partook of that delightful experience as well, before returning to our hotel, where we enjoyed a couple of night-caps before making our way upstairs to our room with the four-poster bed – but no manacles!

Early on Sunday morning, we were again in Swanage. They had a different engine in steam, but that has nothing to do with it! Once at a seaside though, one must look at the sea. The emphasis being on the word 'look'. How parents could let their children paddle or swim in the sea is beyond my ken. The beach was covered in stinking seaweed and the sea itself looked very dirty. When we arrived home in Ash Vale, I ferreted around and came across a cutting extracted from the *Mail on Sunday* earlier this year. I hasten to add that for the two weeks following publication of this article I scanned the pages of *MOS* to see if there was an apology on offer. There wasn't, so I take it that their findings are not up for dispute. The main gist of it was that in a survey of 320 beaches, over half were contaminated. Swanage beach was found to contain bacteria. The sad thing is that we used to consider UK guidelines – on anything – to be of a much higher standard than Europe's. Now, our beaches, like our water, fall well below EC safety limits. Oh, the sands of time.

You can see, though, how our wildlife and fish stocks are being depleted. The whole place is riddled with filth. There is no pleasure in going to the seaside. We visited Lee-on-Solent for the day. Dogs' muck, broken bottles, cartons, crisp packets, discarded clothing and even more unsavoury things which only Claire Rayner would discuss at teatime, were on offer. Another of those 'Sunday' treats from my youth, Climping, was on the agenda as a destination a few weeks ago. Again, we must have stayed about five minutes. Horses' and dogs' muck was everywhere. I cannot understand the local council. I see that the Government's watchdog, the Nature Conservancy Council, having completed a two-year study, stated that 155 estuaries are under threat. It is not just reclamation, or greed, housing development (greed) or the building of marinas (greed) but pollution which affects birds by the million. Mud-flats are disappearing in the same way as hedgerows – at a vast rate of knots.

Also depressing is the constant discussion over whether to mine the Antarctic out of existence, or designate the area as a world park. On the one hand we have rare penguins, whales and all manner of wildlife and on the other, we have billions of barrels of oil and large quantities of minerals. There is no competition, Greedy Bastard PLC will doubtless win again. The only problem is that victory will be very short-lived. As you are well aware, I don't believe in a God, but I am a firm believer in Mother Nature. She will get her own back. I wonder if Aids... It makes you wonder whether the dreadful standard of education is Government sponsored to ensure that the next generation cannot read about what is happening, let alone *where* it is happening.

Earlier this year, that good Education Secretary, Mr K. Clarke, blamed badly organised staff who were using trendy methods. This was twelve years after having come to power. If successive ministers do not have the clout to do something, who has? He wholeheartedly blames the schools, but why has nothing been done before? We have had a whole decade of falling standards. Mind you, one doesn't stand a chance if one is of the traditional persuasion. There is a chap called Professor K Goodman, who states that, 'You cannot teach rules to children.' When you have people with influence spouting out crap like that, there really is no hope. Our Ken had stated that, 'We must make certain that spelling is properly tested at all levels and in all subjects.' It was then announced that marks would be lost for bad spelling in GCSEs. That would have pleased the majority of parents, but hang on. The NUT was not going to play ball so easily. Mr Doug McEvoy, its General Secretary, said in reply, 'There is a danger that children's confidence will be endangered by over-emphasis on spelling in subjects such as history, science and economics.' What he is really concerned about is his members' ability to implement the recommendation properly. How can someone, presumably with an interest in education, consider bad spelling in *any* subject to be acceptable. To me, it smacks of trying to short change, once again, the taxpayers who pay for their children's education. The above happened in early January.

February 12th brought us a survey concluding that 'Britons are among the worst educated in Europe'. Only 22% of Brits hold degrees, against an average Euro figure of 30%. Students make up 3% of the British adult population – less than half that in Europe. That tells us something, doesn't it?

March 3rd saw an article in the Press about a school in London that had been teaching English in the modern vogue. Seven and eight year olds cannot spell or read their own names. A whole page was devoted to this subject. Something will be done now, surely.

March 15th. In another London school, teachers make children recite unsuitable poems that are about violence, murder, vandalism, etc. These children are in a junior school. I am fairly sure something will be done now.

March 17th. Frank Smith (who?) is being praised by Glenys Kinnock. Mr Smith advocates *not* teaching children that there are 26 letters in the alphabet. This is probably so that they won't be too upset by the fact that they only have 10 fingers and 26 is a long way off. This chap, Smith, originally hailed from London, but is now based in Canada. He spends his time touring the world, giving lectures on education. He lectures to teachers – and they apparently listen. He contends that 'testing is a harassment for children and it is biased.' 'Kids', he says, 'should be enjoying themselves when reading. If children have problems learning to read, then they need *less* instruction, not more.' I can imagine teachers lapping up that sort of recommendation. They would be positively creaming at the lack of discipline this cove is encouraging. Still, with a bit of luck our Ken can do something. When I was writing *From Where I Sit*, I read an article and commented on it as well – so what is new, I hear you say! This concerned European teachers coming over here to fill the gaps left by disillusioned Brits.

March 27th. Less than two years on and what we all knew would happen, has happened. These European teachers have found that to appear friendly is to be taken advantage of. Over 1300 teachers have arrived on our shores, the vast majority have experienced failure due to communication problems, difficulties

in control, lack of fluency in English and instructions being mis-
-heard or unclear.

What was I saying about discipline. A Labour controlled council – Humberside – is refusing to back schools who insist on children wearing uniforms. Apparently it is against party policy for schools to enforce a uniform on its pupils, so the school and the parents' wishes count for nowt, as they say 'up there'. I wonder if Ken knows about this one.

April 4th. Schoolgirl mothers are to be helped by being provided with crèches – ahh. Humberside again. Some teachers are to be moved to four special centres in the county. These will cater for around 100 kids with sproggs, so that they can continue with their GCSEs. They will also take lessons in child-care, transport will naturally be free. Are they trying to encourage something that will 'end in tears' for most? Perhaps Ken's busy.

April 7th. This is rich. A Ghanaian lady who came to our country 30 years ago is to send her children back to Ghana, so that they can be educated in a style reminiscent of the British system during the 1950s. This state-run school in Accra sets its store by discipline, uniform, homework, timetables, etc. All the aspects of learning which we have discarded. They also have a very high standard of passes at 'O' and 'A' level. Twelve other children have already been sent to this school from Britain. Does this also not tell us something? Oh, yes, they also use the cane. Perhaps Ken's asleep.

Up to date, now. Langham School in Haringey, London, is situated in a rundown area. Actually, it is near the infamous Broadwater Farm Estate. The headmistress (I know she is officially a headteacher, but I prefer the older title) has seen the number of pupils rise from 600 to over 900 since she took over two years ago. Mrs Green, a Jamaican, has got to grips with the problems at her school, with successes in English and French at levels hitherto unattained. I suppose the fact that Mrs Green, having reintroduced school uniform whilst banning the wearing of jewellery, jeans and trainers, and enforced rules concerning smoking and swearing has nothing to do with it. I suspect it is all beyond our Ken.

It was a pleasure to read that Ricky Valance, BT's Chairman, considers he is worth every penny of his salary. I am glad he clarified the situation because there was some doubt in my mind and I don't think I am alone. He commented that his salary reflects the success of the company. Last month he donated his £150,000 rise to charity. A 43% rise 'ain't bad by anyone's standards', but to be awarded and accept that sort of rise when you are handing out just 6% to your staff, smacks of being just a little one-sided. We all knew the script, though, we all knew what privatisation would bring. Gold for a few, and higher prices for the poor sods who are paying for the monopolistic services. Giving it away to a charity cuts no ice with me. If I want to give, I will do. I don't want an ex-utility chairman handing out my hard-earned money well, not unless it went to a donkey sanctuary or a massage parlour in Guildford. No, I am not convinced that increases in any chairman's wages should be used to subsidise the government, sorry, I mean donated to a charity. I believe he is giving it to the sick and elderly. It could have been worse. It could have gone to that most fashionable of causes – Aids.

It appears almost an 'honour' to die this way. Freddie Mercury is dead, but he has died a hero. To die of cancer or a heart attack is acceptable, but it is not 'cool' and is not held in such high esteem. Someone said that if Elizabeth Taylor had not supported Aids in such a public way, then it might not have had the impact on the masses that it has. We are now marketing 'designer' diseases. There are many diseases, such as breast cancer, multiple sclerosis, motor neurone disease, to name but a few that kill a far greater number of people than Aids. We live in a time, however, when being 'bent', irrespective of sex, places you on a pedestal. Not necessarily because of what you are, but because you dare to flaunt it, actually flog it to death is probably nearer the mark.

Princess Di has devoted a lot of her time to Aids-related 'do's'. She has visited clinics, hospices and premières. She has attended receptions and conferences. She has sat in hospitals comforting those suffering from it. Elitist disease, or what! We have just witnessed the release of *Don't Let the Sun Go Down on Me*, by Elton John and George Michael – what is he doing on it? – *Bohemian Rhapsody* is to be re-released, so that will probably go straight into the charts at No. 1. All profits from this little revival will descend straight into the coffers (should it be coffins) of the Terence Higgins Trust. Churches are seemingly responding in their hundreds to letters sent out by the Archbishop of Canterbury and Cliff Richard to make Aids a focal point – don't they mean 'fuck-all-point' of their Sunday services this weekend.

Besides those who were infected through blood transfusions or dentistry, I really cannot muster much enthusiasm or sympathy for a cure. The only heartening statistic is that despite all the hype, the donkey sanctuary obtains more money from public donation than Aids marketing.

A couple of weeks ago, visitors and shoppers in Aldershot were confronted by a quilt that had been put on display to mark Surrey and East Hants Aidslink at the local left-wing theatre. The quilt is part of a world wide project 'promoting' the names and stories behind the statistics. A founder of Aidslink was accompanying the quilt. His 'partner' died of Aids in 1989. I still think of a partner as being the other 50% of a business – silly me. One of the panels on this quilt was designed by the Aidslink founder in memory of his 'friend'. He says they became lovers in 1987. Frankly, it makes me want to throw up, the quilt is used to educate people – patronising bastards – and is often taken to schools to teach 5-14 year olds about bereavement. I would have liked to have told children that if you don't want your name on the quilt, don't sleep with other men. Seems reasonable to me.

I suppose men with that bent (and I do mean bent) look on the quilt as a giant security blanket and a headstone all rolled into one. As well as offering confidential advice about HIV and Aids, it offers a 'buddy' service. This is for those in need of emotional and practical help. That translates into nosey bastards, getting their fizzoggs in and boosting their own egos. Oh, yes, you will like this. Aidslink also incorporates 'Body Positive', a self-help support group for those diagnosed as confirmed cases and lining up to be heroes. The icing on the cake is that Aidslink is now a charity and has been launched by Virginia Bottomley. How nice. She could not have a better surname for an Aids cause, could she, although I would like to see the fund renamed the 'Bugger-all Aid', more appropriate, I think, don't you?

Now here is a case for genuine sadness. That very fine actor, Donald Houston, died last week, aged 67. He had become a recluse in Portugal during recent years, but I remember with fondness his fine portrayals in films during the '50s and '60s.

You know, I can't imagine being a Samaritan and sitting, listening to everybody's troubles. I think the Samaritans do a wonderful job, some are cut out for it and others are not. If I was on call when someone rang to say they wanted to discuss problems with their children, debts, illness, etc. I would be all tea and sympathy. If, however, it was someone suffering from Aids, I would have to ask them how they had got it before I could feel sorry for them.

My sympathies do go to the Samaritan in America who earlier this year got more than a little upset with a suicidal caller. This chap kept phoning continually, often several times a night and always wanted to speak to the same Samaritan. In the end, it all got too much, so he visited the depressed soul and slashed the man's wrists for him. The Samaritan was charged with attempted murder and the 'death-wish' fellow survived. Well, as long as they are both happy.

Talking of happy, the romance between Deborah and – let's call him Rob – is still going strong. Hardly a day goes by without a letter or postcard being shoved into the shoebox that doubles for a letter-box. Deborah has always lived in a world of flowers, fairies and cuddly animals. Eighteen years on this earth without ever joining the real world. She certainly appears to have found a soul-mate. Although this young man is six years older than her and has lived abroad, his attitude and outlook is very similar. We know a little more about him now. He comes from a very close family who live in an impressive period dwelling in a small village on the 'right' side of Farnham. Rob has got a car, although it is off the road at present. The parents have a Mercedes and a Saab, to which he has access, so at least Deborah does not have to be seen in 'tat', let alone public transport. Being chauffeured around in up-market cars, she is never without electric windows (which weighs heavily with me). Having met Rob now on a few occasions, he certainly is a very pleasant young man. Not shy, but not overpowering either. It wouldn't do to have two like that – I was referring to Maureen, not me! One never knows, Rob could turn out to be the biggest arsehole in Christendom, but he is white and middle-class, so he is all right by me!

The really good news is that Wogan is going to end its run next year. What has happened to lightweight interviewers? There does not seem to be anyone out there. Jonathan Woss is unbearable, but appears to be well liked by some. He is loud, brash, speaks badly and lands plum jobs. Terry Wogan spends half the show building up his next artist and the other half interrupting them. Aspel is probably the only male that comes to mind as being 'quite good'. Frankly, I think Sue Lawley takes some beating – and if she does, I want to be first in the queue! I didn't know I was going to say that, it just came out.

Just when you feel able to cope with the name Terry again, the other one gets released. Oh, well, you can't have everything.

There was a nice little article in one of the nationals a few weeks ago which interested me. A female Liberal-Democrat candidate was being urged by the Tories to do the honourable thing and stand down. Her crime was to issue a cheque which bounced. Now, of course, the cheque should be honoured, but if all Tory candidates 'stood down' every time a little financial problem was made public, I doubt if they could muster half the field they intended to. Talk about a cheap jibe.

For those of you in Carlisle, Dumbarton and Aspatria, you may be lucky enough not to suffer regular invasions from itinerant travellers, masquerading as gypsies. Here, in this part of Surrey and North East Hampshire, we are not so well blessed. Just so as we know who we are talking about, there are a lot of families from gypsy and travelling origins who have settled down over generations in this area. All they want is a quiet life, they are no trouble in pubs and are perfectly acceptable. Guildford Borough Council, like any other authority, has to provide its quota of sites. Every large conurbation has its 'nice end' and its 'not so nice end'. Just like women, really. Julia Roberts has a 'nice end', whilst Bella Emberg does not! So, when the 'travellers' invasion' occurs, there never seems to be the urgency to evict that would be forthcoming, should it be Clandon or Effingham that were being infected sorry, affected.

So, our continual problem with gypsies parking illegally runs true to form. It appears that while regulations can be introduced seemingly overnight for the slightest indiscretion should you be a motorist, gypsies are above the laws and beyond the powers that be. During May, around fifteen gypsy caravans arrived in the neighbouring borough of Rushmoor, and camped on land beside the scout hut. To add insult to injury, they blocked the entrance to the hut with tarmac and rubbish. Parents of the beaver scouts had to find alternative accommodation while the local council spent taxpayers' money trying to evict the 'no-marks', as they say in *Brookside*. In the meantime, wood had been taken from the hut and the surrounding area, which is used for games and became totally unusable. Needless to say, both parents and scouts suffered abuse and intimidation on their visit. The council meanwhile was pursuing the idea of getting the land listed under the Caravans Site Act, which would enable them to evict the gypsies quicker.

A month later and the council was admitting that it could have acted sooner. This comment comes as another batch of gypsies settle on the land. Forgetting the legal fees for a minute, the actual cost of clearing up after the bastards ran to several thousand pounds. They should have installed barriers, but the work was not done fast enough. I would have thought the parents and scouts deserved better. They have had their meetings interrupted by the loathsome little oiks, who should be in social care, while the poor sod of a taxpayer ends up with the clearing-up bill as well. Still, I expect it is society's fault.

I am convinced that do-gooders have a lot of clout on local councils in the same way as those whose only interest is financial gain and those who do not want projects of an 'unsavoury nature' to be built or erected near them. Our borough, Guildford, has approved the building of a hostel for the homeless in the middle of an award-winning private estate. Whilst I accept that the 'award' was definitely over the top, being private it is still only a couple of points up on the ubiquitous council estate. Of all the areas within the Borough of Guildford, where this development could have taken place, Ash Vale has been chosen. The council's decision, of course, was taken despite hundreds of objections from local residents, but then the council knew best – and, of course, they don't live here!

Following on from that, Ash Parish Council, which comes under Guildford, owns an area of green land called Carrington Lane Recreation Ground. It is roughly triangular in shape, the pyramid end of which is to be 'knocked off' and used for a roundabout when the new bridge replaces the existing level crossing over the nearby railway line. This will take place within the next couple of years. The open space itself is given over to football pitches, tennis courts and a general exercise area. It is bordered by some nice trees and bushes, possessing a generally rural air about it. Some fifteen months or so ago, the Parish Council floated the idea of selling off for development a large parcel of this land. Yup, you've got it, retail stores and commercial activities with the carrot of a sports centre for the locals – but little grass.

At the time of the announcement, a fighting group were formed called the Carrington Recreation Ground Action Group – CRAG. They sought the views of local councillors and an exhibition was mounted in the local stable (must stop saying that), I mean the local recreation hall, of course. I visited the 'do' at the time and was mildly amused by the maps that had been used. The whole area was awash with open spaces. In fact, the award-winning estate I mentioned a little earlier does not appear to have been built. It was more than a little one-sided. I asked two councillors how they felt on the subject, both were non-committal and said it was for the local populus to express their feelings by voting in a referendum, which was duly held. I have never heard of a councillor not having an opinion – let alone two councillors. Still, the referendum was duly held, and a large majority said, 'No, leave it alone.' The council came out with the financial sop that if the land was sold, the Parish Council would not need to levy a parish rate – extra poll tax – for a long time. The carrot did not, I am glad to say, have the desired effect. The four Liberal-Democrat candidates who were eventually elected in the local elections I mentioned earlier, all pledged to support the 'status quo'. However, despite the overwhelming view for retention by the local people, the council could not resist appearing to be in the big time by enlisting a consultancy to produce a feasibility report. This has now appeared and at a recent Parish Council meetings' Question Time, members of CRAG suggested that there was more than a hint of bias in favour of development and asked for reassurance that, having been elected, the gang of four would not change their minds and would still be against the change of use. I believe this confirmation is still awaited. Time will tell.

The *Aldershot News* dated 29th November did not produce any reason for joy – unless you wanted the telephone number of a new massage parlour that had opened in Aldershot and was making itself known under the Personal Column. Far from the heady days of 10,000-seater grounds and underground car parks, it appears that Aldershot FC face being wound up because they owe the Inland Revenue £92,000. Aldershot's cash problem is a continuing one. Having survived a winding-up order in 1990, they appear to have bumped along on the bottom of the financial ladder, and not much higher in its league positions.

That story was followed by one on Sunday trading and gypsies. Now, Sunday trading continues to be a thorn in my side. If, however, it is for sexual pleasure and depravation, then I will put up with it, but altering the traditional British life for greed really pains me. All of the large stores are expected to flout the law and open on Sundays until Christmas. What is the betting they continue opening in the new year as well. A good indication of the attitude and downright disregard for the law was epitomised by a spokesman for Tesco's, who said, 'We are aware of the risks of prosecution, but we will deal with that if and when it arises.' If it arises? There should be no question of it not arising. Earlier this year, Sunday trading laws were deemed 'virtually unenforceable'. That was when the Appeal Court overturned High Court Orders to Wickes and B & Q. The two councils who brought the actions have effectively been 'warned off', as the cost of reimbursing the two chains for loss of profit could run into hundreds of thousands of pounds. Whether anyone likes it or not, the law as it stands should stop these large stores from opening, but the threat of European involvement is paramount. To be able to run to Europe every time a decision goes against you shows the monetary obsession these companies possess. I can understand the local council's trepidation. If they enforce local by-laws, they risk having to pay compensation, should the European court overrule them and find in favour of Greedy Bastards PLC. Did the people who voted to stay in Europe consider this kind of incursion into our legal system all those years ago?

The final story concerned Hart Council. They govern Hartley Wintney, Yateley and Eversley. Already two gypsy sites are operating within their boundaries, now Hampshire County Council want a third. I don't suppose for one minute a spare acre of land could be found at Dummer, home of the Fergies.

A couple of letters have recently appeared in the *Mail on Sunday*, regarding articles on Aids. One was from someone who said she had close, personal friends who were homosexual, but would never consider giving a penny to Aids appeals unless she was sure it went to those who deserved it, i.e. haemophiliacs and innocent victims. She goes on to add that the Princess of Wales would be better employed helping those suffering from incurable diseases that were not of their own making.

The second letter makes the point that so-called stars and celebrities make too much of Aids support, when five times as many women die of breast cancer each year. The writer questions whether a disproportionate amount of time is channelled into Aids support. As I said earlier, you cannot over-act or over-react with breast cancer, but to die of Aids or know someone who has, appears to be heroic. I find it all arse about face – well, I would if the star who dies through his own fault gets the accolades and his inheritors a lot more through increased record sales than the poor sod who received the death sentence through a blood transfusion and is merely a passing news fill-in.

There is more than a school of thought – more like a university in fact – that contends that Aids was a product of experimental work used in connection with malaria. You never know, do you, but perhaps one day we will. I personally still think it is Mother Nature's way of getting her own back on promiscuity and deviants. No, I don't take it personally, even though I don't know where I was when the Swinging Sixties gripped everyone else with free love and peace. Oh, yes, I do, I was standing on Platform 8 at Clapham Junction, train spotting!

All I want for Christmas is my sexist doll

We are getting awfully close to Christmas and according to the Treasury, the recession which we merely dipped our financial toes into is now showing signs of easing. What a coincidence, as there will be an election within six months. This year, our money is unbelievably tight, so we are not sending any cards to anybody. We are buying, well, all right, we will use up last year's remnants to physically give to those fortunate enough to be at our home when we (a) can find the cards, and (b) have a pen handy. That is what Christmas is about, giving. I have got it right, haven't I? With a bit of luck, there won't be too many people who will balance the 'sents' with the 'receiveds', so we might still be on next year's list. By that time, we could possibly be a little better off and afford to join in the annual game of let's throw money at the Royal Mail. I cannot wait for this farce to be over, and, yes, I know I'm a crabby old sod. Maureen and I are going to give each other an IOU for £1 million, well it is the thought that counts. One of the best gifts I have seen on sale is the one dubbed as 'worst taste present' by some women's group – and I thought I was miserable. This present comes in the shape of a female doll. The idea is for frustrated other-halves to pull it apart. It has detachable head and limbs. They are officially called 'Tear-apart stress dolls'. A Muzz Kilbride of Birmingham, or was it Ms Birmingham from Kilbride? Who knows, who cares. Anyway, she of the MGB club, no, not the Abingdon sports car, the Misery Guts Brigade, said that these dolls were an insult to thousands of women assaulted each year by their husbands and boyfriends.

Even better, another Ms, this time the co-ordinator of Birmingham's 'All women against injustice', whatever that is when it is in a refuge, described the toys as a spin-off from pornography and rubber blow-up dolls. Strange gal. This isn't the only instance of sexual neurosis that our beloved country has witnessed this year.

In March we heard of another West Midlands town that was

going to ban Thomas the Tank Engine books from its libraries, due to their content being sexist.

April's Fool saw Swedish lingerie firm Hermes censored for a most inoffensive and humorous advert which attracted 78 complaints, so what happened to the millions that were not the least unhappy or concerned by their little offering? Well, of course, their opinion did not count. The problem is that most feminists don't possess the big tits that are carted around and paraded by those they secretly wish to emulate, so acting in very much the same way as a spoilt brat, they try to stop everybody else from being pretty. You see, it is easy to define, you don't need psychologists for that lot, plain jealousy, that's all.

At about the same time, Hunslet Boys' Club in Leeds was being pressured – no, blackmailed – into changing its name to the Hunslet Young Persons' Club. They must not only be seen to be toe-ing the line with regards to the council's sex equality policy, but more importantly, any dissent or refusal to change the name would have meant a cut in the club's grant. I wonder if the residents of Hunslet considered this type of behaviour by councillors before they were voted into office?

So here we are, near to Christmas, and all they find to argue about are stress dolls. It is also anniversary time. Fifty years, to be precise, since Pearl Harbor was bombed. Both the Americans and the Japanese governments are refusing to apologise for their action and I can sense a change in the feelings of the Japanese people. Over the years they have kept a low profile towards mentioning the war, but recently odd titbits I have read have indicated a strengthening of opinion. It probably stems from their near world domination of the economy. This recent uplift in monetary gain and confidence probably enables them to 'justify' their past actions; indeed, alter the history and basis of the war according to Nipponese interpretation.

Yes, you are right, that was a bit deep. Anyway, as I sit here at the breakfast table, eating my Weetabix (3), I learn that John McCarthy has had bestowed upon him the honour of 'Doctor of Letters' by his old university. His father and girlfriend, Jill Morrell, sat in the crowd and he was cheered by a crowd of undergraduates. The Vice Chancellor, Professor David Dilks, said Mr McCarthy had brought great credit to Hull University. He has, great credit to the country as a whole (or do I mean hole?). If the fact that had he not been in the wrong place at the wrong time, he would have been just another 'old boy'. By all means invite him back and give him a little trophy, like a map of Beirut or a piece of middle-eastern pottery, but you cannot become a Doctor overnight. It seems that if you want someone famous to visit you nowadays, you either ask them to open your Aids Fund or you offer them a doctorate.

With this in mind, I have come across the perfect Christmas present. Taking up a fair few column inches in the *Daily Mail* is an advert headed, 'Now on Video'. At around £10.99 I can buy 'Hostage' – you have to read this with an American accent – starring Terry Waite, Jackie Mann, Brian Keenan and John McCarthy: naturally, everyone's favourite, 'Tel', is the first name mentioned. Naturally enough (again) his persona in the form of a photograph takes up about a third of the video cover. The other three are reduced to 'edged' snaps. Mr McCarthy has managed to get one of his outstretched arms out of the surrounding border and across good old Tel's chest. You are not still reading this with an America accent, are you? Strewth! You have to be told everything. The video is apparently available from all leading stockists and shows exclusive ITN footage. It tells of the long days in captivity, the campaigns going on back home, the alleged 'Beirutgate' (my phrase) and finally the emotional homecomings. I expect that includes all the fly-pasts, hangers-on and the rest of the world who were involved, how bloody sycophantic.

Here's one that the home video fraternity might like to keep in the album. Essex University are culling rabbits. It is all a bit rum, as they say in ex-army officer clubs. As a group of adults and children arrived for Sunday service at the church which borders university land, a Land Rover appeared. Two men got out and started clubbing the rabbits, some only yards from the church porch. This killing has been going on since March and several hundred rabbits have died in this fashion. Where do they get the people to do it? The service was abandoned as so many people were upset by what they had seen, not surprising really. A university spokesman, who remained nameless (naturally), said that 'no rabbits were destroyed inhumanely', so that is all right then. I hate to think what these people consider to be an inhumane death, perhaps they are Japanese.

Well, family life is showing all the usual signs of the pre-Christmas menopause. William has had one, well, actually several, of his hyper periods. He cannot sit still for a minute. The manipulating little toad uses every trick to wreak havoc in the house. 'Come in and have some lunch,' Maureen might say, a fairly innocuous request, you may think. 'I'll eat it later,' will be the reply. Okay, we can buy that. So when he enters the kitchen and says he is starving, there shouldn't be any problem. If William has a friend or friends in to play, he is told that if he wants to eat, they must either go outside or go to someone else's house. That is when the trouble starts. His reaction is so volatile and illogical. He will say something like, 'Oh, good, they will all be playing while I am inside', as if you are trying to force feed him. We quantify the position. 'Well, if you want to eat, everybody else has to go outside. That is not unreasonable.' By those very words you find yourself trying to justify your actions, even though you know you are right and you shouldn't be debating the situation. Either Maureen or I will then add that he doesn't stay in anyone else's house while they eat their lunch, dinner, tea, etc. Then comes the emotional twist. 'You don't want me to eat, you want me to starve, don't you?' The conversation now degenerates into a slanging match. 'Right, go upstairs to your room. Go on, I am not being spoken to like that.' William stands by the door in the kitchen. 'No, you can't make me.' I start screeching 'If you are not upstairs by the count of three, I will ring Cleveland Social Services.' This threat is of some benefit. He stamps on every step as he slowly wends his way upstairs. On one occasion, he turned to the dog whom he had met at about the half-way point. 'I wouldn't stay down there with them, you will catch something.' I stood at the bottom of the staircase yelling, 'Don't be so bloody rude.' The dog continued its way downstairs, quickly past me and out to the back garden. William trod the last few stairs and slammed the door of his bedroom, but not before he had added that downstairs was diseased and it was much better to be starving upstairs. The script is basically the same for all of his tantrums. The end scenario certainly is. For all his threats to leave home and never come back, he is still here. Perhaps the diseased ground floor isn't so unpalatable after all!

He is just about to break up for Christmas, having completed his first term at the new school. We had a word with his teacher at the parents' evening recently and she seems a lot happier now with regard to his behaviour. We both like her approach, friendly but firm. He started off by trying to create an impression and encouraging other children to misbehave. William was sent outside the classroom on a couple of occasions. His teacher told us that she had a short, sharp talk and reminded him of a few basic rules. Behave and join in the classroom activities, or stay outside in the corridor. He decided to toe the line – well, until he comes home anyway.

Amongst the many slips of paper and notes which he has

brought home from school during his first term, was one headed 'Super schools'. Photos of athletic stars donned both sides of the folded sheet, while at the bottom were the words 'DP fit for life'. I read the blurb, which informed the reader that super schools is a major fund-raising activity, designed to assist the country's talented children in their chosen sport. I am now aware that money is involved, parents' money. It goes on to say that the emphasis is on fun and enjoyment, rather than sporting excellence. The third paragraph spells out that DP stands for Diversified Products, who apparently are the world's largest suppliers of home fitness equipment. Open the cover, more photographs, a note from the Department of Education and Science saying how glad they are that super schools is operating, it then goes into the 'how does it work' spiel. The child takes part in exercises and sponsorship is invited with target levels, they state £1, £2, £3 amounts. Now here's the rub. Bearing in mind that all this is non-competitive, the reader learns that 'each child will receive a scroll of honour and a photograph taken with their visiting celebrity'. (In this school's case, Kriss Akabusi). Silly way of spelling Chris, but still.

To continue, 'The top fund raiser at your school will be awarded an additional prize' and 'the top fundraiser in each calendar month will receive a special award'. So it is no good competing for sport's sake, but it is perfectly all right for money's sake. Page 3 is the sponsorship form and the back page is lined out for sponsorship. You pay a 'voluntary contribution' that you feel obliged to pay for every school trip your children go on. Now, we are supposed to pay for all the budding Torvil and Deans as well.

You remember my friend who went on the Gender Awareness Course, well they have just received the letter promised to all participants with regard to the feedback sent to them. To be fair to the council, they haven't had a cover-up or flowered up the results. Basically they have admitted that many found the course poor and uninspiring. The comments have been negative, so the council has decided to cancel the remainder of the programme.

As I said earlier, that great annual farce is upon us once again. Everywhere you turn there are gaudy lights and faded bunting limply stretched from lamp-post to lamp-post, much of which has seen better days. Every advert features a sleigh hauled by the proverbial, with a waving, white-bearded, overweight oaf sitting amongst a veritable hoard of supposed goodies. The News Group, publishers of our local papers have Father Christmas in this guise, sliding across the white stuff, having apparently left a quaint timber-built village nestling amid the hills with a church spire as its centrepiece. The odd Christmas tree is peering out of the snow, on a presumably clear night, as there are stars a-plenty. There are no office blocks with 'To Let' signs, or pubs full of warring squaddies. There is no council estate with a queue of Gurkhas desperate to part with £5 for a quick shot at some slut with five sproggs – so it is not Aldershot, then.

I have turned to Page 2 of this Xmas handout, dubbed 'Camberley and District Christmas 1991, featuring Sandhurst and Crowthorne, Bagshot and Lightwater, Morecombe and...' It does sound like a music hall act to me. Under the heading? Yes, another Father Christmas. This time there is a photo of him waving from a sitting room – that's novel. He is surrounded by adverts and articles offering you bargains galore.

Page 3, another Santa with Ho, Ho, Ho printed around his head. Plus more of the same ads.

On page 4 we have a photo of a sledge, Santa, a pony and one of those equestrian ladies in drag with bowler hat – but there is no snow.

Page 5 gives us a full-page advert on behalf of 'Main Square Shopping Centre, Camberley – great gifts in store'. What a play on words that is, breathtaking in fact. Anyway, they wish us a Merry Christmas, which is nice of them and go on to make the point by illustrating a typical Edwardian upper-class family with one of the children holding a wooden rod, on the end of which hangs a lantern lit by candle.

And so it goes on. Every page is headed 'Merry Christmas Camberley' and there is even a photograph of London Road, Camberley, taken at night, showing the illuminations – there's hardly a car in sight. It certainly looks appealing, which just goes to show how deceptive a photograph can be.

I have turned to the 'What's On' pull-out supplement. Let's see what is in this. Well, at the Princess Hall, Aldershot, there is *Babes in the Wood*, starring Dave Lee Travis, so we won't be going to see that! He always comes over as a loud, self-opinionated, egotistical sort of chap, quite unlike me, of course! At Camberley's Civic Hall you can enjoy *Snow White and the Seven Dwarfs*. Not for me, but I am sure the seven dwarfs will enjoy Snow White. This production has Carol Lee Scott in its cast. She plays 'Grotbags' in some children's programme. I always like the way ad men state the name of the one series which made a particular actress or actor a star, even if there was no second run and it saw the light of camera fifteen years ago. Guildford's Civic Hall's offering is *Jack and the*

Beanstalk, starring Dame Hilda Bracket, some girl from *Neighbours* and a chap from TV's *Ghost-train*. No, neither of these inspire me. The Yvonne Arnaud Theatre, Guildford, are putting on *Dick Whittington*, dubbed 'this year's spectacular family panto'. Well, there are certainly a few well-known faces. Patrick Cargill, Dora Bryan, Jonathan Morris from Bread – they have got me at it now, and Louise English, whom I would watch in anything (preferably nothing, but that is wishful thinking!).

The Thorndike Theatre's production of *Cinderella* has more than its fair share of golden oldies – Rodney Bewes, Jess Conrad – thought he was dead – Liz Frazer and Annabelle Giles, who will balance the age scales.

No, I will save my money, although the television has only a few moments worth watching by the looks of things and they are all repeats. *Dad's Army, The Two Ronnies* and *Hi-de-Hi*. The only current comedies to have Specials are *Fools and Horses* and *Birds of a Feather*. Two shows which continue to produce a high standard. If past experience is anything to go by, Christmas versions of games shows always tend to be manic affairs, which leave you feeling let down. I believe there will be a *This Is Your Life* special, no doubt it will have Terry Waite as its subject. The very thought of it makes you wish your Christmas wishbone wish comes true and you sleep for a week. Oh, to wake up when it is all over and find they have counted all those days. No more partridges or maids-a-calling, no more false bonhomie, no more paying through the nose for paper that is ripped off without a second look and then deposited in the fire. All right, I will shut up now. I am expecting a customer to call who is looking for a car and he has been recommended – no, it is not that unusual! They are to be supplied with a AMPTDC. To those of you not lucky enough to have purchased a car from Yours Truly, the letters stand for an 'Anthony Mann Pleasure To Drive Car'. Mind you, what they want and what they get are not necessarily the same thing, but we all live in hope.

An hour has elapsed since I wrote the 'live in hope' bit, which seems to sum it all up really. I live in hope that they might arrive. Not a word, the car has been cleaned and hoovered. It is facing out of the drive, as its front end is tidier than its rear. The nearside is against the wall as that is the one with the off-colour panel. I have done it all according to the motor trade's guide – and no bugger turns up. Ah, well, we will carry on with this I think.

One sad piece of news received this month was the announcement of the death of actress Jill Browne, who made her name in *Emergency Ward 10* and promptly left it there. I was nine years of age when *E.W.10* started in 1957 and I think she was responsible for the first stirring in my loins. Sad that, and only 54 years of age.

Smiley face time now. Councillors in Gloucestershire want to see a ban on hunting over council-owned land. I have no doubt that the pressures on them to 'leave well alone', coupled with the tricks played by the pro-hunt lobby will be intense, but I do hope they stand firm and ban the obscenity. We are not just talking about the odd field here either, but 9,000 acres. That is a lot of land over which to gallop. The anti-hunt supporters, the goodies, have an uphill struggle, but I do feel that more and more people are becoming aware of the disgusting hobby, for it cannot be called a sport. That classification generally presides over an activity enjoyed by both sides, and in this case the pleasure factor is a little one-sided. The last thing most people want is a repeat of the situation we had earlier this year, when activists took revenge on a chap and his wife who were hunters, by literally trying to force them out of their house and having fights with the police, but I can well sympathise with their feelings of anger and frustration.

We have recently seen a film of a fox being dug out of its hole and handed to dogs for them to tear apart. This, of course, is termed 'entertainment'. Despite all newspaper reports that the Master of the Foxhunting Association will be looking into the accusations, I have no doubt that what the public are offered will turn out to be a sham. Nothing will change and any reprimands will be short-lived.

We learn that there is a movement within the church to ban hunting from its land. Now that is a few acres, 155,000 to be precise, or very nearly, anyway. What I don't understand is why the church should be one of the last major bastions for hunting to take place, killing for the sake of it is surely not condoned anywhere in their teachings. I suppose it is God's way of telling you that morality is the key word unless you can make a profit.

A couple of weeks ago... sorry about this, the phone's ringing... I shall have to answer it! It is only 30 seconds later and you have guessed, haven't you. It was the female half of the couple who went AWOL 'Oh, I am awfully sorry we didn't come over earlier, but my husband found a car on the way home, so... sorry... and, thanks for looking.' She couldn't get off the phone quick enough. He found one on the way home? Found what? She could not even be bothered to tell me what her husband had bought, if indeed he had bought anything. A couple of months ago, my local garage recommended a young lady to me who wanted a cheap runaround. She brought along her mum and dad, I showed them a Talbot Samba. They gave it the once-over, drove off to the bank, obtained a banker's draft and returned the same afternoon. They took possession of the car, drove off into the sunset and that was that. Last week, the same garage rang to say that they had a chap in the showroom who had £500 and what had I got? He came over, I showed him a couple of cars and explained the rules. He was white and over 21, so he had no problem in understanding that the warranty was to the garden gate, or 3 yards, whichever was the nearest. He fully accepted that, paid his money and went. Nice and clean.

A couple of weeks ago there was an article in the *Mail on Sunday* which referred to a caged fox found in a hunt's kennels in Hampshire. The hunt say the fox was planted, the league against cruel sports says otherwise. Frankly, I know who my money's on and it is not the hunt. Could you believe anyone who kills for fun?

There is so much sadness attached to animal welfare, isn't there? In June we bought a two-year-old mongrel bitch from the RSPCA in Chobham, Surrey. The little dog had apparently been dumped there as a puppy, taken away by a couple who had recently split up, and decided to hand her back again. She had only been in there for one day when we saw her. She is very much a Heinz 57 variety, black with tan markings. Her rear legs are slightly bowed and the back end doesn't seem to fit the front too well. As someone put it, rather unkindly I thought, it is a typical motor trader's dog, a cut and shut. For those of you not conversant with this term, it refers to two halves of different cars welded together, that eventually end up for sale as a one lady-owner car. That reminds me, my friend in the trade who comes out with the sayings, always tells his customers that the car has a 'titled' owner. This, of course, impresses the punter, as they usually nod to their other halves, indicating that they have a nose for class. Anyway, when they take a peek at the log book, they realise the title is Mr, Mrs, or Miss. Serves them right for being so easily impressed!

How did we get back to cars? Our visit to the RSPCA coincided with their obtaining a large number of beagles who had been involved in smoking and other experiments. I remember mentioning my disgust at this practice in *FWIS*, and received several letters sympathising with their plight. Well, at least the pressure brought to bear on the laboratories by various pressure groups paid off in this case. Many of these poor animals are going to see out a large portion of their lives in completely different surroundings.

It was in September 1989 that the headlines read '79 Beagle Pups in Sauna of Death'. The dramatic scribings did not over state the plight of these and many other animals, destined for a life in torturous pain. I remember that *Today* newspaper played a large part in bringing this obscenity to the public's notice. These dogs had never seen the light of day, never encountered human affection, never seen a blade of grass or chewed on a bone. The 400 seized by the RSPCA are lucky, but successive British governments still license establishments like the one concerned here. They still accept that animals should be used for experiments and it brings not one iota of comfort when you consider that an estimated 12,000 dogs are still used by laboratories, 95% of which are beagles.

The days seem to be fairly cantering along towards Christmas. Every time you turn on the weather forecast, you can be sure of two things. Sian Lloyd will be wearing something totally unsuitable and she, or one of her ilk, will be dismissing the possibility of a white Christmas, but of course, there could just be a smattering of snow – or rain – or sunshine – must keep all the options open!

So, what else was there to look back on? Well, the environment didn't come off too well again, in common with all other years of course. Lord Palumbo won his battle to replace eight listed buildings with a modernistic complex. This sort of decision makes a mockery of listed building status, but then we are talking money, not architecture. The other side of the coin concerned the publication of the plans to rebuild Paternoster Square in London. Again, a demolition site would be preferable to the blocks that currently sit, uncomfortably, awaiting their fate. The idea of having lanes and streets in random fashion with buildings constructed on traditional and historical lines is exciting indeed. I just hope the scheme isn't watered down by the glass and concrete merchants who, no doubt, would like 'another two or three storeys to make the venture profitable'. These extra 'two or three' always turn out to be more. No, if the idea is left to those whose motives are not centred on greed, we might have a chance of restoring some of London's skyline to a standard not only acceptable but engaging and beautiful.

You know, it is not just the 'big' projects which are important. All over the country, there are people trying to save something. During the summer, I read of a couple, Niki Barrett and Simon

Holden, who were doing their best to stand guard, 24 hours a day, over a tiny plant. Somewhere in deepest Oxfordshire, in what is termed an ancient meadow, this couple made sure that collectors (vandals) did not steal a very rare plant – the monkey orchid. Yes, Messrs Barrett and Holden were being paid for their security services, but it takes a fair amount of commitment to live for a few months in a caravan without electricity, in an effort to establish the seeding of this plant. No electricity, huh. No Ulrika Jonssen, no hostage homecomings, no Sandy Gall dressed as a Shi-ite fundamentalist...

Like every other facet of life the Thatcher years have forced upon us, I see that National Trust land and the Nation Parks are being marketed. The aim is to increase the number of visitors, which, in turn, will increase the contributions to the coffers. I bet a lot of people's conception of these beauty spots naïvely presupposes that a particular area is protected from all man's assaults. It seems such a shame that 'selling the product' accounts for 3½ times more money than that which is spent on the management of the land.

An innovative plan to recreate a green England has been proposed. This would include restoration of public footpaths and bridleways. New buildings erected would have to be in keeping with traditional materials and where possible, power lines would be buried. It will be interesting to see if the scheme gets off the ground. I just hope it doesn't die, like Richard Branson's big clear-up.

In Crookham and Church Crookham 'villages', which are close to Fleet, Hampshire – and getting closer by the development – a whole copse has recently been lost under 650 houses. For those of you in Eccles or Cleckheaton, Hampshire is a county in southern England, next to Surrey. Another area of farmland has been made available for the obligatory community centre, which should encourage the growth of vandalism, graffiti and litter, not to mention glue-sniffing, drug-taking and anything else that ultimately leads to Aids. What used to be a farm is now earmarked for 49 houses and flats. The good news is that this creates more wealth for the local council, by virtue of the poll tax – bastards!

Strangely enough, this next little piece comes from 'up there', where motorways are cobbled, and milkfloats carry shotguns. Bootle, to be precise. An interesting article in the People recently summed it all up. The Mersey Docks and Harbour Company, who used to ship in commodities from all over the world, it now houses shipments of cheap imported coal. This comes all the way from

North America and Columbia, and is used to fuel a power station. At the moment between one and two million tons are unloaded, but it could rise to six million tons. This is, of course, at the expense of British pits and the health of local people who have suffered dramatically due to the polluted air from the coal dust, but at least there is the comfort of knowing a lot of people have made substantial financial gain.

I wasn't aware of this, but the government, some few years ago, decided to sell off state-owned historical properties. One, Heveningham Hall, built in 1752, was sold to an Iraqi, and has seen little by way of restoration. The hall has been looted and is suffering from fire damage. The middle-eastern owner has since died. The government has an option to buy back the property, but has declined to do so. Heveningham Hall will now go on sale to the highest bidder, who, like the last chap, may do nothing with it. A picture, accompanying the article, shows how beautiful a building it is. Bet it becomes a mosque.

A couple of amusing snippets have appeared over the last couple of days. One concerned a heading in our local paper, which read, 'Youth stole because of a hole in his sock'. The little toe-rag (double-groan) went into a sports shop with some friends and complained about a pair of trainers. After an argument, he left, the alarm sounded and he was caught with the offending pair of socks. His defence said, 'He saw some socks and knowing his own pair had a hole in them, he took the others while the staff were out the back dealing with the trainers.' He had already admitted stealing food and drink earlier in the day. His defence asked for a sentence to be passed which would help curb future petty pilfering, so instead of cutting off both hands, he was conditionally discharged for six months and ordered to pay £25 costs. As the oik was living on unemployment benefit, probably because he was unemployable, it appears that we, the taxpayer, have paid his £25 for him. How the rest of his sentence is going to 'curb his petty pilfering', Heaven only knows. I couldn't see the relevance myself.

The other story concerned a court, but this one contained itself to 'our side of the fence'. As a court official said, 'This could be straight out of Rumpole.' It is somewhat unusual for a juror to be dismissed for 'interference' but that is exactly what happened at the Old Bailey. The juror, middle-aged and nicely spoken, continued to send notes to the Bench. By the second day of the case, the other members of the jury had got so fed up with his behaviour, they asked if he could be removed –

and he was. It must have been a hoot, the case was proceeding and this chap kept arguing points of law with the judge. At one stage, the judge said, 'I am the judge and the point you raised is irrelevant.' Our thick-skinned friend retorted, 'Well, I think it is relevant.' The court officials apparently thought they might be in for trouble when he turned up on the first day with a cushion and complained about the break being too short.

I would have given a lot of the Midland Bank's money to have witnessed that little exhibition. You wouldn't want that sort of cove as a neighbour, but it is nice to know that someone else has and that his sort are still alive and bucking the system. Just hope he never tries to buy a car from me!

The Christmas festivities are really upon us now. *Songs of Praise* has just finished. It was presented by Debbie Thrower and Alan Titchmarsh, the gardening chappie. Making 'guest' appearances were Gavin Campbell, Gloria Hunniford, Wendy Craig and Kathy Staff, all of whom had a chance to plug their fizzoggs. How many times have I heard Kathy Staff tell the TV audience that she sings in a choir. Now that strikes a chord, so to speak. One choir had a young boy singing a solo section. I sat there imagining all the paedophiles turning up the volume and positively salivating over the screen – and he was dressed in uniform, too! There was a worrying number of adult male choristers sporting glasses and beards – some of them looking decidedly suspect, especially those with balding heads.

I have now delivered as many books as I can to W.H. Smith, Hammicks, etc. so now it is down to the likes of you. Thinking about it, though, if you didn't like *FWIS*, you are not likely to be reading this, are you?

Our local butchers are displaying their usual seasonal bunting. They are also wearing reindeer ears and red noses. On one of their meat cabinets, an employee-cum-artist has applied white spray to templates of angels. They look more like the grim reaper to me.

We are expecting my parents down tomorrow, Christmas Eve. They will no doubt have stopped off at a relative's house for a little seasonal cheer and an exchange of cards, etc. on the way, before arriving laden to the gunwales with goodies for the family, at about 8 pm.

I have just heard a good joke. Question: What do the letters DNA stand for? Answer: National Association of Dyslexics.

You can tell I am bored, can't you. I am sitting here in my office looking round my desk at the many unmade models of railway coaches and wagons that have sat on the shelves for months. Alongside them are several magazines which I have bought and have yet to read, the enthusiasm does not seem to be there at the moment. The lack of money especially at this time of year when the financial pressures are at their zenith, really tend to demoralise you.

I have just been flicking through the telephone directory. I spied what I thought was an entry for a Mr or Mrs Rape Crisis, but it turned out to be an advice centre. Frankly, I was surprised to find it wasn't double-barrelled. There are, however, quite a few coves and covesses called 'Raper'.

The 'S' entries seem to have quite a few good examples of names you would be pleased not to be lumbered with. You could be a member of the select breed of 'Scoggins', or the even more select 'Scoggings'. There is a solitary 'Scroggs', quite a few 'Secretts', a 'Secular', a 'Shackcloth' and also a single 'Shafto' with the initial 'R', he could even be a Bobby. Strange how common names beginning with 'S', like Singleton, Sewell and Sillitoe have an 'H' inserted to produce 'Shingleton', 'Shewell' and 'Shillitoe'. I suppose there must have been a large number of people around with speech impediments, or maybe they were (or are) Sean Connery admirers.

On one page of the Guildford Directory, you can literally go from 'Ship' to 'Shore', taking in a plethora of 'Shoe' type coves. There is 'Shoebridge', 'Shoesmith', 'Shoobridge' and 'Shooter'. One of the 'Shore' entries is a Group Captain – there's posh. I love this one, and there is only one, 'Shuffelbottom'. Mind you, 'Snoddy', 'Snowball' and 'Snuggs' are fascinating examples of the unfortunate. There are a few that could be readily attributed to estate agents and solicitors – not car dealers though, you understand. 'Sly', 'Shady', 'Smoothey', 'Snark' are but four. Then again, you could have ended up a 'Squelch' or a 'Squibb'.

There are not many double-barrels, although one that took my fancy concerned the 'Soper-Dyers', which account for six entries. All these good folk hail from Basingstoke, which is not so good, except for one who resides in beautiful downtown Whitchurch. I can hear the cry being elicited at the local gymkhana now, 'Oh, so you are one of the Basingstoke Soper-Dyers. How nice to meet you.'

Mentioning solicitors reminds me of an event that occurred recently. I decided I needed to write a letter to the Chairman of a bank. I made an appointment at a local solicitors, with a view to getting help in drafting the said epistle. Working on the theory that you only get one bite of the cherry, I wanted to make sure that it was succinct and to the point.

The receptionist at the solicitors asked me the purpose of my visit. I explained and she gave me a time for early the following day. Within an hour of this phone call, the solicitor I was to see rang back and asked a few questions about the case, adding that he would like me to bring along the relevant files. I thought then that as a bank was involved, the old juices were working overtime in anticipation of a David versus Goliath court case.

The following day, at the appointed time, I sat in the solicitor's office, explaining the history of the case. I remember asking at the end of the conversation if he had all the relevant information necessary to form the basis of a worthy letter, to be sent to the Chairman of one of the high street banks. The solicitor enquired as to whether he might keep the file for a couple of days as he wanted to go through them more fully. I had, by the way, previously informed him of my first solicitor's advice, where he concluded by saying that if I was to get anywhere, I would have to take the bank to court.

Our learned friend said he would get back to me, but if I had not heard within a couple of days, I was to ring him. You have guessed. After three days I rang, he wanted to see me. With hopes high, I made my way to his offices. We shook hands and I sat down in eager anticipation. He stated that he had read through the various files and that there was little he could do, unless I took the bank to court – and that he didn't see much point in a letter. I was not that impressed, the only help I had asked for was in drafting the bloody letter in the first place. He said he would send me a bill shortly. He did. £125 plus VAT. I rang and complained. He was very courteous and explained that sifting through files took time and basically time equalled money, but he would reduce the total by £25, as an act of good faith.

I pondered the situation – I was still not impressed. In fact, I was completely underwhelmed. I wrote a second letter to the senior partner, who confirmed that his associate had acted properly and fairly and I should pay up. I did not, and subsequently received a court summons for me to appear within the month at Aldershot Court. The amount required had now been increased back to the original £125 plus VAT, plus court costs and more solicitors' time, making a new total of £175 plus VAT. As it was a small claim, the case was heard, not inappropriately, in a small claims court,with a presiding registrar. I arrived in the waiting room and the usher informed me of a few facts about what to do and where to go. I looked at the list on the wall to see how far down my case was situated. Judging from the number to be heard, most of them concerning repossessions and petty cases, I was not pleased with the standard of clientele with whom I was sharing the waiting room. Most of those attending sported earrings and ponytails and carried bangle-bedecked babies, dressed in attire suitable for the modern-day gypsy camp. Their lurchers and alsatians were no doubt ensconced in an untaxed pick-up that would be lurking on a yellow line somewhere seedy. As you know, I am not biased!

I sat as far away from these people as I could. In fact, the only gleam of middle-class light which appeared came in the shape of my opponent, who entered clutching his briefcase. He spied me from across the room and sat opposite. Group by group, the benefit-laden oiks from the lower orders left to await their fate – usually another chance – smugly aware that whatever the financial implications, the law-abiding citizen would be picking up the tab. We were then alone in this waiting room. It was a bit like *High Noon*. Actually, it was nothing like *High Noon*, but I want to impress on you the dramatic aspect of it all! My adversary laid his briefcase upon his leg, flicked open the two catches and extracted a wad of paperwork from within. As he made what appeared to be copious notes, he occasionally looked in my direction, almost staring through me. At these little intermissions, he would tap his pen against his chin. I felt he had stolen a psychological march over me by at least two points. I retaliated by opening my case and removing from it a folder, which I held open at such an angle, so that its contents remained unseen by prying legal eyes. The folder contained several blank sheets of paper, and the current edition of *Railway Magazine* – which you won't be interested to learn has been purchased by my father and myself since January 1946 without fail. That last piece you have to read aloud (and again) in true 'soppy voice' railway-enthusiast style. Actually, just impersonate John Major and you are there. He sounds for all the world like a 'gricer' that frequented the ramp area of the longest platforms at Waterloo during the early sixties. Although in J.M.'s case he would have been standing at Brixton Station, I suppose.

Where was I? Oh, yes. The usher called out our names, we responded, and appeared very speedily before the registrar, who bade us sit down. The tables were arranged in a U fashion, that is a top table, where the registrar sat, with two sprigs jutting off, causing us to face each other. 'I have read the case, Mr Mann,' said the registrar as an opening gambit. 'Are you prepared to pay the sum asked for?' 'No, I am not,' I replied. He continued, 'Are you prepared to make an offer?' 'Yes,' I said. '£25.' The registrar looked towards the solicitor, who was still making notes, and asked if this offer was acceptable. The said legal eagle shook his head and stated that his practice required the full amount. 'Right,' said the registrar, 'I have to ask both parties in case there is some common ground at which we might arrive amicably. However...' he tailed off. He then asked various questions of me, during which time I stated that when I originally rang, I emphasised the fact that I was without funds and that all I wanted was a letter, which was not forthcoming. I added that at no time was I informed of any charge for his taking files home.

After about 20 minutes and some prodding about the work ethics of the solicitor's practice, our learned friend's case was in tatters. Why had he not informed me of the costs at the outset? Why had he not told me that his practice was on the Green Card scheme, which would have benefited me? This scheme allows a solicitor to give up to half an hour's advice for £10. Why, indeed, had he not done as I had asked and drafted me a letter? The registrar ended his summing up by adding that he thought the solicitor saw a potentially long-running case, until he realised the problems that could be involved and then basically abandoned it – and me. The registrar then sat back and said that he thought my offer of £25, plus VAT of course, was very fair in the circumstances and asked if I could pay the bill within fourteen days. I concurred, he bade us farewell and we left together, walking along the corridor towards the lifts. The solicitor spoke first. 'Ah well,' he said, 'you win some and you lose some.' We got into the lift and I offered my hand, he offered his foot (it was a fair exchange). He didn't really. It is an old Goons joke from an LP I still possess, but it was the only place I could slip it in, as they say. We shook hands and descended to the ground floor, where we emerged unscathed from the jaws of social workers and other unemployed persons. Into the sunlit street we strode and made our way up Victoria Road, towards the town centre. I spoke. 'I have got to collect my car from the bodyshop.' 'Have you had an accident?' asked my companion. 'Oh, no,' I replied, 'what with the cost of court cases I have had to cut out car parks and scrounge parking space from friends.' He smiled and said that he had to go to the cash point for some money. I countered by saying that had he won, he wouldn't have needed to go. We shook hands once more and walked in our respective directions.

Now that is the way a dispute should be handled. No bad feelings, no threats, no nastiness. He even had the courtesy to wish me well in my quest for justice – and financial compensation. No, good English phlegm won the day. Mind you, if I had lost... It was, of course, a hollow victory. I had much rather have paid out the £175 and received the £40,000 this case has now cost me, including interest.

Well, that was a long story, wasn't it. Since I have finished, we have wrapped our presents, placed them under the tree and surprise, surprise, the Taiwanese lights are still bright, despite the tree falling over. The angel has, as usual, been stuffed – and I do mean stuffed – on the very pinnacle of this pine-dropping, seasonal rip-off. She sits astride the uprisen stem, legs outspread, like a squaddie mistress on Para Day.

I suppose I must subconsciously be pleased that there is going to be a break from all this depression – well, it is depressing. I think Maureen has got me a model coach for Christmas. I bet an LNER Thompson 1st Class corridor coach in BR maroon is on the top of many a rugged male's present list. You don't think so? Well, you could be right but it doesn't seem so, a Christmas without an addition to the coaching stock. I just hope I haven't spent more on Maureen than she's spent on me. No, I mustn't think like that. I wonder if I have, though...

I found myself singing *I'm Going to be Strong*, the old Gene Pitney hit, in the shower room this morning. The rendition was slightly marred by the fact that I had a mouth full of toothpaste at the time. I am still trying to fathom out why I'm so happy. It must be the fact that in three days' time this exploited affair will be over and done with for another year.

Definitely got to give some serious thought to presents. Maureen has asked for some suggestions, but the majority I made were improper, and anyway, all the spare batteries have been packed up with William's remote-control car!

Maureen has shown me a list of names with suggested presents pencilled in against them, or if the present has been purchased – penned in. Mum A, Dad A, Mum B, Dad B, etc. I am using pseudonyms, as they don't want to be identified with the book. Well, would you? They mentioned something about holding a certain station amongst their peers and always getting on well with neighbours. I suppose it is indicative of our marriage, but Maureen has not read *FWIS* yet. She is working on the theory that if there are any knocks on our door, she can genuinely say that she knows nothing about their complaint. As if I would let her take flak from a stranger who is being abusive. As if.

Yes, we have made provision for everyone. The mums have got petticoats, plant pots, oven gloves and aprons – all the imaginative type of gifts. Car accessories and railway books for the dads, pottery objects that serve no real purpose, other than to clutter up cupboards twelve days after Christmas have been purchased for Maureen's sisters. We have got jumpers and after-shave for Glyn, a video and animal-free tested make-up for Debbie. William has a *Beano Annual*, a *Broons Annual*, several Transformers, a magic set and a video to look forward to. The dog does very well. She has got some giant bones, chocolate drops, a squeaky toy and a rubber ball.

I am writing this as I wait for Maureen to find one or two things, then it is off to the butcher's to collect the turkey. No doubt we will buy up all the vegetables as if there is no tomorrow and then we will trail around Sainsburys to double up on what we bought in Asda yesterday, just in case.

As usual, Maureen's mum, dad and sisters will be coming for Christmas afternoon and evening, so there will be a full house for a few hours of riotous fun and frolics. Maureen has now purchased all the prizes for 'Bingo'. She has also... I had better go, I have just been summoned.

It is now 11.15 am. Back again. Everything is covered now. We have got the turkey, the vegetables and the aforementioned duplicate pickles, etc. Eighty-four cards and that is not including the ones which William received at school. We must have handed out at least ten ourselves! Next year, when we are hopefully better off, we will send them and with a bit of luck the recipient will have forgotten this blank year when we did not reciprocate. No doubt the second-class stamp will be 20 pence by next Christmas. We have actually got two Christmas cards left. These were found lurking at the bottom of the box, without envelopes. One has a Christmas tree standing in front of what appears to be a Russian Orthodox Church. The card's greeting message says, 'Warm wishes to you at Christmas'. You open the card, to read the following.

'You're thought of more
Warmly Than you'd ever
guess. And wished for
more joy Than These
words can express...
And so it is a pleasure
When Christmas is here

To say 'hope you're
happy Today – and all
year'. Merry Christmas!
Happy New Year.

Who would want to receive a card with that crap, it is nearly as
bad as reading this book – all those capitals in the wrong place. I
know, it is just like reading the first book! .

The second card has a one-eyed, red-nosed snowman, sporting
a hat with holly on it. He is standing amid the falling snow with
a backdrop of blue sky. Curiously, around the snowman's neck
are two bells and a sock. On the ground, about to be buried,
is a shovel and a single shoe. So, we have a card showing a
one-legged, one-eyed, inebriated snowman and I can't find one
support group listed in the yellow pages. The cover greeting in
this case reads:

Know who thinks you're as nice as can be?
(Turn the page) 'This jolly and cute holiday snowman –
                    And me! MERRY
CHRISTMAS!

They must have been printed in Korea (or Billericay).

Hard as I try, I still cannot buy the story they keep spouting out
every Christmas. If there is a God, I presume he is a shareholder in
the retail industry. It all seems so far-fetched. I mean, how dos a
virgin give birth? Was she a hermaphrodite? The son of God dies,
three months later he gets better. Religious buffs are very similar
to railway buffs. Catholics think of their religion as being the only
true faith. The Church of England feel the same about theirs and
so it goes on. They often berate the beliefs of smaller orders, who
is to say that a small group of American Red Indians who follow
a handful of Gods are not the ones who are actually correct. It
is the arrogance which infuriates me. Leaving aside those who
have heard voices – and, in my opinion, that is the prime time
for having them locked up – nobody's actually seen one of these
Gods. There seems to be a greater chance of a discredited city
banker being innocent than there being a supreme creator in the
religious sense.

If the doubt doesn't get you, the hypocrisy will. Phrases like 'At
this time of the year we pray for all our fellow human beings who
are suffering.' They mean that the prayers extend to all sufferers
provided they are of the same faith. I am always intrigued by the

comments made by bishops when referring to a particular priest whose homosexuality has come to the fore within the media. 'Oh, yes,' our good bishop ponders, 'we know he lives with another man and that he is a confessed homosexual, but providing he remains celibate and abides by the rules, he will be supported by the hierarchy.' Well, of course, he will. He has slept with most of them!

Funnily enough, I can cope with all the obsessions, neuroses and crass stupidity which go with religious belief, because as I said earlier, by being an atheist I feel totally cleansed of the whole sordid affair. It is all the little things, daily incidences, that I find lack credibility. How is it that Myra Hindley, whose crimes are well documented, will be helping to deliver Holy Communion to other prisoners tomorrow – Christmas Day. She will stand beside a priest in the jail chapel. Can you imagine what the parents of the children who suffered at her hands must be thinking. Their children were taken away from them in such a vile way, that the names Hindley and Brady will be with them every second of every day. For them it is a true life sentence, far more painful than for those two cocooned in prison. Where was God when these and other children needed him?

What was I saying about Sunday trading? Surprise, surprise, all the large stores have announced their intention to retain seven-day-a-week opening in the new year. The government continues to play down the argument, but I remain convinced that their lack of action is setting a dangerous precedent. Sir Patrick Mayhew, the Attorney General, has stated that it would be inappropriate for him to take action against firms breaking the Shops Act. 'Ministerial sources', whoever they are, add that the government is not unduly embarrassed by the supermarkets' defiance, well, of course, they are not. A lot of money comes into party funds from the profits of Greedy Bastard PLC. They are friends, influential friends, ones you can rely on when you quit political life – or it quits you. Those boardroom offers are most tempting.

Next in line is the humble Mrs Rumbold, minister without responsibility, apparently. Being a female, you would have thought she would have had her ears to the ground at the sharp end, but no, she doesn't appear to wash her hands in any dirty water. She says that the government will not tamper with the 1950s Shops Act, all the while there is a possibility that Britain was breaching the European free trade principles. Now that is a good word – principles. There seem to be less of them here than in the Guinness trial. This sort of farce reduces the elected national government to the status of local authority – which probably sums up the limit of ability those elected can raise themselves to, and that would most probably be when there was a brown envelope in it for them.

Another area of law that I am amazed has not been tightened relates to that which governs squatting. Actually, I shouldn't be surprised. Protection of the law-abiding citizen comes a long way down the list. Twelve years this government has been in power. Surely that is long enough to form committees, discuss the problems, review the existing laws and loopholes and start to play fair with owners of properties who are discriminated against, in favour of the ne'er-do-well. I imagine that the left-wing element are cock-a-hoop with the present system that allows jobless oiks to feed themselves, clothe themselves, inject themselves... and all at our expense, not forgetting light and heat. Usually they manage to obtain gas and electricity by giving false names and then up sticks without paying the bill, leaving that little incidental to the likes of you and I, who will find it incorporated into the price paid for every therm and 'whatsit'. This is, of course, much the same as the poll tax, where the non-payer is supported by higher bills paid by those who adhere to the law. How on earth the law can protect squatters from owners wishing to evict them is beyond me. The owner has to take squatters to the civil courts. Around 11,000 actions have been taken this year, so the solicitors, as usual, do very nicely thank you. To add insult to injury, there is a legal organisation in North London, where else, called the Advisory Service for Squatters, who sell a handbook aimed at helping squatters get as much as they can out of the system, for contributing the least. You can even ring this service. Presumably you look in Yellow Pages under 'Scumhire'. They offer a recorded message, telling you how to obtain all the facilities and give you advice on what to do, should the police be involved. Not least of course, they give you the names of friendly solicitors. You can bet they don't live in a squat!

Isn't it sad, I have just been reading about a girl of 17 who beat her 80-year-old aunt to death with an axe and then robbed her. She has been ordered to be detained for life, not surprisingly. The reason for this act of murder? She wanted to be a model and needed money for cosmetic surgery. You despair, don't you. It would be interesting to know more about her home life and upbringing.

I wonder if the BBC and ITV actually know there is an audience out there. A few years ago they pensioned off Kenneth Kendall, Richard Baker and a couple of others from the 'News' because they wanted 'younger newsreaders'. The news is still read in the same way. The staff they brought in were not inferior, but was the move necessary in the first place? I cannot help thinking that there is a lot of change for change's sake. Earlier this year, Anne Gregg was relieved of her duties on the 'Holiday' programme. Why? They wanted someone younger again. They chose Anneka Rice, who is not even in the same league.

Four days ago, David Jacobs played his last record on Radio 2. Like Anne Gregg, he was one of the best in the market. The BBC are no different from the government in this respect, they make decisions, telling us they know what we want and what is best for us. Look what happened to Margaret Thatcher.

Well, this is it. 8 pm. My parents will be here soon. William is in the vexed state of being hyperactive, while trying to remain a 'good boy'. It is like putting together magnets of opposite polarity, not easy.

Glyn has gone around to his girlfriend's but will be back later, whilst Deborah, who could always be relied upon to stay in and babysit, now seems to want a life of her own. From the lovely little girl who kept herself amused, usually by rearranging her bedroom, she has changed considerably since she has got the boyfriend. The wings are beginning to flap. I was telling my religious friend (R.F.) about the boyfriend. I explained that he appeared to come from a good home, he didn't drink alcohol, and he followed her home in his car in case she broke down in her Mini. I added that he was also quite religious and did not believe in sex before marriage. Similar to me, really, except for the religion and sex before marriage. I believed in it, I just didn't get any. R.F. said that I was surrounded by Christians, which made me feel uneasy. He pointed out that it was nice for my daughter to be going out with someone who valued her for what she was. I smiled, and concurred with his view. However, he brought me back down to earth with his observation. Having said that, when we were that age, all we wanted to do was to get our hands up their skirts in the least possible time and at the least possible expense. Yup, those were the days of exploits that always happened to others and you had to listen about them the following day at school. So, Debbie and Rob are out tonight at a Midnight Mass, so she will be home about 1am. After all I have taught my children about religion and she goes out with someone who goes to carol services – where have I gone wrong?

Well, it really is time to sign off for a couple of days. There are headlights shining in the drive and I can hear the tappits of my father's car. I assume it is my father's car, it could be some irate cove who has come to retrieve the card they sent because they are upset at not receiving one from us. I can hear voices, it is definitely Mum and Dad. So, it is Merry Christmas to all of you who bought the book and sod the rest of you!

Just waved goodbye to the parents. To be honest, it was a very pleasant Christmas. We did the same things as most families, I guess. We ate well and drank well. The kids did well, as usual. I got my coach, two jumpers, the obligatory socks and the even more obligatory Old Spice. I only blotted my copybook once with my parents, as far as I know. Debbie and Rob came back for coffee on Christmas Eve. When they arrived home from the Midnight Mass I was out taking the dog for a walk. On my journey around the block, I passed two policemen standing near the church at the top of our road. I assumed they were waiting to pounce on any drug-pushers, or those committing acts of indecent behaviour. I thought the latter was a trait of all church-goers and, as you know, it is not like me to make sweeping, unsubstantiated statements! All I said when the dog and I returned home was the situation as I had interpreted it, and that the place was awash with God Botherers. Only an innocent remark, I felt. Mum and Dad's faces were set in disdain. 'You shouldn't say that sort of thing when Debbie has her boyfriend here, and him a church-goer.' I replied that it was my house and I could say what I wanted. That cut no ice with my parents. I tried explaining that despite Rob's misguided and naïve views, I still liked him and treated him as an equal. My father accused me of being extremely pompous, condescending and arrogant. Cut to the quick, I was. I thought I was demonstrating my tolerance – apparently not.

The rest of the holiday went off without any fuss and I am now sitting in my office writing this and eyeing my stock book, which tells me that I have sold just three cars during December. A diesel Orion, an Escort and a Panda. In short, we have a Montego Estate with a dodgy gearbox – but if you are a member of the public, it's fine – they are all like that. There's a black Panda which I bought at the end of November and I still can't shift it. I paid my bodywork man £150 to tidy up the paintwork, but it still looks a heap of crap. It is not that what he has done is substandard, it is the fact that the car is basically as rotten as a pear, and in less than two months, it is all starting to 'bubble' again. Well, it is a Panda. The only other car on the books is a Metro, which we are using because it is taxed. You know, that little addition to the windscreen weighs very heavily with me. So that is it, stock to the value of £2,600 and an overdraft of £15,000. Sounds about right, doesn't it?

One good thing happened over Christmas. The number of dogs brought into Battersea Dogs' Home was only 86 for the three-day period. Perhaps people are getting the message about buying pets as presents without realising the consequences of an unwanted gift.

One facet of our lives that has continued on a downward slope has been race relations. It has been smouldering away for years, coming to a head occasionally and then dying down until the embers are fuelled the next time. Brixton, Tottenham, St Pauls, Toxteth, spring to mind, and there will be more. It will always remain just beneath the surface, all the while successive governments attempt to cover over the cracks without getting to the nub of the problem. I appreciate it is a lot easier not to bother. The attitude seems to be in line with that of local authorities when it comes to moving on travellers. As long as they are out of your patch, it is all right. Like everything else in this country, decisions are made only for the short term. Governments are basically gutless, the last thing they want is to bring a controversial subject out into the open. It would be nice, however, if someone in authority thought about asking the indigenous population of this country for their views. What do they think of the race laws, the CRE, our immigration and refugee policy? The CRE might just find that there are an awful lot of people out there who have no axe to grind with coloured people, their argument is with the do-gooders, who appear to champion the 'rights' issues that do not leave them equal with whites, but with an advantage. Positive discrimination as they like to call it.

In March this year, which has only got a few hours left, one daily paper printed an article about Britain's first black QC. The headline reads, 'Be a shop girl, said teacher'. There have been hundreds of pupils over the years who have defied their teachers' expectations and suggestions, taking the bull by the horns and making it to the top. Because this young lady is black, the article and photograph take up a quarter of a page. She and her nine brothers and sisters became part of the first black family in Walthamstow, apparently. You might have expected the article to comment on parents who had ten children and the financial burden placed on taxpayers to support them, but, no. Our newly appointed QC says that there was some prejudice when she first entered the law and there is still a lot of change required, well, there would be. The article goes on to say that fourteen years after she was first called to the bar, the legal profession is still dominated by white, middle-class men. Is that such a surprise? I would query it if it wasn't. Now we come to the crux of the matter. 'Only six per cent of the total 7,306 barristers are from ethnic minorities and only 1,040 are female.' This sort of article always angers me. It is not that it is biased, it is what it sets out to do. Am I supposed to feel embarrassed or guilty that there isn't an equal number of black or Asian QCs, not to mention an equal number of women? Am I supposed to be shocked by the 6% figure? I think they should have sold the space to advertisers.

Here's a short article printed a few days later, Hackney Council are running an advertisement in a local paper, asking, 'Are you a lesbian of Afro-Caribbean descent? Have you experienced a loss or a bereavement? Are you missing someone special? If so, then this six-week course may be for you!' Hackney, whose poll-tax payers are financing the above farce, said it would introduce courses for white people some time in the future. So where is the equality in that?

That piece of enlightening bias came shortly before details were announced that an 'Ethnic Communities Development Officer' had been appointed by the Scouts. The officer, a Ms Ross, will no doubt manage to do what years of scouting has failed to attain and that is to segregate children of different backgrounds and of different colours so that everyone must think about their own origins and disown the white, middle-class christian (with a small 'c') teachings. I expect this Ms will be happy when there are a number of packs exclusively Muslim, with their own promises, a number of packs for Afro-Caribbean who can be patronised by her kind, while the honest endeavours of traditional scout leaders, whose only rewards are the satisfaction and development of those in their care, come a very poor second. No doubt they will be relegated to assistants, due to their poor grasp of equal opportunities and lack of knowledge concerning colonialism, slavery, etc. They can't leave anything alone, can they.

The end of April brought the Rev. Al Shapton and his minders to our shores, where they criticised this country and its white population. At least he went home.

September was to be a bleak month for racial bias. It was the turn of Everton Football Club to get the boot. They have only had one full-time black player on their books. That makes for bias apparently. The critics ignored the fact that the club have been unsuccessful in their recent attempts to sign some black players. That, of course, wouldn't make good reading and would only serve to weaken an already weak case and they wouldn't want that. I have no doubt that Everton are just like any other club, wanting the best players available, regardless of colour. Are we to impose a minimum number of black players in each team? What about Asian players, they seem to be very few and far between. Does the blame for this lie in the hands of a racially-biased white population as well?

At about the same time, it was also the turn of the hotel industry to come under scrutiny for a cheap story. The dear old CRE, luv 'em, commissioned a survey – when don't they – and came to the conclusion that the hotel industry was failing to recruit sufficient ethnics for their liking. Frankly, unless the percentage of black workers was 100% ethnic they wouldn't be satisfied. Actually, that wouldn't do either, as the industry would be accused of attracting black workers because of the low wages it offers, so they can't win. In a survey of 117 hotels in Britain, none kept records of the ethnic origin of staff or job applicants. Why should they. More paperwork, just to satisfy that group of smug bastards.

Chairman Michael Day, so that is where he went, said the industry needed to increase the number of managers and skilled workers from ethnic minorities and to liaise with schools and colleges to encourage more youngsters to consider hotel work as a career. Why? Surely a hotel should go for the best applicant regardless of colour – not a little unlike Everton FC. Still, the good and knowledgeable Chairman said the CRE would be advising major hotel groups of a programme of action and I have no doubt it will. The power these bastards have is frightening.

The harm done to society by the CRE, the Ms Ross's and others with a 'coloured conscience' is well illustrated by the following story. A lady teacher, an Asian incidentally, not one of those awful white people, called one of her pupils 'a little monkey'. You, the reader, were doubtless described in those terms at school, or in the home by your parents when you were young. But that was 'before'. The mother of this child, who incidentally is single and has two other children and lives on state benefit (just thought you would like to know that) attacked the teacher. She hit her in the face, punched her in the chest, pulled off her glasses and smashed them against the wall. That, of course, is a great advertisement for parental understanding and tolerance. No 'let us sit down and talk this thing through.' Not of course that there was anything to discuss in the first place. Oh, no, an inoffensive saying that has been with us for years is taken completely out of context, the affair blown up out of all proportion and the only winners are the flag wavers for ethnic advancement. Some advance, you really need that kind of behaviour in front of a classroom full of children. Still, without the CRE we wouldn't be able to 'enjoy' that sort of neurosis and the teacher wouldn't have been assaulted. No doubt Mr Day and his ilk will consider the price well worth while paying as the child's mother has been made aware of another word, in which lies 'deep-seated racist overtones'.

A further and worrying aspect of racial obsession took hold earlier this month. The headmaster of a local school in Hartley Wintney, Hants., decided that the school Christmas play would be about the incarnation of a Hindu god. Thankfully parents complained and the play was cancelled. With dismay I read that Hampshire County Council backed the headmaster and said his actions were in line with the council's policy on religion and multicultural education. The school concerned has *no* Asian children. This report saw the light of day in a couple of national dailys, but as you would expect, there was quite a bit in our own local rag. One letter, from a lady residing in the said village, summed it up. She said that parents who withdrew their children were not racially biased (as they had been branded, an obvious course to follow) but in fact considered Christmas to be a Christian festival. She went on to ask if one would expect a Muslim school to put on a Christmas play at Ramadan, or a Jewish school to perform an Easter play at Passover. What about Hindu children re-enacting the nativity during Diwal? I have never heard of that one, but that is the point, whose bloody Christmas is it?

Well, that is it then. I shall sign off until the next wave of inspiration takes hold, which will be next year – a couple of hours away. I shall now sit down and watch some television. I hope it provides more entertainment than that transmitted over Christmas. Besides the comedy repeats it was a disaster. *Only Fools and Horses* and *Birds of a Feather* were total flops. Taking characters out of their environment is usually a recipe for disaster and these two were no exception. So that is it, another one over with. Another year in which the bank did its best to make me a statistic, but we survived – and without any handout. As Del Boy would say, 'This time next year we'll be millionaires.' Well, I have faith in the Man from Lamont. Look how he took in that poor, young lady, clad only in leather and whose luggage consisted of rope, canes and whips. A man with that much compassion can't be all prat.

A New Year, and it's honours time again

Well, I did it! I stuck two fingers up at tradition and went to bed at 11 pm on New Year's Eve. Half an hour was spent reading The Visitor's Guide to the Great Western Society's Museum at Didcot, and I was ready to succumb to Mr Sandman's potion. It did cross my mind, fleetingly, that the other half might be disposed to a bit of Percy Filth and wake me up, but, no, she apparently managed to stay awake throughout the whole video recording of 'Marnie', and then came to bed determined to nod off without any disruption. Twenty odd years of marriage certainly alter your attitudes and priorities, some of those years being distinctly odd! Gone is the wispish form of more youthful days, I now possess a more, a more... 'contented' build (no, not fat). The flowing hair that once covered collars and about three inches of jacket, is shorter, but still there. All right, it is greying at the sides, and yes, at the back as well, and also a little grey showing through on top. All this could be dismissed as acceptable 'bearing in mind one's age'. I prefer to think of it as the next stage in my life, where I become distinguished – as opposed to extinguished – where my physical appearance conveys experience, dominance, smooth self-assurance, with just a hint of boyish charm in that warm smile of mine. At forty-cough, and now an internationally famous author, whose rags-to-riches story has captured the heart of millions, I should be holding court with the intelligentsia, exchanging theories on wide-ranging subjects, catching the eye of pretty young things in short, pleated skirts, desperate to spend a little time in the company of someone they would remember fondly as being their first love.

Meanwhile, back in the real world. Last year I was asleep at the witching hour, but in circumstances, that could only be described as partially successful. Maureen and I fell asleep in front of the box and we woke up nearer 1am. This year, however, I am more satisfied.

We spent New Year's Day at the out-laws, a tradition I am happy to continue. It would be a nice touch, though, if the Yorkshire puddings were thought of by the chef (mum-in-law) during the preparation, and not at the end of the main course. That, however, is another tradition. Years of meals at Maureen's mother's have witnessed absent gravy, forgotten boiled potatoes, salt in the sugar bowl, and so on. To be fair, it is always a single item per meal, and she always makes allowances for my being picky about vegetables by offering sweetcorn with everything.

I am sitting in the office writing this as the credits roll at the end of *Taggart*. No doubt I will be able to see the episode during the summer, when it will inevitably be repeated by way of a 'classic', or 'another chance to see', etc.

On the way up to Putney I asked Maureen if she would like to have a look around Kingston. This suggestion was, of course, accepted with some surprise and not a little suspicion. It is not like me to suggest shopping, but on the assumption that a leopard never changes its spots the motive was that I wanted to visit W.H. Smith and Waterstones, to see how they had got on over Christmas with the sale of *From Where I Sit*. I actually spoke to WHS yesterday, but their Book Manager was not available. The young lady to whom I spoke said she would be in today. I expressed surprise that they were opening on New Year's Day, but she added that Woolworths were opening and she was convinced that Waterstones would likewise be trading.

Having bade farewell to the elder two children, we beat a path for Kingston, armed with some games to play later with the elders, and William, who could aggravate them instead.

At every traffic light we stopped at during our epic travels around the shopping centre perimeter, I tutted and bemoaned the newly constructed office blocks that dominate the area. By the time we parked (outside Waterstones) Maureen commented that it wasn't worth coming and could I please shut up about the bloody buildings! My irritation was compounded when I discovered that the Book Manager at WHS was still off with 'flu, and Waterstones, contrary to advice, was closed. Still, there was the Market Place and Bentalls to look round.

The market was dirty and heaving with waste paper. Woolworths was full of space – I have never seen such wide aisles – and Next, housed in a beautiful building, looked closed. Actually it was, but only for the Bank Holiday. Whoever had authorised yellow sheeting to be placed over every window with 'SALE' signs daubed over them wants certifying. It makes the shop look like one of those short-term Christmas lets... still, if they are happy.

We followed the merry throng towards the new Bentalls building, *not* an improvement on the former, graceful lines, but we were unable to compare the present interior with that of the previous. Inside the entrance were staff stopping the poor sod who wanted to pay cash, and allowing in only those with store cards for preferential treatment. What you really need in times of recession is more credit to be doled out.

Back we went to the car, up to Putney, where we had an excellent roast (without Yorkshire pudding), a few games which ended in cries of 'cheat', and another visit was over. We returned with William and an exercise bike, kindly given to us by Maureen's mum. I thought we might be able to do a swop, but she said that in that case, she would keep the bike and we could keep William. Ah, well.

I am just going to break off now, and have a look at the papers, since Maureen has just brought in a cup of tea.

'Why Only the CBE' was the heading that greeted yesterday's *Sun* readers. I use the term 'readers' loosely. Apparently, that is not enough for four British hostages, Messrs Mann, McCarthy, Keenan and Waite. Why give them anything? It is such a farce. Mr Cooper and Mr Richter, also held hostage for long periods, are not included. Did they suffer any less? I think not. For me, Terry Waite took over the mantle from Eddie Edwards as 'Pain in-the-arse-in-Chief'. It has been said many times over the past months, that he *did not* have to keep going back. To my mind, he found a niche that enabled him to find excitement and satisfaction without having to pay financially for it. Against all advice, maybe for egotistical reasons, maybe not, he went back once too often. A lot of people I have spoken to feel that he may have been carried along on a wave of media euphoria at his successes and considered himself above the fate that befell him. Faced with reality, was he not more than a little silly? In the words of the great bard, 'Bugger that for a game of soldiers'. Whilst on the subject of Honours, the 'keep it in the family' ethos seems to be as prominent as ever. The Queen's winetaster, personal servants and the Balmoral gardener all received awards. William Rogers, one of the founder members of the ill-fated SDP won something, so did Sue McGregor, a Radio 4 presenter. Why them? I can understand recognition being given, if it must, to people like Magdi Ycoub, the transplant chappie, but Trevor McDonald? I can't believe it... oh, yes I can.

Gary Lineker, OBE, has been receiving increased recognition

over the last couple of years for being one of the nicest people in football, indeed, within the sporting world. From what I have seen, the comments appear to be totally justified. A more modest chap you could not wish to meet. His reputation as a fine sports man, as well as a player, without any bookings in 13 years, have helped to earn him the title of 'football's ambassador' throughout the media. Now, though, with the anxiety he and his wife must be feeling over their baby, the 'family man' has appeared to take precedence, and rightly so. I just hope the national dailys' craze for building people up and then getting bored and trying to dish up the dirt does not take hold in this case.

You can envisage a tabloid headline on a day Kate Adie was not dripping in blood and dung. 'Lineker Pit-Bull Fight'. Then again, at the extreme end of the tabloid press you might see 'Exclusive, Lineker is an Alien Being, Lineker seen in his true colours – or colour'. Ah, well.

Media terminology does not help either. Another recipient of an award was Liz McColgan, described by more than one national daily as 'supermum'. Lots of mums work and run a family. Which reminds me, do you ever watch *You've Been Framed*, with Mr Beadle? After a few video antics have been shown, and I have yet to be convinced about the percentage of genuine cock-ups, the camera returns to mine-host, who is sitting with the person who was the main subject of the last clip and refers to him or her as a 'star'. They are not stars, they just happened to feature in something mildly amusing, or were part of a put-up job for financial gain.

The increasing use of American-orientated hype really bugs me. *You've Been Framed* offers £250 for every clip shown, which is unnecessary. Take the nought off and a token gesture should be all that is required. This obscenity is compounded by an audience vote for the funniest entry, when the winner receives £1,000. It should be sit-back-and-enjoy-it entertainment, but it has become a competition.

I suppose ITV feel that financial inducements of that magnitude are necessary – maybe they are right, but it seems that the grabbing society is being fed once again.

It was sad to see Prince Charles, one of the few Royals who appears to really care *and* speak out about the environment of this country, continuing to hunt. A comment by anti-bloodsports campaigners that it was sickening for Prince Charles's children to hunt at such a young age is absolutely right. If those hunters had any balls at all, they would let their offspring watch an animal being torn to shreds. At least the child would know the true reason for all the country hacking that has preceded the kill. He can then make up his own mind as to whether it is sport or sadistic, perverted violence.

There is no reason why they should not dress up in traditional garb, down sherries and sod off at a canter, but why spoil it. Some cove has written to today's *Daily Telegraph* – you will like this. He says that on Christmas morning, he had a cow dying in considerable pain and she had been, quote, 'a respected and faithful servant'. The vet had visited the farm but the animal had not responded to the medication. The only alternative was for her to be destroyed. The farmer rang five abattoirs, all of which were naturally closed. So far, so good. Now for the sycophantic bit. Our rustic man decided to ring the local hunt, who 'responded immediately'. They 'painlessly destroyed the animal and made no charge'. He goes on to ask most oddly, that 'if hunting were abolished, would the anti-hunting fraternity provide an alternative service?'

Well, of course the huntsmen responded so quickly. Heaven forbid the thought of missing a 'kill' which did not need chasing. Strange letter, I thought. Perhaps he just wants to rub shoulders with Prince Charming.

Christmas Day was, as usual, followed by Boxing Day, which saw around 400 hunts taking place across the country. Prince and Princess Michael of Kent were dressed to kill, like all their sadistic friends, for the Beaufort Hunt. A local hunt near us, the Surrey Union – sounds more like a canal – failed to find a single fox, but at least one of the huntsmen was kicked by his horse and had to go to hospital. There, more good news!

I still cannot see the difference between the hunting set and owners of pit-bull terriers, other than accents and money. The hunters would be horrified to witness a crazed, vicious dog, tearing into a child, at least I think they would be, but they quite happily egg on a crazed, if not naturally vicious, dog to tear into a fellow animal. I suppose the social junketing and the social ladder-climbing tend to numb the guilt which should be there, especially if you can boast that you rode shoulder to shoulder with – wait for it – a Royal.

The article to which I referred earlier said there were about 50 riders in the hunt that Prince Charles joined. I can imagine there being all sorts of people trying to muscle in on the jolly jape. A bit like *Songs of Praise*, really. Have you ever seen so many Church of England churches swollen to the gunnels during one of those televised farces? All the blue rinse set, desperate to get their fizzoggs on the box. All the relations at home exclaiming, 'There's our Freda over there, no, over there on the left... Oh, she's gone.' Then they sit there leaning forward, glued, for a view of someone they have seen not an hour since – as they say in *Coronation Street*. They put it on video tape as well. Hubby's had to double-check before, during and after the programme, to make sure that the TV channel is matched by that on the video. This will be one to keep in the family video album.

I took a bit of flak from motorists about comments in the previous book concerning speed governing. My view was, and still is, that *all* cars should be fitted with governors so that no-one can drive at more than 80 miles per hour. I also maintain that the production of all engines over 2,000cc should be stopped. Today, I read of an actress/model who was nabbed whilst driving at 90 mph. It seems such a waste of an already overstretched police force. Patrol cars, unmarked cars, radar traps, etc. and all for the almost exclusive role of catching speeding motorists.

A letter to the *Mail on Sunday* last year was illuminating. A chappie from Kent was awarded the British Empire Medal. Whilst commenting on this honour and his personal delight, he was not a little miffed to discover that he would not be attending Buckingham Palace to receive his award. He suggests that this amounts to discrimination against 'ordinary people' who the public consider to be the most deserving recipients. He adds that whilst personalities, sports 'stars', etc. turn up, some for the second time, he and his ilk are relegated to a Town Hall bash. I know what he means, and it goes to show that you can't please all of the people all of the time. So working on that theory, you might as well give nothing to anybody and save everyone a lot of time and expense – well, I wasn't lined up for one anyway!

Talking of discrimination, there was a case of alleged bias against an Asian chappie who claimed he had been hindered in his quest for promotion with a regional police force. Now this may have been true, but one other certainty in life, besides the fact that you will always pay income tax, is that in a case like this, the Commission for Racial Equality will always back you. Needless to say, they did in this instance, and the PC was awarded £8,000 compensation. Apparently it was not enough. Is this what it is *really* about – money? I contend that in every race dispute which gets to court, the coloured or Asian claimant now has an advantage before the kick-off, regardless of the rights and wrongs of the case.

There was a survey carried out last year which asked coloured people their opinion on various issues. Inter-racial marriages, the adoption by whites of coloured children, voting patterns, etc. A whole page was dedicated to the survey in the *Mail on Sunday*. Didn't see one the following week for non-black readers!

You see, the problems are deep-rooted, very deep-rooted, and this oppressive obsession is becoming dangerous. Last year, a five-year-old white boy was put on school records as a racist. He was paraded across the playground in front of other pupils, so that his peers could see that he was a 'bad boy'. What sort of people are we dealing with here? Whoever they are, they seem to possess a lot of clout and influence. The reason for this humiliating action was due to his calling an Asian child a 'black' in an argument. The kid is five years old, for Christ's sake. Would a coloured lad be made to suffer in similar fashion for calling a white 'Honky'. No, of course not.

Strathclyde Regional Council, when asked, said that the teacher was following guidelines set concerning racial incidents. The rub is that not only do we see the teacher either going along with these guidelines because it is her job, or because she believes in them, but she has the backing of every relevant department. It seems that these establishments are riddled with troublemakers, desperate to cause sensation, and all at the expense of a child's feelings – a white child.

You may remember that during the Gulf War, taxi drivers in Stockton (Teeside, not Cleveland) were told to remove Union Jack stickers because it might upset Muslims. In Birmingham, a market trader was asked to take down a Union flag from his stall for the same reason. Out of 550 stalls in this market, 80 of them are Asian owned. So what happened to the views of the other 469 English traders? Well, they weren't Asian, were they!

Being torn between two cultures can cause such heartbreak. I remember the case of a young Asian girl who was raped four times by a chap who ran a temple in London. Because of her culture, she could not tell her parents and had to confide in a schoolteacher. That isn't right, is it. Her parents, when told, wanted to keep it quiet because of the shame it would bring on the family. I think 'sham' is more appropriate, but still, what of the feelings of the daughter and other women he was alleged to have raped? All because of a culture.

It is smiley face time now. A friend of mine runs a small business supplying security guards to industry and large retail chains. One chap had been seconded by a local food store and he was in his second week's employment. I have to tell you that he lives some 40 miles from this store, which is situated in Guildford. This particular morning he did not arrive. The manager at the store rang my friend to enquire about this chap's non-appearance. The said friend made some phone calls to check, and then rang the manager back to confirm that he had left home in plenty of time and could not understand why he had not arrived. About an hour later, the store manager rang again, to say that the doorman had seen the security officer drive in quickly, stop, and then turn around and leave. A replacement was found and quickly despatched to Guildford, to replace the lost cove.

Some time later, my friend received a telephone call from the missing guard, who told him that the previous evening he had bought a takeaway curry, which had given him a gippy tummy. All the way up in the car from the wilds of mid-Hants, he kept suffering from wind. Several times he had stopped at toilets, 'just in case', but, no, wind it was. Having arrived at the store and thinking that one final burst might end his inconvenience, he let rip – only to find that he had made a slight error of judgement!

Now badly stained trousers never seem to go hand in hand with a professional image. Do farts have lumps, or what!

It is only a few days into the new year, and it has started off no better than last year. When you read of the crimes committed, especially against old people, it makes you wonder about the kind of home the offender goes back to. The punishments do not fit the crime. One case that made me extremely angry concerned a young mother who was all but raped in front of her two children. Their pet puppy was killed by the boot of the aggressor, and this lady's 15-year-old son was sprayed in the face with ammonia. Initially the purpose of the break-in was theft. Even when sentenced, the defendant raised his fist in a salute to relatives and friends in the public gallery. His sentence? – 13 years. He should never be let out again.

There was also a 75-year-old spinster who was raped by an 18-year-old. We have all read about the policeman, 20 years of age, who was battered with an iron bar. Another policeman of 21 was killed by a sawn-off shotgun. There is no respect. Another 'person' hit a middle-aged mother almost to the point of death with a 2 lb hammer in a public car park – he received 15 years' imprisonment. The lady is now partially paralysed.

Locally, a young lad of 17 happened to be in the wrong place at the wrong time. He and a friend were talking to a cashier at a petrol station when two men entered, one armed with a shotgun.

Both lads were told to lie on the floor whilst the cashier handed over a paltry £70. For no apparent reason, one of the lads was shot in the back. He died on arrival at hospital.

A lady of 83 suffered a fractured skull, black eyes and crushed ribs after she was punched, kicked and beaten. The thugs got away with her pension book – brave, weren't they?

The list is endless.

Another blow for justice was when a couple had their convictions quashed because it could not be proven as to which of them had killed their baby. They both blamed each other – they were both as guilty as each other. Don't tell me they did not know what was happening. They are both free now.

The last couple of years have been marked by prison releases. The Birmingham Six, the Guildford Four, etc. Vast coverage was given on the TV news, radio news, reviews and interviews, but nothing about the atrocities that the victims suffered. Regardless of where and with whom the blame lay, it must have been hurtful to see such coverage when you are still grieving the loss of family or friends.

A rural environment does not protect you either. Last August, in the Ayrshire hamlet of Barrhill, two lady workers were tied up and robbed at the village hall, which doubles as a post office. The harm these oiks do. The ladies may not have been harmed physically, but what a terrifying experience it must have been, and will doubtless stay with them for the rest of their lives.

Even children aren't immune. A young lad of nine was robbed of his £1.10 pocket money. Two men held him up, one pushing a pistol into his stomach and making him empty his pockets. Just £1.10, you can't believe it, can you? These are just a few of last year's cases which I have picked out at random.

The year actually ended with a mentally handicapped chap being shot in the face by a mugger with an air pistol – for 40p. As the witching hour drew nearer, a lady of 83 was injured by two robbers for £10, and a 74-year-old had acid thrown in her face. The offenders have been caught and are 22 and 17 years of age.

Where did it all go wrong? Hampshire Police Farce (sorry, Force) admitted that crime was up by more than one fifth. In real money this means 21,130 more cases! After the announcement of the figures had been made and detailed analysis shown, there came the familiar call that the public could do more to help. We should all fit alarms, lock car doors every time we get out, not leave doors open at home, as it 'makes it easy for the criminal'.

They also advocate greater use of the Neighbourhood Watch scheme.

The emphasis is always on *your* help. The detection rate in Fleet, Hampshire, was just 26%. Great, isn't it? Mind you, the motoring offence figures look good. Forty-three mph in a 40 area, illegal parking – another two crimes solved. I am more convinced than ever that you have got to bring criminals to heel, where it hurts most. In *From Where I Sit* I advocated, some people thought jokingly, that the standards of British prisons should be based on Risley. I still stand by that. Judging by the number of letters I have received in support of this view, and the lack of improvement by 'being nice', I see no reason to change my mind. It is not just a case of having your house or car broken into, it is the everyday changes that were unheard of a few years ago. The number of beggars who have attacked passers-by – simply because they just passed by. There is a growing number of 'steamings'. We have had it on the Underground where vicious thugs, having issued threats, assault the public and steal valuables. We now have groups racing through crowds, grabbing jewellery as they go, or pouncing on taxis at traffic lights and robbing both driver and passenger.

Another aggressive tendency is being demonstrated as you wait at major traffic junctions. Some intimidating person appears in front of your car, wishing to clean your windows. In some cases they don't ask, but start, in the hope that you will pay them, if only because you don't want to create a scene. There is very little difference between the beggar and the windscreen cleaner, except that the cleaner is armed with a chamois and knife, whilst the begger just has a knife – bastards.

We also have to contend with young thieves – joyriders – who are a danger to everyone. We must not upset the little loves, though. In Exeter last year, convicted teenagers were being given free driving lessons. A probation officer explained that by learning to drive properly, they will gain self-esteem and enjoy themselves. So we are paying to teach them to drive at such a high standard that they won't be caught next time – great, isn't it!

I can still remember the case in Liverpool a couple of months ago when a girl of 12 was killed and her two friends injured. They were knocked down when collecting a 'penny for the guy' by a Mazda MX3 which had been stolen by two youths. The court was told of their remorse and sorrow, so that is all right. They have cut short a young girl's life, ruined the lives of family and friends and they offer 'remorse and sorrow'. This should be offering their lives. Instead, they will be taught how to be artistic and enter Open

University courses at the public's expense. Then, of course, they will be helped by Nacro, the do-gooding service for wrong-doers. Oh, the injustice of it all. I have no doubt the local priest would have seen it as God's will.

We even have a Camberley insurance company director stating that motorists should be more responsible by making it harder for thieves to succeed. He goes on to say that 'joyriders' will be deterred if alarms are fitted and that with one in three car owners making claims, premiums will continue to rise, unless everybody makes the effort to protect their vehicles. When the world and his wife have locked, padlocked, alarmed, sat Dobermanns in each seat and the car thief is as extinct as the dodo, will insurance premiums come down – will they, heck as like (as they say in Lancashire).

Once again, the emphasis is on the poor sod in the street, forking out continually, but when will it hit the thief's pocket? If he is underage, will it hit the parents or his parents/guardians/ homosexual or lesbian workers/mixed stock, one-legged sack race champions, etc. etc.

You remember my mentioning that Glyn's car had been broken into, well, just before Christmas, we received a visit from the local police to say that they had apprehended some youngsters. They were underage, so they could not be prosecuted. They had, however, been given a moral lecture, which will really help. The good news is, however, that Glyn got his jeans back. I asked the policeman whether, as the children had admitted taking the goods, their parents could be made to recompense my lad. Apparently not. Why is this? If one of our children stole anything, both Maureen and I would consider it our responsibility, as parents, to reimburse the victim, or victims, for any damage. Are we alone? The little bastards involved in Glyn's case apparently came from 'good' homes, but I would be interested to know if they lived with their real parents, or not.

Good news now. The look on the faces of Wrexham's team as the final whistle blew will be remembered for a long while. 2-1 against Arsenal. My father has always supported the Gunners, but I could never take to them. The North London side did not deserve to lose on pure footballing merit, but they became lax and forgot to play until the final whistle. So many players become petulant when things go wrong and Arsenal were no exception. It was with great pleasure that I witnessed their demise.

In this case I was naturally biased, because the underdogs were Welsh, but I am convinced that this way of thinking is part of a Librarian's make-up. It is always the David and Goliath factor which influences my views. If Liverpool are representing England in a European competition, I root for the Merseysiders. If Liverpool are playing Luton in a First Division match, I hope the Hatters win. Should Luton be playing Halifax in a Cup Match, then it is the 4th Division side that would be cheered on, and so it goes. The same could be said for shops, small independents versus the 'super' supermarkets.

These large food chains cannot accept a competitor in an area at the expense of their own outfit, can they. You can bet your bottom dollar that as soon as Tesco, or any of them, gain planning permission to build on yet another field, Safeway, Sainsbury, M & S and Asda all follow. Which brings us back to Sunday shopping. We are now well past Christmas and the lack of involvement by local councils and, even worse, the government, is frightening. Such must be the power of the EC and the retail groups. If shops want to open until, say, 9 pm on weekdays, then fine. The opportunity for shops to make more money and for staff to earn a bit extra in overtime is all to the good. The crime rate may also be helped by the extra use of high streets and shopping malls after dark. Sunday, however, should remain a special day. I repeat what I said first time round, 'You will miss it when it has gone.' I cannot understand the logic. There is still only the same amount of money to go round. It can only lead to higher prices. Small shops, just holding their own, will fall at a further rate. The market domination by these giants will increase, as will their influence and clout not to mention their prices. The politicians, however, remain sitting on the fence. They are not in charge of the country's destiny any longer.

It was strange to read that Brian Keenan, the ex-hostage, will be returning to Beirut in April. He stated that he has a morbid fascination for the place, well, he must have.

Another good start to the year was the news that the number of NHS dentists in some parts of the country is so low that – wait for it – helplines are being set up to advise patients about the locations of dentists who still practise. They will be about as rare as rocking-horse shit soon (that is motor-trade terminology, usually reserved for a Skoda that has fetched over £2.50 at auction).

This is a hoot. Four hundred male employees are being sent on a course to instil respect for their fellow – or should it be fellowess – female colleagues. They are to be instructed on the evils of sexual harassment – remember, please pronounce it harass, not har-ass. I blame Frank Spencer for this Americanised intrusion! Anyway, they will also be told that it is wrong to make jokes about women. They will be shown videos about women working in non-traditional occupations. The organisers hope this will stop them making remarks about women being unsuitable for certain jobs. The council concerned is, surprise, surprise, Islington, in London. They are also planning to sack workers (they mean men) who pester colleagues of the opposite sex for a date. This all follows a court case in which an eighteen-year-old was awarded £15,000 compensation for being forced out of a job because of sexual harassment. At £15,000 a go, I would be happy to be forced out every week. My complaint is that working from home, you are slightly restricted by possible contenders. Ah, well. I will put on my Kylie Minogue video!

Last August, in an edition of *Wales on Sunday*, a Gwent Police Superintendent was advocating the banning from sale of all toy and replica guns. He did add that if they were still to be sold, then proof of identification should be produced first. As he said, if you are the one looking down the barrel, you can't afford to take chances. He made the interesting point that during the last ten years, armed robberies have tripled, and so have the sale of toy guns.

A psychologist was also asked for his views. He believed that increased news coverage of armed attacks led to a rise in the use of both real and replica guns. He added that power is a very big influence and holding a gun makes you feel more powerful. There must be a lot of deranged adults about, as I would not feel like that. I probably did when we played 'Wagon Train', but then I was eight years of age.

With this in mind, it was interesting to read about the incident that has just happened in West Yorkshire. A man in his 30s pointed a gun at a policeman through the upstairs window of a house. The police shot the man and he died. So what happens? The police (as usual) have to justify their actions. The Police Complaints Authority commence their investigations, whilst that most bland and ineffective of Home Secretaries, Kenneth Baker, is urged (yet again) to ban the sale of replica guns.

Apparently, giving three warnings to someone brandishing a gun, replica or real, is not enough. I suppose the do-gooders expect a policeman to walk up and inspect the said armament to check whether it says 'Casdon' or 'Merit'. It used to be 'Chad Valley' in my childhood. Personally, I would like to hear it spelled out loud and clear, that if you are holding what turns out later to be a replica gun, you will be treated as if the instrument was real. We might just be able to save a few bob from the time and effort wasted by complaints authorities looking into the moans and gripes of relatives who are determined to blame the police. It is funny how the chap with the gun is always so blameless.

Bearing in mind that in this latest case the police took away a number of replica weapons from the chap's flat, a solicitor was already acting on behalf of the family and confirmed that legal action was being considered – now there's a surprise!

Well, Deborah's romance still seems to be in full swing. If he visits us for the evening, we are in bed before he goes, but at 8 am the following morning when the post arrives, there is an abundance of cards and letters. Being artistic, okay, slightly eccentric, these items are not stamped with either a first or second class stamp. Oh, no, nothing so normal. We (I say 'we' because I read the postcards first – after all, she is my daughter and I am just protecting her – or being nosey). Anyway, the GPO must love him. Twenty-four one penny stamps arranged around the border of the card. Another variation is to have one penny and two penny stamps alternating, so that a pretty pattern is created. Not for my daughter a 'seaside type' humour card. She receives pictures by Monet, seascapes, landscapes, dolphin smiley faces, stating undying devotion and unrequited love. Let's face it, anyone who addresses the card to Miss Beautiful, Gorgeous, Biggest-blue-eyes in the Whole World, etc. etc., is going to have the rest of their scribings read by parents who are curious to say the least! Frankly...

Glyn's relationship with his young lady is continuing. I say young, it is bordering on cradle-snatching, but she is a very nice girl. He brings her back most weekday nights and they watch TV in what was the playroom until there became a more pressing need for somewhere for the two elder ones to go. There is nothing worse than having to sit in the same room as parents, is there?

We moved William into one of the larger bedrooms which now doubles up as a playroom, complete with computer, so the 'gang' tend to congregate upstairs, which keeps them from under our feet. Mind you, why is it that when one child wants a drink, all the others feel thirsty as well?

This self-styled Moslim Parliament is a bit of a cheek, isn't it? Who the hell do they think they are? Their proclaimed leader, one Dr Kalim Siddiqui, said that as people broke the law by refusing to pay the poll tax, or opening their stores on a Sunday,

Moslims might feel justified in withholding taxes because funding is not available for separate Moslim schools. He views this as discriminatory. His parliament's opinions apparently reflect those of this country's two million Moslims. Are there really only that few? Judging by the media space allotted to them, I would have thought they accounted for 50% of the population by now.

Prat of the Month award goes to a chap in Cardiff, who was too lazy to heat up the water to make his baby's feed. He mixed lager with the milk and gave it to the seventeen-day-old child. The baby was admitted to hospital with alcoholic poisoning and the said prat was sentenced to eight months' suspended jail sentence for cruelty. I would have had him sterilised.

Young William's grip on life shows no sign of abating. When told that he could not go to the cinema to see a particular film because it was rated 18, he said to Glyn, 'Well, you can take me and tell them that I have got a disease which makes me short for my age.' It makes a change from his usual response, 'I'll get it on video, so there.' This type of comment is generally followed by blowing a raspberry, while standing with hands on hips. This action is then followed by a whack across the back of the legs. He has always appreciated a well-informed discussion!

A woman is suing the promoters of a trade exhibition because they did not allow her to take in her three-month-old child. She is, not unexpectedly, being supported by the relevant equality quango. This woman lectures, she has actually been termed a senior lecturer (there's posh). The subject is 'human resource management', so it is not a proper job. As a spokesman for the exhibition said, 'Exhibitors pay a lot of money to hire floor space and would not take kindly to damage or grubby hands on the products and stands.' And why should they? This woman, however, insists that the rule is discriminatory. Her solicitor (didn't take long to hire one) is claiming damages. You actually get the feeling that the legal bod was probably briefed beforehand, in case a confrontation occurred. If it wasn't over a child it would have been something else. I suppose it is a boost to the ego. Anyway, that's another one against the wall. She can stand next to the lager-feed chap. They seem well suited.

Sad to see that Richmond Ice Rink closes this month. Generations have enjoyed its facilities over the years. It is warming to know, though, that some awfully nice property development people have bought the site and are replacing the famous landmark with flats.

There was an article recently about a male au pair from Iceland, who is working in this country illegally. This is because *au pairs* are defined as 'unmarried girls between the ages of 17 and 27'. I read through the article twice. Not once was there a comment by the Equal Opportunities lot supporting this chappie, so proving conclusively that the bias is one way only.

After the last few years, where cones have dominated our roads, it is now the turn of the hard-hat brigade. Everyone, male and female, being interviewed at outside locations where a building site or factory is within a ten-mile radius, appears to have one, whether it be power stations, bridges, railway stations, you name it, the donning of such headgear seems necessary. It is just that the wearer assumes an air of importance (in their eyes).

Since the heady days when I was a milkman, unfettered by an excess of weight (I was a pretty trim 10 st 7 lbs actually) the ravages of time, trauma, pressure, William and all the other excuses have caught up with me. This last Christmas I felt particularly bloated. The Saturday after, I weighed myself – it was not pleasant viewing. I topped the scales at 13 st 12 lbs. This is all right if you are over six feet, but when you measure 5' 8½" – always remember the half – one is a little on the heavy side. Now I know I am not pregnant, so the New Year resolution was to trim down to 11 st 7 lb. I appreciate that I will never recapture the youthful figure that cut such a dash with young fillies in the swinging '60s, but just being able to see my willie when I am having a pee will suffice!

I decided to cut out fried breakfasts, indeed, all fried food. Sugar, cereals, cheese, sandwiches have all had to go. I cut out sugar in my tea three years ago, but although it took me around six months to accept the taste, I can no longer stand the sweetness of sugar in any hot drinks. My downfall, or part of it, is my love of sugar sandwiches, made with real butter and thick-sliced bread. We are now three weeks into the diet. On the first Sunday weigh-in, I stood in at 13 st 9 lbs. The second week, 13 st 7 lbs and last Sunday, 13 st 6 lbs. So that is the equivalent of three bags of sugar lost over three weeks. Well, it is better than a kick in the futtocks!

Oh, I forgot to mention, I have cut out the red wine, as well. I haven't missed the fried breakfasts, nor have I missed the late-night doorstep cheese sarnies. What I have missed is real butter and sugar sandwiches. I was the last member of our family to eat unsalted butter, as opposed to the greasy muck I now spread from one of those unappetising punnets, bedecked with garish yellow. Yuk!!I am sure it is healthier for you, but it makes you feel ill just looking at it.

You remember what I was saying about gypsy sites, well, at the moment Guildford Borough Council is evaluating 13 sites for use by gypsy families. Some of the candidates are at 'the nice end', most are around here. I am sympathetic to the view shared by many that the inclusion of certain areas is only a sop. When the final site is chosen, it won't be among the green-swards of Send, Clandon or Effingham, you can bank on it – not the BICC I grant you – but the others should be okay. Watch this space.

You remember my friend who has turned to religion, well, he came out with a classic the other day. We were talking generally, you know, the way men do, and the subject turned to sex. I jokingly asked if, bearing in mind he will no longer work on a Sunday, he still continued to hand out a portion of helmet (as they say in Homerton). 'I may have turned to God,' he said, 'but I can still use my knob-end!' Succinctly put, I thought. Ah, well, it must be God's will (or willy).

Recession – what recession?

Some farming chappie has just been killed whilst out with his local hunt, the morning paper declares. He was thrown off (or, as they would say, 'orff') and his steed fell on top of him. Hope the horse was all right.

Our local paper has reported on a man who held up a petrol station with a replica gun. His defence at the trial was that he had argued with his girlfriend when she had told him to go out and get a job. Surprise, surprise, she is pregnant and is already a mother of two other children, one of which has been fathered by this fellow. What sort of life have these children got to look forward to?

I have only one comment to make on the following story, which appeared in the John Smith column of *The People*. It concerns a bank employee on £33,000 a year, who stole the thick end of half a million pounds from his employers. His sentence, described by his wife as 'right and just', was two years' suspended imprisonment. Why? This thief apparently belongs to the Methodist Church and is a devout Christian. There must be more to the story, because, if not, this greedy bastard is definitely a member of the right club. I cannot see a non-believer getting off so lightly. Frankly, I think the let-off is discriminatory, in fact, it is 'atheiest' (groan)!

Talking of groans, did you hear the one about the two dyslexic skiers who were deliberating whether they should zig-zag or zag-zig down the slopes? Having arrived at the top, one said to the other, 'Look, as we can't be sure I will ask at the kiosk over there.' Off he goes. 'Excuse me, but can you tell me whether one zig-zags or zag-zigs down the slopes, as my friend and I haven't been for a couple of years and we cannot remember.' 'I don't know,' the man replied, 'I'm a tobogganist.' 'In that case,' said the dyslexic one, 'I'll have 20 Benson & Hedges and a box of matches'!

So, Scarborough has lifted the ban on homosexual conferences being held there. They reckon it would have cost £6 million in other conference business if they had not bowed to pressure by other groups and trade unions. For seventeen years the ban has been imposed. For seventeen years it has been a 'nice place'.

Wasn't it pleasing to read that a thief (not joyrider) who stole a Metro and raced it at 90 mph, forcing a lorry driver off the road and killing him, has been given 12 months' youth custody. Twelve months? Words fail me. I expect the news comforted the grieving family no end.

Do you remember initiative? A lady, 78 years of age, lost her purse on a bus in the West Midlands. She managed to reclaim it within 20 minutes at the firm's offices. She was charged £5.80p plus £1.05p. The £5.80p was 10% of the amount she had in the purse, and the £1.05p was calculated as part value, due to the purse being made of leather. A West Midlands travel oik said that they were 'only following government guidelines' – a 'Jobsworth', in other words.

This lady was 78 years old and handicapped, for God's sake. Who are these people? What worries me is that someone considers them employable. Then again, fancy living in the West Midlands in the first place, to most people it would be the last place

An eleven-year-old and a twelve-year-old commit burglary at 3 am in the Barnsley area. After their arrest, the eleven-year-old stated that he had burgled previously with a thirteen-year-old, having stolen goods worth over £5,000 and a car. So where were their parents?

I don't like to see any business going to the wall, but the possibility of Hutchinson and Partners ceasing to trade will not worry me unduly – actually, I will gloat. Max Hutchinson is the architect chappie who criticised Prince Charles for interfering and wanting architects to mimic 18th century architecture, instead of building for the future. I have always found it somewhat unnerving that the word 'interference' should be used. It implies that criticism and comment are taboo unless you have got the 'right' qualifications and probably belong to the right club as well. If what has been thrown up over the last thirty years has been designed by his sort, and is considered 'building for the future', then I consider any views and comment from the man in the street to be more valid than the egocentric whims of these purveyors of glass and concrete monstrosities. Judging by the photograph of him in the paper, a haircut would improve his appearance no end. (Bitch, bitch!)

You probably know of my dislike for the Japanese and anything they stand for. Now I can say that without any fear of my comments being labelled racist, they are yellow, not black. It makes you shake your head a little when you read that Berwick-on-Tweed Council is planning a Japan Day on 16th February. This celebration is 50 years to the day since the fall of Singapore. Many people are still alive today who suffered personally at the hands of the Japs as POWs, or are related to those who died horrifically. How anyone would want to make *any* day a Japan Day is beyond me, unless you are about to toady with the offer of a greenfield site for a new factory offering back door imports and the obligatory golf course – for Japanese members only, of course.

I see that an Asian edition of *The People* has been launched. That should see another forest eradicated within a few weeks.

During the last two years, I have travelled around the southern half of England, the Midlands and Wales quite extensively. The change in certain areas is quite dramatic over a relatively short space of time. There is a huge increase in the rate at which another section of single road has been upgraded to dual carriageway. There is a growing number of intersections on motorways, new bypasses to bypass the old bypass, etc. The effect on the countryside is devastating. One half-mile section of road improvements goes unnoticed because of the benefit to the local community, but add together the areas of land affected, the amount that is 'levelled', the trees that are cut down, the hedgerows that are churned up, and the end result is the destruction of irreplaceable woods, fields and meadows. Each 'road improvement scheme', however minor, is nibbling away at another edge of this country's resources. The sore is getting larger.

Arrival at your destination is so often a let-down as well. When you eventually reach the town which you set off to visit some time previously, the majority of them have had the heart ripped out in an effort to create a traffic-free precinct – what a wonderful word. Pedestrian areas, walkways, arcades, they all look alike. It is not that I am against modern shopping centres just because they are modern, it is what you get as a punter which concerns me. It is the same multinationals, selling the same wares. It is the conformity of it all.

If, on your journey, you stopped off at a Crappy Eater or a Shittle Lef, sorry, Little Chef, the food will be the same wherever you are. It is not bad, but just the same. It is the lack of choice, where have all the Greasy Spoon Cafés gone? Town councils seem to be competing with each other but for the wrong reasons. Healthy competition should be encouraged. There is every merit in providing a clean town with nice shops. The planners seem to be controlled by the monopolies, however. Everything is built around the giant food chains. Newly developed town centres, precincts, etc. regardless of geographical area, are all supporting the same multinationals. You can bet that wherever you go, there will be a Sainsburys, Tesco, Safeway, Comet, Halfords, Texas, Do-It-All, etc. This list is endless, but it is always the same list. Shoe shops, variously named, are all owned by the British Shoe Corporation and where have all the independents gone? There are very few privately owned greengrocers left in these centres. Privately owned butchers are pretty scarce. It seems so shortsighted to provide the *same* facilities. I would like shops which reflect local tastes, traditions, etc.

Newsagents are another area that has not gone unnoticed. The corner and high street shops seem to be gobbled up at a vast rate by the Martins, Dillons and Forbuoys of the world. Once they are acquired, they change hands again. It is like a newsagent merry-go-round. All are small things in themselves, but eating away at the very fabric of our society. I suppose it goes to show how small the world is getting.

Now here is a good example of what I mean. The Shropshire town of Market Drayton still has a cattle market. What is more, it is situated in the town centre. The good planners, however, have an idea about relocation. They want the market moved to a site currently used by a tenant farmer. This chap's farm covers 150 acres. The council want 30 of them. We have two problems here. One, the idea of moving the market out of the town centre is because a prospective developer – yes, you knew it was coming – is being courted by the local council to build a supermarket, housing estate and swimming pool on the present site. Local people have questioned as to whether another supermarket is required, they currently have two anyway. They also feel that the market adds to the attraction and character of Market Drayton. Secondly, the farm is destined to lose a large percentage of its acreage and is quite unique. It works on a system of producing permanent pasture which means that 150 cattle and 100 sheep can graze throughout the year without being brought in for the winter, and without the need for hay, but then, that's regress!

The farmer has studied crop rotation for many years, written a book on it and should be hailed as an innovator in his field (well, not just his field, but anybody's – another one which just came out!). Anyway, the long and short of it is that while another retail giant makes Market Drayton look like Bracknell, Gateshead,

Redhill, etc. the country loses a rare slice of arable land free from pesticides and chemicals.

It is Sunday and I have just weighed myself. Thirteen stones, two pounds. Going down!

Dounreay Nuclear Processing Plant have just announced that after eight weeks of searching, just over 6½ pounds of highly enriched uranium is still missing. Well, I have looked in William's pockets, and he hasn't got it. He is learning, he earned a Brownie point the other day as well. We were in Aldershot, when he commented on a girl who had just passed us by. 'Dad,' he said, 'that girl must be common.' I enquired as to the reason for this procrastination. I didn't say that to William, of course, but I had to put the word in somewhere! I haven't bought Roger's Thesaurus for nothing and yes, I know his name is not really Roger, but it seems more English and homely and it lends itself far better to classical sayings. Have you ever heard anyone speak of 'wishing to give a girl a good Rogeting'? No? Exactly! Anyway, William answered that the girl had tattoos on her arm so she *must* be common. It is nice to know he is grasping the rules of social class.

Thought you'd like to know, Guildford Borough Council are still sifting through the list of candidates for the gypsy site.

It was reassuring to learn that members of the Quorn Hunt who possessed guns are not to be charged. I wasn't aware that having a plum in your mouth entitled you to immunity. I notice that the donations made to the League Against Cruel Sports has doubled over the last twelve months. Equally pleasing was the news that Paul and Linda McCartney have purchased 84 acres of land in Exmoor with the express intention of protecting deer from huntsmen. Naturally, there are farmers who feel that this move jeopardises the existence of the herd, as hunting is now banned from these acres. Smacks of sour grapes to me.

You know the way our government keeps telling us how good the NHS is, well, the following puts it all into perspective. In the massive Dryburn Hospital, Durham, two women were recovering from an operation. Both patients required pain-killing treatment. Because the system cannot afford it, only one pain-killing machine was available. The question was asked, 'Which woman should get the treatment?' The answer was provided by the toss of a coin. The winner received the benefit of modern technology, whilst the loser had to have injections. These machines cost £4,000. Makes you glad we give Ethiopia umpteen millions, doesn't it?

Sad to see the membership of the Women's Institute is in constant decline. No doubt this news will bring joy to the feminist brigade. Let's face it, the majority of WI members are white, married, middle-class ladies, who live in respectable areas. They are interested in middle-of-the-road, non-aggressive subjects and they generally speak very nicely. No, we can't have that.

Two Geordies, aged eighteen and nineteen years, who admitted spraying graffiti on local trains were jailed for twelve months. They asked for seven more offences to be taken into consideration. The sum involved here was £20,000. Bet they weren't asked to pay for it, though.

I find it interesting that Germany should be trying to stop Czechoslovakia from selling off state-owned borderland exclusively to Czech nationals and not to expelled Germans. The area concerned has been populated by Germans for about 700 years, but after the war three million Krauts were sent packing. The authorities in Prague said that they had no intention of selling border land which could, in the future, make national boundaries questionable. Germany is at it again, I am pretty certain that by the year 2000 they will be out of the EC and NATO, and pushing out their borders once again. If the 'Great Bear' remains a fragmented group of states jockeying for position in the political arena, then I think a German initiative will be even more probable. While the Georgians, Ukrainians, Latvians, etc. are all squabbling over who has the right to push the buttons, the general populus could wake up to find that another army of jack-booted soldiers has just walked all over them. Having said that, the Ruskies and other derivatives might find the discipline something of a comfort, after all this freedom they have recently suffered.

It is a strange case of justice when a father and son get sent to prison for swearing at a judge and the drink-driver of a car who has killed their respective daughter and sister gets three months. Swearing at the judge would be the least of their worries. Apparently, just after the defendant was sentenced, he smiled in a smarmy way, indicating that he knew he had got away with it. I am not surprised that the father 'snapped'. Any normal father would have done the same. Three months? How can the sentence be so lenient? He should have been given life.

Aren't people funny? Maureen and I were watching TV last night when an advert appeared on the screen plugging an article in a tabloid about Simon Weston, the Falklands chappie. Now, like everyone, we have admired his courage, fortitude, resilience and basic guts, after what he has been through, but to go back and meet the Argentinian pilot who was responsible for all the grief he and others have suffered is beyond us. I am not blaming the pilot either. He was just doing his job as he saw it. 'Ill-advised', 'let down', etc. are the comments I have read from comrades and friends, who are also quite surprised. No, I am afraid he has lost a Brownie point for that. It all seems a little sensation-seeking. If my son had died on that ship, the last thing I would want to read about is the pilot who made it all possible, smiling faces and hand-shaking between the pair of them. No, it is definitely out of order.

I was relieved to see that British Telecom's profits for the three months to 31st December, were £759 million. The thought of Ricky Valance not being able not being able to award himself a huge increase in salary would have made me feel unwell and guilty at not taking more advantage of their over-priced facilities – greedy bastards!

Well, we have survived the first month of the new year. The only car that we sold during January was the Montego Estate. I received a call out of the blue from an old friend of mine who used to live in Wokingham. He uprooted the family and their three dogs and set off for the wilds of North Cornwall. He bought a plot of land last year, on which remained the outer walls of a barn. These four walls, all three foot high, have been enough to allow him to apply for planning permission. They managed to pay off the bank, with the proceeds from the sale of their house, and are living in a mobile home, which isn't entirely mobile, while they scratch enough income to keep them afloat to buy the materials to build their new home. I hope they succeed. Anyone who takes that sort of risk deserves all the luck they can get. Anyway, Alan rang to say that he was stuck and wanted something large and reliable. I said Maureen wasn't for sale, but he corrected me by saying he meant transport back to Cornwall. He came over that afternoon, bought the car and bade farewell. I haven't heard from him since so I wonder if the 'Anthony Mann Pleasure To Drive Car' actually got him home. Is this another name I will have to cross out of the address book?

So, we are just over two months away from a general election, and every newspaper is printing the latest opinion polls. Personally, I still think it will be a hung parliament, but Mr Ashdown will have to provide one or two commitments. There seems to be so much waffle flying about, it is difficult trying to pluck one Liberal/ Dem. policy out of the air. I still think they will end up with about 25% of the vote, just forcing the Tories out of office. Labour,

I feel, do not represent that much of a threat. As I said before, there is nobody with any real personality or leadership quality, with the exception of John Smith, and I just don't see a victory being on the cards for Neil Kinnock. It will be interesting to see how the wives fit into the puzzle. Will they be paraded, presidential-style, or as the other half. What an awful thought. They could inflict themselves upon an unsuspecting public in true Nancy Reagan fashion. A friend of mine's wife is called Glenys, but the only Norma I have ever known was a Vietnamese pot-bellied pig – which reminds me...

A friend of a friend wanted to buy a Vietnamese pot-bellied pig (or two). He read an advert placed in his local Exeter paper giving details of some young ones that would shortly be available. Ray, the friend of the friend, rang and made an appointment to see the lady who placed the ad. The directions she gave him sounded idyllic. Some few miles out of Exeter he arrived at the lane leading to this 'dingly dell' type house name which he had been given. The result could not have been further from the truth. The place was more akin to a portakabin, or two. The lady who had advertised the pigs was not yet home and it was her mother who answered the door. Ray was ushered into the 'house' and along a passage to a sitting room. As he walked along the passage, which was by all accounts very dark and dingy, something flew over his head, screeching. Back it flew again. He said it felt as if he was being dive-bombed. Into the light of the sitting room, but not the sanctity, the bird, a parrot, flew in and continued to zoom around. She asked Ray to sit down. He did. Everywhere he looked there were parrot droppings. Unfortunately, he had already said yes to a cup of tea as he had entered. He was perusing the scene when the mother came in with the tea on a tray. Milk and sugar were in attendance, along with copious doses of parrot droppings. Apparently, he 'couldn't see the sugar for the shit', so he declined his usual two spoonsful. She left him to his own devices for a minute, long enough for him to deposit the tea into a nearby plant pot.

When the mother returned she was accompanied by a large chap who resembled the village idiot, being introduced as her son. He continued his seated wait for the pig-selling lady to arrive. He became aware of something moving outside the house. Eventually a head appeared and pressed itself up against the window. It was a coloured chap who, on being spotted by the mother, was promptly referred to as her other son. After what seemed an interminable age the daughter arrived home. She appeared quite normal and showed Ray the piglets. A deal was struck and Ray returned some few weeks later to take delivery of his purchase. He declined tea and quickly made his way to the coast where he has a job as a warden. He has since purchased another Vietnamese pot-bellied pig, a male this time, naturally called 'Norman'. Norman and Norma have since successfully tickled each other's fancy and produced a litter of 'Normettes'. Don't say I don't have any sense of romance.

While some new eras dawn, on many the sun goes down. It was a pity that the old Stock Exchange has finally closed its doors after 200 years of tradition and those selling incomprehensible packages will now be doing so through video screens.

Carla Lane seems to be getting herself quite involved with animal welfare. She has just taken it upon herself to save forty Canada Geese that are not welcome in Battersea Park. So far she and a small team have managed to capture sixteen of the birds. These will be sent to parks in the north for resettlement. All this is necessary because Wandsworth Borough Council is concerned about the amount of mess generated by the geese which walk the pathways within the park. They have taken it into their minds to shoot the offenders. It must be me, but I can think of far worse things that go on in a park, like being ripped-off over the price of an ice-cream or hot dog, putting money into a machine which decides not to work or finding half the flowers have been stolen. That is not to mention vandalism or assaults. If I could shoot someone just because they were having a crap, I would have a field day!

It is not just the geese I feel sorry for. Mike Tyson is another. Mind you, if he were standing in front of me, I would say he was innocent even if he wasn't. For the eighteen-year-old girl he is alleged to have raped to say, 'going to his room at 2 am was not an invitation for sex' is an all-time classic. Any red blooded – or blue blooded male with those minority heterosexual tendencies, whose girlfriend says she will come back to his place at that time of the morning, is going to think he is on to a winner. This young lady in the Tyson case even stated that she sat on his bed to watch TV in his room, as she couldn't see too well from the chair in which she was sitting. Couldn't she move the chair? Still, being female she has got an excellent chance of winning the case. Yes, I know the girl failed in her action against one of the Kennedys, but then it *was* the Kennedys.

Some cove in Nottingham fed live finches to his pet snakes. He has been found guilty on cruelty charges. He has been fined £1100 and ordered to pay the RSPCA £2,500 in costs. What this snippet of news doesn't say is whether or not he is still allowed to keep pets. Other than the usual ego trip, I equate snakes to rottweilers in the 'Common Man's Pet League'. I cannot see any pleasure or satisfaction in restricting the movement of a non-domestic animal that should be slithering around some sand-dune. Bet our guilty foe has tattoos!

Unusual to see that Australia still has something in common with us. They appear to be having problems with the ordination of women in much the same way as the C of E over here. In these days of equality, and Equal Opportunities Commissions, support groups and other quangos, how do the churches manage to get away with it. It just goes to show the power they have, not to mention the land and money. New South Wales State Court of Appeal has just ruled that women cannot be ordained until there is a full court hearing, which won't take place for several months. So they are about as quick as we are in finding a solution. It was a year ago that Dr George Carey, the Archbishop of Canterbury elect, said that the ordination of women would go ahead. On that tack, I would think most people outside the church would be with him. However, he spoilt his comments for me when he went on to say that he expects the same standards from homosexual clergy as that from those who are married – no sex outside of marriage. Well, as queers cannot marry in this country just yet – well, not unless there is a new EC directive I don't know about – he has got no chance. I have never heard of two men with 'these leanings' living together purely for the company, hobbies, religion that they share. Still, such is the power of Dr Carey's faith – or his naïvety.

Neither Maureen nor I have been overly excited, but then you are not going to be when you have been married for twenty-two years. I digress. Neither of us have found the new dom-sit-com called *As Time Goes By* to be very imaginative. Both being fans of Judi Dench and Geoffrey Palmer, we looked forward to its arrival on the screen. Only watched the first couple of episodes. The daughter doesn't come across as being very realistic. The whole concept feels jaded and somewhat dated. It seems to be a very poor variation on the theme of *A Fine Romance*, which starred Judi Dench, alongside husband, Michael Williams. Modern comedy offerings are usually lacking in originality – and laughs. Besides the Tuesday repeats of *Dad's Army* last year, it has all been a bit flat recently. We rather like *Hope It Rains* with Tom Bell, which ran for six weeks and appears to have drowned in its own water. The *Brittas Empire* also had some good moments, but occasionally bordered on the manic. *Keeping Up Appearances* with Patricia Routledge looked a good bet, but was spoilt by the dreadful overacting of her nymphomaniac, hard-drinking sister, Rose. The other sister, played by Judy Cornwell and Onslow, the brother-in-law, were quite superfluous. Frankly, they could cut out half the cast and run on Hyacinth, her long-suffering husband, who plays a blinder, and the next door neighbour, played by Josephine Tewson. Some of the best lines are uttered when Hyacinth is on the telephone, that is when the true art of comedy shines through. As I have said before, many times, I will be happy when they repeat *Hi-di-Hi*, *It Ain't Arf 'Ot Mum*, *Porridge*, *Just Good Friends*, *The Likely Lads*, etc. There is very little good American comedy with the exception of *The Golden Girls* and *Roseanne*.

What is it I keep saying about 'the family' being under attack from the trendies? Today, we have a girl of twelve years, a Welsh lass, who has been raped by, not one, but two stepfathers. One, aged 28, and the other, a former stepfather aged 29, took the girl to the same location on different occasions and raped her. As I keep on saying, children need both parents – their real parents. This young girl has been let down too many times.

With Aldershot Football Club's bank account being frozen, and the Inland Revenue filing a winding-up order, their future does not look very bright. Like everything else, where continuity comes a very poor second to money and egos, the team have suffered boardroom upheavals and managerial changes. Only a few years ago you could find people talking about the Shots and saying they were afraid to win too many matches in case they got promoted. Now we need to win a few just to get off the bottom and survive. The continuing financial struggle does nothing for the playing staff's morale or the spectators', come to that. It will be a sad day if they follow Accrington Stanley in being unable to complete a season.

Talking of money, it comes to a pretty pass when someone as respected as David Plowright, Chairman of Granada TV, is asked to resign because he wants to place quality before profit. He has got no chance with views like that. Goodness knows, there is little enough home-grown drama, be it ITV or BBC. Forever following American traditions, we will no doubt be deciding the fate of a series, comedy or drama, on the audience figures. I would love to know how they are arrived at. I have never been surveyed, and I don't know anyone else who has ever been asked about their viewing preferences. Frankly, I expect it is all fixed, like the sale of records. Those figures have been tampered with for years by unscrupulous people with greed as their motive. If TV viewing figures were genuine, Beadle wouldn't be in the top 100, would he?

Here we go again, a teenager has been accused of beating his stepfather to death with a cricket bat. This act was the culmination of an argument about the mess created by some puppies. You will note 'stepfather', won't you.

Only slightly less obscene is the case brought by Sarah Keays, who no-one can say anything about, because she sues people like it is going out of fashion. The article which she seems to be less than amused about, appeared in the magazine *New Woman*. They headed their little spiel 'Laughing all the way to the bank'. Now I know it is crude, but I think it is a wonderful title, worthy of the *Sun* any day. We all know what the press is like, but what worries me is the amount of pound coins which will be dished out in compensation when she wins her case, 'cos win it she will.

A little announcement gave me cause for the proverbial wry smile. You surely haven't forgotten my 'Sunday openings' ramblings and what I said about the present situation being the thin end of the edge. Well, Sainsburys have announced their intention to issue new contracts to staff, terminating their 'double pay for Sunday' clause and rostering them for regular Sunday work at a premium – but not double rate. You would think Sainsburys could afford it. They give the meanest price cuts of all the large combines with regard to food approaching its sell-by date. See, another edge of British scruples has been nibbled away.

Next time you are following some arsehole in a BMW who is hogging the middle lane and driving with one hand, because the other is holding the mobile phone, spare a thought for England. Every area of the country needs masts and antennae for transmission use. At the moment, the legal height is a maximum of around 49 feet. I say around, because the article quoted metres (there, I have said it). Anyway, the government want to raise this figure to nearer 65 feet – and all without planning permission. So sod the disfigured countryside, because the profit and increased income from VAT at 17½% is invaluable.

We have got some more news on the gypsy site saga, which I will come to in a minute. First, however, do you remember my mentioning the King's Head Public House, the one that has been around since 1850? There, I knew you would remember. Despite all the protests, letters and comments by historical societies, the building is now about to be flattened. Surprise, surprise, the application to build 23 flats on the site was won on appeal. One of those Department of the Environment nobodies, a Mrs Natalie Eaton, came down for a couple of hours from the big city and decided it wasn't of such historical or architectural interest as to be worthy of saving. She commented that she had taken into account the views of some local residents and Ash Parish Council, that the building had historic interest and was considered a local landmark. She obviously wasn't going to be swayed by those who live here, so that is that. It really doesn't matter what local people want, does it. Twenty-three flats equals a lot more poll tax and less government support. Don't tell me these inspectors are not pressured to make the 'right' decision.

It is, at the time of writing, a particularly lean period for the brewing industry. As we have mentioned before, the greed of the breweries has played a large part in the fall of beer sales. I have never witnessed so many public houses with 'To Let' signs appearing over the doors. There are more closed houses than I have ever seen. One established traditional pub which changed hands under the farcical government scheme to create more competition was closed almost immediately. In June, the 'Anchor' in Tongham closes its doors for the last time. The landlord and landlady have been there for twenty-four years. No mean achievement for one tenancy. Not only is the Anchor a pleasant building to look at, but it also retains a barn, situated alongside the pub, and only just back from the highway, creating quite a rural air. Surrounded as the site is by trees, a quiet, pastoral scene can be appreciated by those whose motives are not conditioned by money. If, of course, your motives are of that ilk, then think of the site as it will be. A building has been here since 1745, a licensed premises since 1849. We will, however, be able to watch the extension of a recently built estate continue on its sprawl unabated. This will no doubt be viewed as 'cleaning up a corner', not to mention the poll tax again. It will all be for the good of the community and Greedy Bastards PLC.

Rushmoor Borough Council are looking for a new top dog, a Chief Executive, no less. The post is worth £50,000 a year. This money-conscious council has spent £10,000 on advertising the post and the front runner is thought to be its own Director of Environmental Services. It will be interesting to know if he gets the job, won't it.

At precisely the same time as this £10,000 advert came to light, the same council announced that it would no longer be subsidising meals-on-wheels as they could save £13,000. If they stopped allocating monies to the TTT (Town Twinning Twots) they would be well in. Then again, why look after your own, people who have always paid their way, when you can ingratiate yourself with foreigners and act out your fantasy as an international prat. This council, like many others, still hasn't taken the hint that the majority of people feel the same way. They have now decided to strengthen links between their borough and some place called Sulechow in Poland. It is not as if the Poles are in the Eurovision Song Contest, which reminds me, how come Israel enter year in, year out. Perhaps they think they are European, they certainly never admit to being Arabs and I can never see the difference myself! This all started because one of Rushmoor's councillors was a Pole. He set up one of the many 'Help Poland and every other eastern bloc country who needs feeding association'. From that tenuous link they have decided to embark on a full twinning arrangement. Why do they bother? Oh, I remember, if you can manage to pick up a little business as well...

I only veered slightly from the subject there, but it was still local news, so you shouldn't moan too much. What was that? You bought the first book and you expected this one to be better? I have got half a chance of selling you a car!

Anyway, ever onwards, the gypsies. That list of sites stretching right across the area controlled by Guildford Borough Council had been narrowed down a little while ago to just five sites. Three of the five are in Ash, now there is a surprise. Is Clandon there amongst the other two? No. Is Effingham? No. No, it is down to Ash again, along with a possible site in Guildford and one tagged on the end of a council estate in Normandy – which for those of you in Mytholmroyd, Etruria or Clitheroe, is the next village from Ash. It is a travesty of justice that the estate was built where it was anyway. It is slap bang in the middle of a very pleasant area with commanding views. Not really ideal for those whose vision extends only to their tattoos and greyhounds. I am totally against council houses being built where there is a nice view. I feel it is all so wasted. It doesn't seem right that people graft away to pay a mortgage on a house that overlooks another similar property six feet away, while those whose doors and windows are repaired, painted and generally cosseted can draw back the curtains and survey fields of unspoilt agricultural land. I have noticed that about so many small towns and villages. No doubt there will be someone who disagrees!

Anyway, local councillors were making the usual squeaking noises to the committee concerned and the local paper, just to cover their rear, but we all know the scenario. By the new year, councillors had organised a public meeting and asked for 10,000 signatures to be on the petition that would be handed to Guildford Borough Council, in the hope that someone would act in Ash's favour. By the end of the first week of the new year, our esteemed MP, Mr Cranley Onslow – I will spell his name correctly this time – was backing Ash's corner.

The beginning of February saw our neighbouring council, Rushmoor, being granted possession of some land it was going to develop. The site, once used as an old people's home, will soon be 32 two-bedroom flats – more poll tax. At the moment, the site is a sight. The so-called travellers have been there nearly two months and the place is littered with rubbish, looks awful and the local residents have to put up with the foul language being uttered at all times of day and night. Still, what better way to spend your poll tax than cleaning up after these bastards. A week later, the council were once again applying for a court order to remove travellers who set up camp in an Aldershot park. At the same time Hampshire County Council were announcing their five short-listed sites, three of which are close to Farnborough.

Meanwhile, back in Surrey. The 3,357 residents of Ash who signed the petition were disappointed. Another surprise. Guildford B.C. – Borough Council not 'Before Croydon' – decided to site the gypsies at Ash Bridge (in Ash), one of the three short-listed areas. The irony of this decision is that the land Guildford B.C. have allocated for the gypsies is currently used by mobile home dwellers. They, in turn, will have to have their homes remobilised for the journey of just over a mile to their new site. They, of course, don't want to move, but are being moved because the council have decided that is where the gypsies are going. I don't understand anything any more.

All the above tales of woe give credence to the view that everything is predetermined by councillors. The initial list of sites is just a front. Every councillor in the area, the local MP and 3,300 who signed the petition are apparently wrong and their views count for nothing. The whole thing stinks and to move existing mobile home dwellers who have lived on a site for years and do not wish to move, to another site just because you want to use the site for gypsies, begs a reasonable explanation, but nobody has been given one.

One piece of information that came to light recently was the fact that the poll tax has cost four times as much to collect as the old rates. One million pounds in fact for one borough. Now work out how much money has been wasted on collection throughout the country and we have enough to keep several hospital wards and schools open for years. It is actually easier to throw it down the drain. The council tax will soon be taking over, but don't be fooled that the new system will be any cheaper to implement. New systems need new computers and the likes of IBM will be rubbing their floppy discs with glee. I rubbed mine the other day, but Maureen said you can be arrested for doing that in Safeways!

So, Mr Whiplash is still insistent that we are coming out of recession, which is good, if not predictable news, seeing as it is now less than two months before the election. Unfortunately, this tends to fly in the face of comments from industry and commerce. Oh, and the unemployment figures. Then again, they are not that important if they don't back up your argument.

It has just been revealed that 1990 saw the highest immigration into Britain since 1964. Two hundred and sixty seven thousand came and two hundred and thirty one thousand went, making a net increase of thirty-six thousand people. That is a hell of a lot of mouths, homes and land – and benefit. Breaking the incomers down into categories, the largest number, some 108,000 were returning to Britain after a spell abroad. The next largest group comprised 38,000 from India, Pakistan, Africa and the other Caribbeans. Thirty-two thousand came from Canada, New Zealand and Australia, while another 35,000 legged it from Europe. British citizens going abroad accounted for 135,000. The phraseology 'British citizen' could mean anyone and the figures are not broken down into ethnic groups for this statistic. Got to go, Maureen has just called me for tea. It's Toad in the Hole. It is also Friday and one of the rare nights of good comedy. Three programmes, in fact, and surprisingly, two of them are on ITV, *Watching* and *Second Thought*s. Then it is over at 9 pm to the Beeb for a repeat performance by Victoria Wood. The Channel 4 programme *Whose Line Is It Anyway* receives rave reviews in the press, but I must confess to sitting stony-faced on the two occasions I have watched it. I feel it is too clever for its own good, not unlike many adverts, and aren't there a lot of them these days? You tend to find yourself making tea during the programme because it is the shorter of the two time slots. I have never understood the Guinness adverts, or that series of ads for lager. I have left out the name because I can't remember it, but it is a Pilsner. That shows how much the advert has influenced me.

Social Security are currently running a series of TV adverts aimed at would-be claimants. They are being asked to contact the DSS, so that they can receive a 'disability living allowance'. If people are entitled to it, fine, but to spend money advertising the fact that there is an undisturbed pot of gold available seems a terrible waste. Why does the chap who tells you about it have to be so po-faced? He has a slightly aggressive style and he is badly spoken. Why did they use this chap? Is he supposed to be indicative of the disabled at large? Or is it that by appearing common with a chip on his shoulder, he will strike a chord with the undefined? I know not.

I am not at all impressed with the adverts for sanitary towels. It is bad enough sitting eating your breakfast or dinner when on the screen flashes something absorbent with wings, but to endure 'luvvy, darling' Claire Rayner being her normal ingratiating self really puts my back up. The other morning I was just about to stuff my face with toast and marmalade (Tiptree, of course – we don't buy rubbish!) when Dr Hilary Jones started to discuss female discharges. I would have much preferred battery discharges, but I accept that the subject is probably lacking in audience appeal. Now he is one of those chaps who is just bloody perfect! He has got sickeningly good looks, good physique, nice diction without being plummy, and can get away with an effeminate name. (No, I didn't mean Jones.) What the TV hierarchy cannot do is leave well alone. Mr Jones is another one who has been 'got at'. His hair is groomed to the point where he looks like a character out of *Thunderbirds*. They did the same with Alan Titchmarsh and Bob Holness. The snooker player, Terry Griffiths, has also been hairlifted. It doesn't suit any of them. In fact, the end result is an unsuccessful attempt to make personalities look younger than they are. Thank God for Patrick Moore!

If you read *FWIS* you will know of my love for the Welsh Valleys, where as a child I travelled a lot on either Red and White or Western Welsh buses. Occasionally it would be Crossville Services, but the former were the regular mode of transport. It is with regret that 24 years after Red and White merged with Western Welsh, the company that grew from that association, National Welsh, should now be in the hands of the receiver. Bus depots have been sold off and it looks unlikely that the name will survive. In the fifties, Western Welsh possessed some beautiful six-wheel buses in its fleet, a far cry from the boring single deckers that are the mainstay of operators throughout the country today.

Here we go, another nibble at the edge of our society, another tear in the fabric of our nation. Durham's Chief Constable has admitted his doubts about his police force's ability to control crime at the present time. This sort of news will no doubt be greeted with glee by those who strive to reduce this country to lawlessness. Durham is not your average inner-city area, but as we have seen before, a rural environment is no protection from crime. Thefts of all kinds, some 32,300, are up 25% on the figure issued a year ago. There were over 6,000 home and 7,000 other burglaries on top of that, up 23%. Northumbria police are training another 200 police to deal with rioting. Who would have thought it possible, even ten years ago, that we would be in the state we are now, with no apparent will to halt the slide.

Well, I have found another couple of candidates to be shot at dawn – sooner, if possible. It seems that a chappie called Ken Collins, who is a Labour Euro MP – no, I had never heard of him either, but then you can't call being a Euro MP a proper job – has had a tantrum. He is upset because the Foreign Office Minister with Special Responsibilities for Europe (that's not a real job, either), one Mr Tristan Garel-Jones, referred to the French as frogs. Where has the petty Mr Collins been all his life? They have always been frogs and that is on a good day. To most of us they are sheep-killing French bastards, who only want to know us when Germany's calling. The innocent and naïve Mr C. goes on to say that Tristan, as his friends call him, also used provocative language to describe Scotland. How else would you describe it? He is accused of uttering the phrase 'pouring subsidies down the necks of celts'. So? We then have Alex Salmond, leader of that continuous non-event, the Scottish National Party, suggesting that Tris (as his wife calls him) should be dismissed from office. He says it is not appropriate to have someone who hurls abuse at both the Scots and the French as a Foreign Minister. Frankly, I think they make excellent credentials and should be compulsory. After all, what else should you do with them? If Mr T., as his mother calls him, continues in this vein, I think he should be heading for a promotion spot very soon. 'Snitcher' Collins has, you will not be surprised to learn, written to the Prime Minister. Well, he would, wouldn't he. Then again, anyone who could be that petty is destined for a successful career in Europe.

Mock surprise time. Mike Tyson has been found guilty – I can't help thinking there is more than a little doubt over the decision made in this contest.

The Broadcasting Standards Council yesterday upheld two complaints against ITV, about the programme 'Baywatch'. It stands accused and apparently has been found guilty of promoting unacceptable stereotypes and is unsuitable for early evening viewing. I would have thought the latter was more appropriate to the tampon adverts. The 'unacceptable stereotype' refers to young things in bikinis. What is wrong with that? I expect a lot of girls are like that in California, so they will be stereotyped. Anyway, whoever those two were who complained, I bet they weren't male and I also wager they weren't young, good-looking with hour-glass figures and turned-up noses. Jealousy will get them nowhere, whereas diet and plastic surgery may well do the trick!

You know my faith and respect for anyone who dabbles in the world of honking (sorry, banking), well, the Bank of England's Governor, Mr Robin Leigh-Pemberton, is not best pleased that Kent County Council want to instal a gypsy camp on one of his acres of land near the M2. On the M2, would of course be acceptable to most of us, but it is a bit rich when a local authority can implement the 1968 Caravan Act and tell Mr Leigh-Pemberton, 'We are taking your land under a compulsory purchase order.' Now I am aware that he has got another 1,999 acres still to his double-barrelled name, but it is not on, is it. I don't suppose Kent County Council's powers extend to France, do they. It just occurred to me that with the Channel Tunnel completion fairly imminent, there might be some boundary changes.

The Tories will have a rough ride through the election, I feel, as unemployment has now reached 2,600,000 and the number of homes repossessed last year totalled 75,500. So that must be a few less Tory supporters, I would think. Still, as the wise one known as Lamont says, all the signs are that we are on the road to recovery. Ruin starts with an 'r' doesn't it. I wonder if that is what he meant?

NHS prescription charges went up today to £3.75 a shot. Now that is a bloody scandal. The have-nots, who don't want to work, but can always be found smoking and drinking, continue to get theirs free, of course. The poor sod like you and I will continue to pay. I say you because I am pretty darned sure no-one from the lower orders would be reading this. Well, not unless it had been stolen and they had been told it was about badger-baiting, rioting and being given instructions on how to hot wire an XR3.

We have had a couple of good ones in the announcement column of the *Daily Telegraph* recently. A Lt Cdr A.C. Morse is to marry a Miss E. Taggart, and the Todd family, you know, Fiona and Conrad, the Kuala Lumpur Todds, have had a daughter,

'India Paloma Hannah', beautifully colonial, don't you think?

Aldershot FC have another 'mystery' backer who is going to save the club. That must be the fiftieth this year. Talk about lurching from crisis to death-throe.

Now this *is* sad. Unfortunately, it also reflects the present downward trends I keep on about. An 88-year-old man is having to shut down the gardening club he has run for 40 years, due to continued vandalism. The sheds they use to store gardening equipment have been broken into four times in the past month, the last haul being worth over £700. The club actually existed to help would-be members and enthusiasts with techniques, hints and equipment, but these lousy bastards have stopped all that – and the do-gooders want to ban smacking.

This is a nice 'get out of jail free card'. A local grocer has complained to Rushmoor Council about his day's takings since Sunday opening started and has asked why the council is taking no action against Greedy Bastards PLC – my words, not his. He seems to be more polite than me, which may surprise some of you! Anyway, the answer given by Mr Stephen Taylor, Head of Rushmoor's Legal and Estates Department, is that 'We cannot bring a prosecution unless we have a specific complaint and witnesses willing to give evidence in court, and as far as I am aware, this has not happened.' He goes on, 'Even then we would have to be confident that the law has been broken and at the moment, the issue is far from clear.' He added that at the present time, there were a number of test cases going through the British and European courts and until they were resolved, it would be unwise to prosecute. This last quote takes the biscuit, though. 'If we don't know what the law is, we can't say whether it has been violated.' The law, or lack of it, seems to be totally on the side of GB PLC, doesn't it?

February 14th has turned out to be a depressing day. It should have been one of joy, of relief, but, no, the gutless and uncaring MPs were in the majority and threw out Mr Kevin McNamara's backbench bill that would have finally put an end to the hunting obscenity. Of the three party leaders, only Neil Kinnock voted in favour of it. John Major-Balls voted against, whilst Paddy Pantsdown naturally sat on the fence and abstained – which shows real leadership qualities. How can he *not* vote on an issue like this? The pro-hunting lobby have come out with some prize statements during their 'shock horror' campaign. There was a letter from the Duke of Rutland, who should know better, asking what would happen if hunting were banned, to the remaining hounds? Would they have to be put down? Talk about scaremongering. Then we have the Campaign for Hunting saying that it wasn't possible to remove one thread from the tapestry of rural economics without unravelling it entirely. Very nicely put, but complete twaddle. Some fellow called Stephen Hastings, a former Tory MP and more importantly, Master of the Fitzwilliam Foxhounds, said the bill would reduce the countryside to a slum. How is that? With these people galloping around it cannot be described any other way at the moment. A letter was sent to all MPs asking, sorry, demanding, them to proscribe animal welfare organisations under the Prevention of Terrorism Act. We, of course, are to take these animal murderers seriously. It seems ironic that the ones who kill for sport suggest that those who wish to stop it are nothing more than terrorists. Methinks they doth protesteth too much. There was a letter printed in the *Wales on Sunday* newspaper. Some 'person' called Steve Loveridge of the British Field Sports Society said that the bill, shorn of all its gimmicks, is nothing more than an old-fashioned anti-hunting bill. So what is wrong with that? He goes on to say that banning hunting would not save a single fox's life. His tone becomes sinister when he adds that the number of foxes killed would have to be increased by other 'methods'. I think the BFSS should be taken to court under the Trade Descriptions Act, and made to alter their name to the British Field Murder Society.

I can do no better than refer to that most learned and honest of MPs, Teddy Taylor, member for Southend, which is strange really, you know, being a Scot, but never mind, there has to be the exception to prove the rule. He has admitted to being neither for nor against hunting, and decided to go out to hunts, ask opinions and see for himself. This act is, of course; uncommon in itself, as MPs rarely seek the views of others, and even more rarely, for an occupation that professes to care, bother to get off their back benches and visit the scene of a crime. I found it reassuring that he received, with few exceptions, nothing better than contempt and at worst, such vicious hate mail from hunt supporters. The majority of the British public are against fox and deer hunting, so how did the bill end up in the wastepaper bin? I suppose it was a case of too many friends in high places, too much tit for tat, too many favours being called in, too many planning applications, too many contributions to party funds...

I am sitting at the kitchen table, jotting down these notes. Maureen and I are just having a cup of tea, and coming to terms with the facets of romance that never existed in our day –

I am assuming you are in your forties. About an hour ago, I was in our bedroom getting dressed, when I gazed out of the window and spied the postman walking up our path. He was carrying some post in one hand and a banana in the other. He rang the bell. I went downstairs, opened the stable door upper section and having told the dog that he was a 'friend', he handed over our mail and the banana, complete with franked stamps stuck to its skin. It was addressed to 'Banana Woman'. There was a lot of waffle and it was signed 'Mango Man'. The postman didn't say anything, he didn't need to. He just smiled in a sympathetic way, he obviously had children of his own. Debbie came down about half an hour later. Despite my comments that, as a father, I would prefer my daughter to be called Guava Girl or Lychee Lady, she just laughed and took the banana – and the rest of her post upstairs. I mean, a bloody banana!

Glyn is going to one of his regular night spots tonight, so once he goes out early this evening, we won't see much of him. In fact, anything of him until about lunch time tomorrow. He has changed his job within the last couple of weeks and now works for a large retail food chain. Whereas in the fast food industry, everybody appears to be either school-leaving age or waiting to go to college, here he is mixing with men and women of all ages. This should help his confidence no end, and hopefully will be the start of a promising career, even if they do open on Sundays.

We are taking William stock-car racing this evening. He has been good for eight consecutive minutes, so that is definitely worth a reward. We are only going down to the track in Aldershot, so we just hope we don't see anyone we know. I am led to believe that the 'greyhound' types frequent the place. Fortunately, neither of us are snobs!

Aldershot Football Club are still holding on. They play fellow strugglers Doncaster Rovers this afternoon, at Doncaster's ground, so that will be one match nearer the end of the season. I suppose they might even earn a point. Hang on, it must be flying pig time.

We are off to Horsham in a minute. There is one of those old-fashioned cheese shops in the Carfax – that's the main square – which offers a superb selection of goodies. Further down the road from that is a corner shop, selling all sorts of rice, baking accessories and ingredients, dried fruit, sugars, etc. A veritable cornucopia for the kitchen enthusiast. It is a fair division of labour in our house. I tell Maureen what I want to eat and she makes it! Well, I tend the garden, actually I tend to look at it. So it is off in a south-easterly direction we go, our trusty Mini being our mode of transport today. I hope it starts. Great, isn't it, in 1983, we had an 'A' plate car, in 1992 we are scurrying around in a 'T' plate Mini. That bastard in Spain has got a lot to answer for, not even a holiday this year. Ah, well.

Maureen came back from her local WI meeting the other evening and said, 'I can knock another two names off the list of people I know who haven't been to Disneyland.' Yes, I can say quite unashamedly that I would love to go to America, full stop. Not that I would go on most of the rides, as I hate the thought of my stomach churning for the rest of the day. I wasn't impressed with the 'boat' ride at Chessington, and there was no way I was going on the Magic Carpet ride. So, having gone to Disneyland, it would be the more sedate activities that I would participate in. I remember being stuck at the top of a Big Wheel and promised never to lie or be nasty again, if only I could get down in one piece. I did get down, but the promises evaporated immediately. Well, fancy trying to do a deal with God when you are forty-two years of age and scared shitless – or, for those in Bromley – poo-less. One hundred feet up in the air. He surely didn't think I meant it. Ah, she's ready, it seems like only twenty minutes ago she said, 'I'll only be a minute.' She has probably been trying to start the car. Just checking the pockets, door keys, overdraft facility (cheque book), bank card, Network South East discount card, in case the car doesn't restart in Horsham. Anything else? Yes, the dog is in its basket, the windows are closed. I'll see you later.

A bright, sunny, Sunday morning, it is, to be sure – see how international I have become about Southern Ireland. Still, no matter. It is 8.30 am, breakfast is a-sizzling and I have promised faithfully to start digging that vegetable patch. At the moment it resembles a bumpy lawn – which in fact it is, but armed with a spade and fork, I will yet make this saw's ear into the proverbial. More likely, of course, I will end up in here at the desk painting some coaches and wagons, which have been sitting on the shelf for months, and sod the garden. Let's face it, all this writing is a bit one-sided. Have you written to me saying how much you agree with this and that, or how you are going to grab me by the short and curlies because you don't agree with something else? As long as the pleasure is mutual, then it is all right with me.

'Man of the chapter' award goes to a gentleman called Eddie Wilde. He is a storeman, working for British Aerospace in North Wales. He spends nearly all of his spare time caring for badgers. Mr Wilde has constructed sheds for hospital use and runs for them to exercise. Road victims and those caught in snares are taken by him, or to him, from members of the public. No fuss, no social-climbing – and no pay to show for it. Just love and affection for a creature which has suffered and still suffers at the hands of man.

Just before I sign off, did you see that the Black and White Minstrel Show in Rotherham, Yorkshire, went ahead as the White Minstrel Show. The cast were asked not to don their blacking in the interests of 'racial harmony'. I would have thought that little piece of neurosis was in the interests of 'racial harm'. The management added to the farce by commenting that they feared the show might breach race relations laws. The manager, one Terry Dobson, who made the decision, has obviously been sent on 'awareness' courses, or is he just the proverbial wet blanket, as they would say in Sevenoaks, Kent. I ask once more, 'Whose bloody country is it?'

Eau dear, water can the meter be?

There is an article in the Sunday Telegraph about water privatisation. Now this subject is a very sore point with me. Until we moved into the new house, we, like everybody else, paid our water rates half-yearly. Nobody told us that we would be put on a meter. The only indication came when we received a bill explaining that we had used so many units, plus, of course, the cost of the obligatory standing charge. Mid Southern Water Co. is now owned by the French – which really sticks in the throat. Anyhow, I rang their office and the young lady I spoke to was most helpful, explaining that since the poll tax (that again) was being introduced in a couple of months' time (April 1990), rateable values were no longer being decided locally, which meant that all new houses built after April 1989 were to be supplied with metered water. She seemed genuinely surprised that we did not know and offered to send us a booklet explaining the situation and telling us how to calculate water usage. I asked her where the meter was situated, as I knew the whereabouts of the gas and electricity cupboards, but knew not of any water meter. I was told that the said imposition was located at the end of the lane, under the pavement, access to which was by lifting up a metal cover and peering into the unknown, well peering at a dial anyway (back to the dramatic angle, I am afraid). I queried as to why the meter was not on my land. She said that the pipes in the lane were the responsibility of the house owner. The water board, as was, tap in their meter at the first point of public land. The fact that the gas pipes and electrical wiring come down the lane underground and are the responsibility of the respective companies cut no ice at all.

Following the call, I went and checked, and sure enough, with the aid of a screwdriver I managed to prise open the cover and there beneath was a bright red meter whirring around like a good 'un. The booklet arrived, we studied it. Ingratiating bastards. The first line on the inside page reads, 'Mid Southern Water Co. welcomes you to your new home' – gives you shell shock more like. I want a cheaper service, not a welcome, the dog can do that! The further we read into the booklet, the more outraged we felt. It tells you how much water you use when flushing the toilet, bathing, showering, washing the clothes, using the dishwasher. It gives a table in every equation. Get this. 'If you bath every day, your water usage is likely to be high.' It seems as if they are encouraging people not to use water, but you can't win. If less water is being used, they will put up the price of the cubic whatsit and you will still pay through the nose to fund yet another jolly time being had by the Chairman and all the ingrates. Along with this expensively prepared colour booklet comes a list of charges. This starts by explaining why they needed to increase their rates over the level of inflation, and then try to soothe the poor sod who is paying by telling us how cheap water is. Next, it tells you where to write should you wish to express your views on 'Our Service', 'Charging' or 'Metering'. What it doesn't say is that it would be a bloody waste of time, as you won't change anything and you would be even more stupid for thinking you could. Now we come to the stun-gun. The annual standing charge for this piece of machinery that no-one asked for is £48 for your water and another £25 for getting rid of it. What a rip-off. £73 per annum before you turn on the tap. After this we learn 'how to pay' – with a mortgage, I would think. Then there is a short section on 'Customer Care', which is followed by the biggest cheek of all, headed 'For many children in the third world, water is a matter of life and death'. I wish people could stop blindly referring to the phrase 'third world'. It seems to be a catch-all for everywhere east of Java, or is it Melton Mowbray? It matters not. Anyway, they are asking you for a donation. Elephants, lions, giraffes, all need water, but they didn't include them. I know who I would rather save, and they don't breed so quickly.

We paid up and looked unhappy, as they say in Merthyr Tydfil, and if you lived there you would look unhappy. Not another word was heard until September last year, when we got a bill for an astronomical amount. I rang the offices, spoke to someone who was, as before, very helpful and visited their premises with said bill clutched very firmly in hand. The offices have changed considerably since it was the local Mid Southern Water Co. Now privatised, answerable to shareholders and the French, a fortune had obviously been spent on the new structure. It is actually a pleasing design, but I question whether it was necessary to provide such quality stone flooring, or the giant fish tank in the wall, or the wooden surrounds, not to mention the reception desk that is so large, ten people could work from it. Words fail me, well nearly. A large revolving door that seems to be typical of those that are all the rage in Sainsburys and Asda stands as the central entrance point, guarded wither side by push-pull types of conventional design. Superb quality, no atmosphere and a clock that didn't work. The lady whom I saw was very courteous and appeared genuinely interested when I said that the bill was the first example of correspondence we had received in eighteen months. I pointed out that the bill had not taken into consideration an episode some six months previously when a valve, their side of the meter, thank someone, split and the water fairly gushed out while the meter digits worked overtime. Our lady receptionist investigated, but I had already written the script – which was correct – it was the computer's fault. In due course we received another bill with the agreed amount duly credited and a paying-in book for monthly instalments. Since then, the outlet union (there's technical, as they say in Llanwern Steelworks) has split again. This, of course, not only wastes more water, but uses up a lot of their engineer's time that was never relevant before. All because of the bloody poll tax. By Christ, that woman's got a lot to answer for. Since then, we have received another bill, this week in fact. The consumption tariff has increased by almost 50% in a year, so Greedy Water Bastards (French) PLC are doing very nicely, and still getting complaints about the quality of their eau – too many frogs, I suppose.

Good news for Aldershot. They only lost 1-0, a distinct improvement over some recent results.

The stock car racing was good entertainment, certainly better than watching a Grand Prix. The only problem was that once you had seen all three types of races... stock cars, minis and buggies, the rest was very repetitive, appearing to be retakes of previous encounters, minus those vehicles that had succumbed to the paddock in the centre of the race track. The clientele were, however, somewhat lacking in the finer graces. Rubbish bins were rarely used for depositing the remains of the hamburger, hot dog or polystyrene coffee cup. There were a number of children with Grade 1 haircuts (I believe that is the terminology). They ran hither and thither, not really interested in the races, in fact climbing the wire fencing that separates cars from spectators held far more appeal. William seemed to enjoy it though, and to be fair, the hot dogs were not awful.

I have decided it is too cold for gardening, so I shall paint these models that have been sitting gathering dust. Television doesn't look too inspiring this evening. On every TV guide or supplement that is appearing, one name seems to be prominent – that of Miss Hannah Hauxwell. Hasn't she done well? I watched, like many others, the programme about her which was televised a couple of years ago. The simple lifestyle she had managed to continue was refreshing and humbling. She wanted for very little, but now, I can't help thinking she is being exploited. I could be wrong, the slight possibility of which you are no doubt dismissing with consummate ease. Sean Day-Lewis, in his review of the series *An Innocent Abroad*, 'feels she and those around her retained their dignity and that TV has done her proud'. Talking of Day-Lewises, there seems to be a plethora of them these days. It used to be Troughtons and Dotrices. Every drama, every comedy in the seventies had their share of various members of the afore-mentioned families. Every decade has its names, however. Now it is the turn of the Cusacks, Day-Lewises and Bonham-Carters.

More statistics. Another 320 coves and cove-esses have put up their hands and admitted to being either bored, petty or frigid. The Independent Television Commission have stated that they received the above number of complaints about an advertisement for Citroen cars, where an attractive girl is kidnapped and later let go, unharmed. The main cause of complaint is that the advert is frivolous and irresponsible. If complaints were received about Vespre sanitary towel ads, I wouldn't be at all surprised. Frankly, that is the last thing I want to know about. Even the poor old British Safety Council have come in for criticism. A poster depicting a caricature of Madonna with accentuated breasts housed in coned sheaths is apparently beyond the pale. The wording in the advert says 'Protect your assets – Madonna does'. What is wrong with that? It is a play on words, or, in this case, a play on tits – and wouldn't we like to, and why not, as Barry Norman would say. 'It was in the worst possible taste, and the most sexist example of advertising I have seen.' These were the words used by Cardiff City Council's Personnel Officer. He has banned the poster from the City Hall and all other council premises, because it contravenes the city's Equal Opportunities policy. How? Does he mean there should be a man by her side with a coned sheath covering his willy, or is he complaining that a small-breasted girl should also be in the frame to compensate for Madonna's mammaries. Not surprisingly, this petty little man who's grovelling for anti-sexism brownie points has complained to the Equal Opportunity Commission in Wales. I bet he was the school 'snitch'. The good news is that the British Safety Council say they have no intention of withdrawing the poster. Whilst feeling sorry for this officious official, like others of his kind, I worry about the power he is able to wield.

Do you remember the days not so long ago, when race wasn't mixed with religion and education? Last year a disagreement between a coloured teacher and a white headmistress erupted into a full-blown fracas, which ended in a race case. The ins and outs of the case are irrelevant, but the fact of the matter is that the headmistress was described as being 'subconsciously racist' in the tribunal's findings.

As I write this, there appears to be a power struggle in an East London school. Its intake is mainly Asian children, but the teachers and headmistress are white. The school governors, Asian, don't like the set-up. The governing body suspended the headmistress. She, in turn, has been reinstated by Kenneth Clarke, still the Education Secretary. A quarter of a page has been devoted by the *Daily Telegraph* to an article on some long-haired chap called Muhammad Haque, who runs an organisation called the London Collective of Black Governors – isn't that slightly more than 'sub consciously racist'? According to the article, our long-haired foe sees racism everywhere he looks. Kenneth Clarke is apparently a racist, so moderation and reality aren't going to get a look-in here, are they. Mr Haque came here twenty years ago from Bangladesh and is obviously only concerned with his 'people'. He wants to see two school governors removed. These are the two white governors imposed on the school by our Ken, then he wants an apology. What about the children? Nobody has said anything about them. The case continues.

Have you noticed how the land between an existing arterial road and the new dual-carriageway, built to relieve congestion, then becomes an infill for housing, office or commercial development. It is as if the sanctioning of a new road to enable the existing traffic to flow more easily signals the green light for further decimation of green land. It rolls on, of course. The greater the development, the more the need for a further by-pass. Everywhere is being opened up, being made more accessible, but what a price the countryside pays for this progress.

Last week, around 500 people protested against the extension to the M3 which is being built, sorry, driven, through Twyford Down in Hampshire. The route is 400 feet wide. That is a lot of land lost to concrete.

In Wensleydale, aggregate traffic is about to be lost by British Rail to the roads because they are unable to agree costs with British Steel. As well as the large number of quarry trucks using the roads within the dales, this action will see another 90 joining them. It is outright madness for these sort of decisions to be made. It cannot be justified, but then we are back to money. What little value those in power place on their country's future.

Having just finished writing the above, I have just discovered that not only are they still serious about widening the M25 to four lanes, but consideration is being given to building a series of parallel orbital roads to take local traffic. The Royal Society for Nature Conservation says that 81 important wildlife sites, and 47 ancient woodlands will be either destroyed or severely damaged. Still, who is going to listen to them, the RSNC are only concerned for the future of the country.

What constitutes all the nasty and grabbing side of Britain is at least balanced in some small way by reading that Frinton-on-Sea, Essex, is to get its very first fish and chip shop. I only went there once, as a lad, with a friend for a week's holiday. If I remember correctly, the lady we stayed with was a family friend of my friend's mother. I will give you a bit of time in case you have to read that last sentence again. It was on Frinton's promenade that we two lads watched a Spitfire and a Hurricane fly overhead to an inland destination. I remember thinking what it must have been like to witness the homecoming of 'our boys' after a 'sortie with the hun'. The imagination runs wild when you are about ten years of age, doesn't it. My imagination still runs wild but I have yet to wake up next to Emma Samms, Lysette Anthony or Jan Francis! I was going to add the name of Kylie Minogue, but the kids would laugh. No, sod it, why can't I face the world and be honest. I have still got an ageing, lecherous crush on her, especially if she is dressed in schoolgirl uniform.

Meanwhile, back in Frinton-on-Sea, a quote has just been uttered by Lt Col Roger Attrill, Secretary of the 800-member Frinton Golf Club, and I relish his words. 'Frinton', he says, 'prides itself on not having these things. A chip shop will cause a bit of a comment. People will be concerned if this sort of thing is allowed to go ahead.' The chap who is opening this subversive establishment said he had already been told to leave town, but was prepared to take the brickbats and open at Easter. He did add that it was only a fish and chip shop, not a burger kiosk – and even he wouldn't dream of that for fear of being lynched. It is reassuring to know that in a small town so close to the great metropolis, they still ban radios and ball games from the promenade. Topless sunbathing and nude bathing are also prohibited. In fact, only recently has it relaxed the ban on buses and coaches.

Here is a case of injustice if ever l heard one. An eighteen year old from Bristol stole a van and drove it at a thirty-two year old chap who had just foiled an attempt by the same example of pond life to steal a car. The man was thrown over the van's bonnet and hurled onto its roof. He fell to the ground and died six days later. The court heard that the said eighteen year old had 30 previous convictions for car-related crimes and showed no remorse or conscience. He was sentenced to nine years' youth custody. He should *never* be released, he should spend the rest of his life in jail. He murdered someone needlessly, he should pay. In less than six years he could be free. On the assumption that capital punishment will not be reintroduced all the time we are ruled by weak, gutless over-feds, the least we can do to him and his ilk is to punish them when they are inside. I have said it before, and I will say it again, no TV, no snooker or table tennis, no variation in food or diet. Just give them the most basic sustenance to support life, no hot drinks, just water. I would force them to work twelve hours a day, the rest being given over to rest and the minimum of exercise allowed by health experts. When they are not working, they would be in solitary confinement. No visitors, no communication with the outside world. I would make people like them suffer. The mask of arrogance might just slip when they reflect on what the rest of their life holds for them.

Once again, an innocent person, attempting to uphold the law, has been killed. Once again, a family is given a lifetime sentence of regret and sorrow, while he still has his freedom to come. Why wasn't he already behind bars? Thirty previous offences, doesn't that tell the powers-that-be anything? Still, he has got NACRO, who no doubt will be fighting for his cushioned corner. They will hand out endless reasons for the situation this oik and others have found themselves in and probably blame white, middle-class society for their undoing.

I half expected some correspondence, in the form of letters to the editor, to follow an article in the *Daily Telegraph* concerning a private club in Handsworth, Birmingham. The club concerned was no doubt cited because half of the local population are black, and the club's 400 members are white. The old tried and tested method of selection has been overtaken by time and zealous campaigning. No longer does a prospective member of a club need a proposer and seconder, oh, no. This tradition has been filed under 'Reasonable behaviour and fairness'. A change in legislation has been brought about by the Commission for Racial

Equality and Claire Short, that champion of the oppressed, for whom a life sentence in Handsworth would be welcomed with glee by the vast majority of the population. With the blessing of the courts and the CRE, the new system introduced means that an applicant needs only to produce an outside reference to qualify for a three-month probationary period.

Once again, this form of legislation only serves to 'irritate' the racial issue, not help it. You won't see any more black people enrolled as members of white clubs. Members will, however, go out of their way to make sure their club stays white. Why? Because they are being forced to make a stand, they are being pushed into a corner. The private club is the last bastion of free choice by the members – black or white. As one of the club members pointed out, 'There are clubs and pubs up the Soho Road, they don't say whites are not welcome, but just you try going in one.' What concerns me is the arm-twisting, the persuasion that accompanies a CRE enquiry. You can smell the overtones of power that is all-embracing for a club experiencing a visit from that obscenely over-funded quango. One Peter Oteng, who travels with the really important sounding tag of 'Senior Social Policy Officer' for the CRE in the West Midlands, visited the Handsworth Central Club and told their committee that the aforementioned 'proposer and seconder' system of selection was, quote, 'potentially discriminatory' and they would have to look at it again. When told that they would welcome decent black and Asian people to the club, the CRE representative said that they should target a few and get them in. If that happened, the CRE would 'back off'. 'Back off? back-off?' It echoes the sort of threat uttered by Nazis, they too were idealists. There is also the not-so-little matter of a discrepancy over the number of so-called unsuccessful candidates that the CRE are happy to tell the world about. They say that 31 people from ethnic groups wanted to join the club, but failed. Only four could be contacted by the *Daily Telegraph* and all denied having approached the club for membership or complaining to the CRE. Perhaps there is just a tad of desperation creeping into the CRE's case, after all, it costs money to support the title of 'Senior Social Policy Officer'.

A couple of days after this article appeared, a letter was printed in the same paper commenting that the club concerned had been landed with costs of £15,000, while at the same time, £750 million of taxpayers' money was to be invested by a black housing association. The writer asks what would happen to any housing association that declared itself to be devoted to whites?

Does he not have a point? In mid-February, the CRE's top-dog, Michael Day, wrote his letter to the *Daily Telegraph*. As I read his ingratiating spiel, I could visualise his hands gleefully rubbing together in sickening satisfaction at the disservice he had done to the country. Once again, those obsessive, flag-waving (Union Jack not included), single-minded nobodies had succeeded in nailing another load of metal into the coffin of freedom. Mr Day stated that 'the judgement represented a significant advance – though its implications may disturb those who hold a narrow view on the multiracial society and set limits to the practice of equal opportunities. Public opinion now accepts that an explicit colour bar is repugnant and it is, of course, illegal.' Pompous arse! Who does he think he is conning? Does he never talk to ordinary people who continue to wonder why their opinion has never been taken into account. I would like to know just who this public opinion of Mr Day's is. Other than those working with him and under him, who breathe hypocrisy and live for their biased goals, he seems to find very little time for real people. If, however, by his use of the phrase 'multicultural society' he means there are more people having a free ride, then we agree on something.

The 'London Collective of Black Governors', the 'Society of Black Lawyers' plus advertisements aimed at 'black lesbians only' continue to add weight to the view that the CRE is here purely at the behest of anybody non-white, to promote them in favour of the white indigenous population, and place the position of these people at a disadvantage when phrases like 'positive discrimination' are used by 'blind-eyed Mike' and his cronies.

Meanwhile, back in Aldershot, I see that another 'mystery backer' has been found for the football club. The big mystery is that their names are never revealed and no cash is ever forthcoming. I have no doubt that next week's news will reveal that someone else is waiting in the wings. Mind you, we could do with someone waiting on the wings, and up front and in goal...

Now this is music to my ears. You know the way Rushmoor Council toady to their continental comrades in France and Germany, well, attempts to make contact with their French twin 'Meudon' have failed. These two unfortunate places have been twinned since 1973. There was supposed to be a meeting between Meudon's mayor and representatives from Rushmoor. It had to be postponed at the last minute due to the French chappie being in Canada. Had he heard that the Germans were calling round, collecting land for the umpteenth Reich, or did he crack at the thought of the possibility that he might have to make a return visit to Rushmoor, home of Aldershot FC and an increasing number of Social Security claimants, unmarried mothers and fast-food takeaways. Still, it could be worse, his town could have been twinned with Islington or Camden, and that *would* have been worth running away from. The great thing about these twinning committee people in Rushmoor is that they keep trying, or maybe they can't take a hint. It was the committee chairman, a Mrs Linda Montgomery, who attempted to flee – sorry – finalise arrangements. (I was not looking at my notes, and found myself in her place.) Anyway, try as she might, she couldn't locate her frog, who appears to be the only one with any sense. She phoned everywhere, poor love, at the taxpayers' grant, of course, and then found he had gone Mountie-side up. Councillor Marsh commented that the council were getting nowhere fast and that ties (or strands) should be broken with the French town. To be fair this is the one moment in a committee's life when there should have been universal agreement, but no. One councillor replied that he thought they should 'keep forging ahead, as we have a mature relationship with Meudon'. Next, one of the double-barrelled heavyweights stepped in. Lt Cdr John Town-Clear blamed the recession. So the bad state of the economy is responsible for gallivanting off to Canada, is it? Even he went on to say that Rushmoor must try to rekindle the relationship. At the end of the meeting, the 'ayes' had it. In almost total harmony they agreed to write to the mayor and ask him why he wasn't available and when he might be free in the future.

As I said at the start, if it wasn't costing hard-earned tax payers' money, it would make for good, if rustic, comedy. Isn't this pro-Euro attitude adopted on a local basis the same as that put forward by central government, it just costs more. Hang on, we haven't finished yet. There is another article on page 13. This deals with the simplified systems of subsidies issued by 'Twin Twots' to organisations taking part in exchanges and visitations. According to this snippet I am reading, there is a councillor who has taken the unusual step of considering the taxpayers' pocket. He says that 'the council has had to make people redundant and those people may feel that money could have been better spent other than on twinning'. So he should be assured of a seat if he stands at the next local election.

A couple of pages on from the above story, was an article about a lad who was 8 years of age in 1972, when the Paratroopers' Mess was blown up in Aldershot. He lost his mother in the bombing.

Twenty years on, aged 28, the story centred on his life during those intervening years. At the time of the attack, the Criminal Injuries Board initially offered him £400 for the loss of his mother. This was later increased to £4,000 after the *Aldershot News*, amongst other concerns, made noises. Yesterday, a High Court Judge awarded Sarah Keays £105,000 damages for libel. Her loss cannot even be measured against that of the Aldershot lad. Talk about over-protection.

These nibbles at the edge of our fabric are still going on. The Football Association have now approved plans to end the 104-year-old Football League. The last thing one wants to see is an elitist division. Despite all the informed claims and comments that international squads might benefit from fewer games, we all know that the only real benefit will be to the clubs' pockets. I can see this exclusive club being flogged to death by the TV company who bids the most. No thought will be given to the smaller clubs, suppliers of so many players who go on to greater things. For them, financial life will be even more acute. Here is another worrying trend, the loss of grounds to developers. It makes football even more anti-social to hive off a town centre site and move to a new all-purpose, green field site. That is where a club's roots are. I feel that if a club has to move it should fold. To most supporters a club is basically dead if it doesn't have its own ground.

No doubt the Premier League will continue to cash in on the fans where the First Division left off. Spurred on by the ill-fated judgement that all-seater stands are to be the norm, prices will rocket. The likes of Umbro, Admiral and Hummel, etc. will rub their hands even more readily at the prospect of introducing their subtle changes to team strips on a more regular basis – like by the game. Not for today's football team is there any pride in donning traditional colours worn by their forebears for decades, possibly generations. No, today's money-, sorry, fashion-conscious teams must be seen to be wearing a new strip, preferably one with a sheen. They all look a mess to me, and cheap.

In the same way as children as young as six are hyped by the media men into wanting, demanding, fashion shoes and trainers, football's moneymen will continue to rip off supporters with merchandise, because they know they have a loyal contingent. Where would all the fat-cat salaries come from without the fans and their pay packets?

Keeping with sport, another act of toadying has just been dished out. Ellery Hanley, the rugby league player, has just been bestowed an Honorary Fellowship by Leeds Polytechnic. So he was born there and he plays rugby for them, what act of public service or heroic action justified this little adornment? Oh, that's right, there wasn't one!

At the start of this book I mentioned the eastern bloc's demise. This must have been an important subject, as it took up two lines. Eight months after I started writing and eighteen months since things took off properly, all we have to show for it is a united Germany that is very concerned about immigration. Russia has been laid bare for the money-grabbers, and is still unable to feed itself. Yugoslavia is in a state of complete devastation. All the factions that were controlled under Communism have escaped, not to build a brave new world for their own breed – based on a free market economy, of course – but to run around like headless chickens. The real beauty of all those cats being let out of the bag is that they can blame every other race, creed, religion. Perhaps if Milton Keynes were liberated...

Talking of liberated, my religious friend came out with a classic last night. To put you in the picture, a small group of about six of us meet every six weeks or so, at his house, to discuss the world and its wife. It is a small debating society, really, where everybody taking part brings some wine and cheese. R.F.'s wife, who is fairly quiet, and not a little shy, has started to throw in her four-pennyworth during the discussions at this 'boys' night'. It was this new-found confidence that prompted R.F.'s comment, 'I am glad my wife is getting involved, the trouble is she will soon have an opinion of her own.' Quite profound, really. Mind you, this is the same man who said to me, jokingly, 'I love my wife, well, I will until the blood test results come back, anyway!'

I had a strange dream last night. It concerned Maureen and I. We were out in the country somewhere, it was quite desolate. The landscape was hilly with quarries that were old and worked out. We walked around the edge of one of these deep pits and came across a narrow-gauge railway station. The rain was falling heavily. The station resembled, but was not quite the same as, Abergynolwyn on the Talyllyn Railway in North Wales. A train was waiting to depart. Although it was fairly bucketing down, we elected to travel in an open coach, along with some other passengers, who must also have been one star short of a galaxy. I recognised nobody, save for one passenger – Jasper Carrot. Down the valley the train travelled, until it reached the end of the line and we all alighted – as opposed to detrained. I don't like that word, it always reads as if you were once good at something and now you are not. A bit like debriefed. I always associated that word with taking down a girl's knickers, not finding out what some ex-hostage can tell you about Terry Waites' whereabouts. Anyway, the dream moved forward to Maureen and I driving away from the station in much warmer and sunnier conditions, back towards the quarries. Incidentally, the car was either an MG sports from the thirties or a Morgan. As we turned a corner, a lorry could be seen wending its way around the side of a hill. The lorry overtook a bus which was stationary, setting down just one passenger – Jasper Carrot again. Maureen pointed him out, he walked across the road and along a path around the side of a hill. We stopped the car and followed on foot. You can tell this is a period dream, there was no other traffic on the road, and we left the keys in the car. J.C. kept looking back as he walked. We kept close but out of sight. Maureen suggested he was having an affair as he looked shifty. I said he always looked shifty, although I could mean embarrassed, after all, let's not forget where he comes from! We rounded the hill, to find that he had stopped to talk to a group of people. There was nothing sinister about them as far as I can remember, no clandestine meeting with a group of nymphs or the ghost of Robert Maxwell. Maureen and I walked up behind them and I was about to ask what they were doing when I woke up, or rather the dog leapt on me and woke me up. It must have been the cheese. Well, I am sorry there is no juicy bit, no ending, no neatly tied-up package or logical conclusion. Blame the dog, not me.

Getting back to quotes for a minute, the one I really liked recently was a line uttered on that most appalling of programmes, *EastEnders*. I can't even tell you who the characters were, but it was two women discussing the rape that one of them had suffered. I assumed they were having a highly charged conversation as the 'un-raped' one exclaimed, 'he invaded your body'. What a peculiar phrase to use, I thought. What was he, a Viking? Not to be raped in that programme is a rarity, I believe. In fact, if you haven't suffered child abuse, physical abuse, mental abuse, rape and torture, you must be either queer, lesbian and/or suffering from Aids – either that or you know a man who is. A very queer man a very, very queer man. Of course, being cast as one of the afflicted, or infected, doesn't preclude you from having a dip in the Mix 'n' Match tray of abuses. In fact, the more the seamier. If that programme reflects life, and there happens to be an after-life, I still want to come back as a Black Box. You always get found, you are always in one piece, you are still working, and as far as

I am aware, there have been no proven cases of Black Boxes contracting Aids.

Well, if *EastEnders* is the dross end of soaps, then I have just witnessed the soulmate in game shows. I happened to be having a late breakfast, or early lunch, when *Keynotes* appeared on the screen. The compere was manic, and the contestants must have been picked to suit. The producers or research assistants must go out of their way to pick oddballs. I deliberately watched three episodes. With one exception, the female contestants were born show-offs. Big in body, with common names or nicknames. All that hugging that went on, merely seemed an excuse to grope. If I hadn't seen the title, I would have sworn I was watching 'Musical Crufts'. I think the games show market has hit an all-time low. They are obviously stuck for ideas. What you can be certain of, if it is a daytime show, is that it will be hosted by somebody who is past their sell-by date, somebody who has upset or embarrassed those in charge, or an unknown who will hopefully remain that way. Having said that, dross isn't confined to the light hours. I once made the mistake of watching *You Bet* with that grinning, bearded chump, Matthew Kelly. How people can switch on the TV and then be entertained by a JCB making a cup of coffee while its operator performs hari-kari is beyond me. Where do they get an audience from? I had assumed that all people with that mentality possessed Sky aerials.

Here is another example of where costs awarded by a judge bear no relation to the loss, let alone any relationship to those awarded to the likes of Sarah Keays or Jeffrey Archer. A motorcyclist was killed by a car driver travelling in the opposite direction on the wrong side of the road. This happened in 1983. The motorcyclist's mother has been awarded £11,700, out of which she has to pay costs which will leave her with £6,500. Six years' fight for that measly amount. You can see why the woman is bitter, and has not come to terms with her son's death. The driver who caused the accident was convicted of careless driving, fined £250 and given five penalty points. Tell me where justice can be found these days, 'cos I would love to hear about it.

The Simms family have a trio of children whose names are not going to be forgotten in a hurry. With the birth of Matilda on the 13th February, there is now a sister for Bertram and Rowley (I suppose the latter is a boy). Meanwhile, in the forthcoming marriages section, a Mr Wright is to grasp the hand of Miss Jacquemine Francesca Anastasia Charrot-Lodwidge, some time in the near future. What a bloody mouthful that is.

I made a note of an article in last week's *Wales on Sunday* about the plight of two horses. I hoped to write a little piece in the 'happy ending' mould. It was not to be. I know nothing about horse-racing, other than the fact that some chap, who has kept his weight down by stuffing his face full of chemicals, whips a horse unnecessarily in order that it will be first and win a lot of money. Okay, so I don't know much about racing, but these two horses, one 30 years of age and half-brother to the famous Arkle, and another, 27 years old, were both winners in their day. However, the time has passed when they could earn money and they had been left alone in a field in the county of Glamorgan. Their only shelter was an old railway carriage. The *Wales on Sunday* newspaper investigated their plight and the RSPCA were called in after a vet had examined the animals. He reported that their ribs were sticking out through their coats, which were in poor condition. The same was said of their teeth and they had cracked and infected hooves. Somebody had made money out of these two when they were in their prime, but it appeared nobody wanted to know any more. So, this week I looked for the silver lining, but no. They had both been put down by their owner. I use the word loosely. Yes, someone did own them. Both the Society for the Welfare of Horses and Ponies, and the RSPCA agreed that with treatment they could have been saved and that it was unnecessary for them to have been put to sleep. It did not go unnoticed by me that the owner was the daughter of the Master of the local hunt.

Animal welfare groups are not overly impressed with the unauthorised horse racing that is taking hold in rural parts of Wales. It is apparently known as flapping. Up to 40 horses race at a time and there are no checks made for drugs or stimulants. This is the perfect environment for those seeking to make a fast buck. It is seedy and tacky. The only real loser here, of course, will be the horse. The Welsh do not have a particularly good reputation when it comes to animals. The number of breeders who I have noticed banned or fined for ill-treating dogs within the principality is very high. They appear to have no morals, only a love of money. The intensive breeding that takes place at some of these so-called farms should be banned.

They are on a par with those who inject animals with chemicals in order to increase their weight more rapidly. I find it ironic that cows are injected so that their yield in milk is raised unnaturally, whilst at the same time the authorities that encourage this cruelty, for that is what it is, monitor the quotas and order so much to be thrown away. This is politics at its most frightening. As I have said before, it is the power these people have. Their ability to pass legislation which never takes into account the animals' lives is very worrying. I would imagine we know nothing really about the experimentation that takes place on behalf of us, the consumers. Cruelty doesn't sell pre-packed food and we can't have that. If they really cared, we wouldn't still be witnessing the appalling sale of battery eggs, quick-grow chickens and turkeys that couldn't stand when they were alive. Most pigs and calves sent to their death for the provision of veal have never seen the light of day. These are issues politicians need to get to grips with, not the level of social handouts that can be claimed by a 22-year-old single parent, who just happens to be on drugs and her five children under seven, with Grade 1 haircuts and earrings.

Nice to see that Kathleen Harrison – and don't say who? – is 100 today. A ruddy marvel, and no mistake!

There is another letter to the *Mail on Sunday* this week from the Chairman of the Quorn Hunt in Leicestershire, trying to subtly placate readers about the video filmed showing a fox being thrown to hounds. He, not surprisingly, goes on to defend the culling, by saying that this action ensures a kill or an 'unscathed' escape. He didn't convince me – did he you?

While the above was wending its way to the newspaper, a nurse, protesting about hunting, was whipped across the face with a riding crop. The Master of the Portman Hunt in Dorset is to face charges for affray and criminal damage. That's better.

A woman has lost her case against her old employers, on the grounds of sexist remarks. Initially, I was quite pleased about the result, but when I read that her boss said she had not been sacked, but left of her own accord, I read on. He added that the employee made 'sarcastic remarks about my positive motivation meetings'. Having heard that, my loyalty changed. Have you ever been on a 'positive motivation' course, or sat through a meeting where some complete prat tells you how to sell the most boring of products? She was probably the only normal person there.

The changing face of London is, I see, to retain one familiar face at least. The Routemaster bus is to be with us for another ten years. They cannot do without them, can they. Having tried successfully to hive off all the routes to one-person operated, sorry, one-man operated (must be politically incorrect) it is nice to see common sense prevail. Whoever decided that the retention of these useful buses would be in the interest of the passengers had better keep looking over his shoulders. Logical thought and customer service have no place in this government's rules, it isn't economical, there just isn't the financial return.

Someone must have felt their ears burning. After my comments about repeating good comedies, I see that *Just Good Friends* is to be repeated, starting tonight. They are apparently starting off with the first episode of the final series. Why not go the whole hog and start from the beginning, at episode one. Yes, I know, it is better than nothing, but it would not have taken a lot of thought, would it.

I see that the Apex Trust, a training charity for ex-offenders, has managed to stave off liquidation, due to its six hundred creditors agreeing to waive debts of £1½ million. How is a charity allowed to use up such huge amounts of money, and not be accountable? I wonder if liquidation would have been avoided if the charity dealt with the needs of victims, rather than the aggressors?

The day is looking up. The owner of two pit-bull terriers has lost his appeal to walk his dogs without a muzzle. Without boring you, and I frequently do, his wriggling over technicalities got him nowhere. He has been fined £300, plus £200 costs, for walking one of his animals in a public place without a muzzle. After the hearing, he insisted that he would still flout the law and continue his unlawful practice. Providing the dogs did not bite anyone, I find his voluntary contribution to the nation's coffers very laudable. You only have to look at the name of his two dogs to get a 'mental' picture of the kind of person a pit-bull owner is. One dog is called 'Tiger' and the other 'Rhino'. Impressive, huh!

Well, February ends on one good note. There will not be a full Channel tunnel rail service before the summer of 1994, so we have still got just over two years of relative freedom left.

Now here is an easy way for an aspiring young female journalist to make a financial killing. You just copy the actions of a Ms (note the Ms) Lisa Olsen in America. She walked into a locker room of a football team in Boston – no, not Lincolnshire, Massachusetts. The locker room was full of players who had just come out of the showers. Remarks were made by the footballers about her 'cute body' and two of them dropped their towels and asked if she would like to interview them in the nude. This journalist then slapped a 'sexual harassment' lawsuit on the team and they were ordered to pay the equivalent of £285,000. Frankly, having seen the photograph that accompanied the article, Miss Olsen, as I prefer to call her, certainly looked a cracker, one I would like to show my vitals to any day, and yobs will be yobs. I just hope they were man enough for the job! There must be nothing worse than trying to impress, by dropping your towel, only to find the shower was colder than you thought.

There is another original, or certainly unusual, name in the births column of the *Daily Telegraph*. To the Fitzgeralds, a second daughter has been born – Atalanta Rose. Sounds like a Second World War bomber, nice enough though. I remember a few years back there was a news reporter, or presenter, in the west of England called Petrel Trelawny. I don't know what happened to her, but her name is beautiful. I am not so sure about this one. Someone further down the column has called their daughter Theodora. I am not impressed with that, or the one a few entries below it, another daughter, Saskia. This sounds like something you throw down your neck, before you hurl the glass against the wall.

You will like this. Riding along on their usual wave of obsessive greed, Rushmoor council decided to charge for parking in the town centre car parks from 6 pm until 11 pm. Now 20 pence may not be much, but it adds up if there are a lot of cars. Not surprisingly there have been complaints. When asked for comment, a chap called Ian Betts, the council's head of engineering, said the idea came from a member of the public, who had written in suggesting that it would enable the council to continue lighting the car parks. Now I can't see that myself. Unless senility is to blame, or the public-spirited soul is an ingratiating sort, it seems a strange thing to do. Do you know anyone who offers the council money? I bet he or she does not own a car. This head of engineering goes on to say that if they do not charge for the night-time use, those that frequent the car parks during the day are subsidising those who use them at night. They do not like poll-tax payers subsidising those who do not pay year in year out! They are also employing a patrol officer to check that everyone has paid, so there's more expense. It just does not ring true, does it? Since when has the council listened to the suggestion of one person? They don't usually give a toss about the opinions of the public even when there is a 6,000-signature petition to back up the view or feeling over a particular item. The key word of course is money.

Well, here we are, Sunday, 1st March, St David's Day, and it is belting down. I have just looked up my stars in the Sunday People. It says that I feel excited on the one hand, and a little apprehensive on the other – well, that's keeping my options open. It goes on to say that I have a chance to express my opinions in no uncertain terms, so I will be writing a few more pages then! My romantic life is going to buck up and there will be a new moon on Wednesday and I must be guided by my intuition. We will wait and see.

Oh, God, he's here. Page 25 of the Supplement, under the heading 'A Pink Chancer'. It is Eddie Edwards. Eddie the Eagle limbers up for 1994 – I thought they had dropped him. Seven pictures of him in different exercise positions, with an inset of Lizzie Webb. Two of the most irritating people on the same page, the rest of the month has got to be better, not least for selling cars, as only five sold during February and the bank manager is visiting us for a 'chat' this month.

What about the BBC's version of *You've Been Framed*. It is called *Caught In The Act*. We watched it once, to be precise, we watched the first five minutes. I had to look and check that it was on the BBC. The compere, although I believe this description to be flattering overstatement, is a chap called Shane Richie, whose diction and grammar are on a par with an East End barrow boy. How low the Beeb has sunk and still not caught on that it isn't necessary.

Aldershot lost 1-0 again, away to Scunthorpe. I went to Scunthorpe once and was amazed to see, on reaching the town boundary, 'Scunthorpe, a Garden City'. I know Welwyn is one, but Scunthorpe?

The English Tourist Board is becoming increasingly concerned about the recently introduced regulations forcing hotels and boarding houses to instal three sinks and comply with a whole host of new hygiene and safety laws. Fine for the over-priced international hotel group, but what of the B & B that Britain should generally be very proud of. Are we to price them out of the market, or see them go to the wall because of the expense necessary. When you read of the changes forced on football clubs due to the overkill of the Taylor Report, the B & B situation, and the MOT changes designed to wrench yet more money from the poor motorist, does it not make you think that this is just another government ploy to increase the coffers through indirect taxation? In every case you have a captive audience. It is pay up, or close up.

You remember what I said a couple of pages ago about the one member of the public who influenced Rushmoor's decision to make money, via evening car parking charges, well, here's another decision that restores your distrust of councillors and councils. The ex-little village of Yateley, which for those of you in Oswaldtwistle or Austwick, is now a sprawling estate in North Hampshire, has agreed to allow a video games centre to open in the main street. This application was opposed by many local shop keepers and a petition signed by more than one hundred people was handed in. Did it do any good? Did it buggery – (typist's note: a very difficult word, buggery, to write in shorthand – not much call for it! Author's comment – No need to make a meal of it, just type it)!! The applicant was the son of one of the councillors, not that it would have had any bearing on the issue, of course, because those elected are upright citizens of impeccable morals, whose only interest is in the electorate – I wrote that last piece under duress! The shopkeepers are concerned about the number of vandals and yobs who congregate at night without the added attraction (if that is what you call it) of a video centre,... but think about the Unified Business Rate...

It is always a pleasure when a jumped-up little arsehole gets jumped on. This particular upstart was logged driving at 148 mph on the M25. He later told police it was perfectly safe and that he had driven at 170 mph in Germany. Frankly, I think they deserve each other. He was banned from driving for six months and fined £700 for reckless driving, so at least he will be off the road until September. His car was a £50,000 Porsche.

March 4th and it is the first real signs of an impending election. The lead photograph in the *Daily Telegraph* shows Norma Major tossing pancakes in Huntingdon and, of course, it is noticeable that we are coming out of the recession, well, according to the Shetland Pony we are. Car sales, home sales, retail sales are all still depressed. The jobless figure is still climbing, but these are all signs of the worst being over.

Another indication of subtle pre-electioneering comes from learning that the government is either funding or arranging loans to various causes. We have just seen £75 million being loaned to the poor, so that is going basically to the Breweries and tobacco companies via the benefit claimant. £55 million for new ships for the Royal Navy and £12 million towards Aids. I think the only amount justified there is for the new ships, at least it will give the public something to look at. If you think I am being hard concerning the £75 million for the poor, let's see who it is gong to. On page 4 of the *Daily Telegraph* is a picture of a unmarried mother with a child in her arms, very touching. She is described as the type of person the Social Fund is there to help. She is 21 years of age with two children aged between fifteen months and three years. She has either been extremely unlucky, has conceived on the basis of queue-jumping for a flat, or basically couldn't give a toss. Whatever the reason, our reported case is the lucky winner of an unfurnished flat in Waltham Forest. She then asks Social Security for a grant so that she can buy a cooker, beds, carpets and other essentials. I am glad to say that they turned down her request for £1,500. They did, however, loan her £271, which is £271 too much. To cap it all, she continues complaining throughout the text of the article. These sprogs did not just pop out, did they, or were they really found under a gooseberry bush. I don't suppose she has heard of working, and she now has a good excuse not to. £75 million going on the likes of her and her ilk – or is it oik? Yes, it is still the land of milk and honey if you are not prepared to contribute. There is many a poor sod who has been contributing to the system all his working life and never taken a penny, so it will be reassuring for him to know where their money is going.

I read a comment that Mrs Major will be seen and not heard during the election. It will be interesting to see if she is allowed to remain in the background. I cannot see that happening to 'there's lovely' Glenys. By the side of Mr K. for most of the time, I bet, or when she is not, it will be because she is giving a speech of her own or visiting high-profile venues. Not one for the background is Mrs K. – and she is not even a candidate. Actually, you wouldn't be voting for a Labour prime minister, would you, it would be the job lot.

Another nice example of the upper classes was found in the births column today. To Janetta and David Ross, a girl, Miranda Eleanor Otter-Barry, sister for Isobel, well, they won't be going to a comprehensive then. Hang on, we can beat that. Marilyn and Luke Withnell have just produced a Persephone. Luckily for her their surname isn't Pratt, although it will still be bad enough having to live with the nickname 'Percy', won't it.

Aldershot slipped up last night (again). They lost to Barnet, 5-0 this time.

Now all you see on television at the moment, and for the next few weeks, besides the tedium of politicians trying to destroy opposition policies, are the polls. I fail to see what possible benefit they are to anyone, save giving a small number of housewives some pin money and lining the pockets of the administrators. Gallup, Mori and all the others should be placed in a political museum and shown to future generations. They would certainly have a good laugh.

Crime and a distinct lack of punishment

It is no wonder that the public have lost faith in the judiciary. There are another two cases of sentences which 99% of the population would consider inordinately light. In case one, a drugs dealer who shot a policeman in the heart at point blank range has been given seventeen years' imprisonment. Needless to say, the poor PC has yet to return to work. The gunman fired nine shots so there is no question of the gun going off by accident, is there. He was convicted, amongst other things, of attempted murder. That one crime alone should carry a life sentence.

The second case concerns the teenage son of a Ford Motor Company director who crashed his father's car. Two school-friends were killed and three others were injured. The youth was sent to a detention centre for two years and banned from driving for ten years. What I find worrying is that Ford, and probably many other companies, allow teenagers to be insured on a blanket policy, just because one of their parents is in an executive position. Even though the company allowed youngsters to drive, I cannot for the life of me understand a father giving the okay for his nineteen-year-old son, who has already been involved in two accidents, to drive a Granada Scorpio, a high-powered car. It was driven at speeds of up to 116 mph by the youth. Ford have now changed their insurance policy, which makes it illegal for anyone under 21 to drive high-performance cars, but was it not crass irresponsibility in the beginning? The convicted teenager will be released at the age of 21, or probably before, and he will be able to continue his life, the others won't. As I said time and time again, if cars were restricted by governors to 80 mph maximum, a number of lives could be saved.

The above news comes just a week after an irresponsible driver was sentenced to five years' detention and disqualified for twelve years. In this accident four people died, as the seventeen-year-old raced against a friend at speeds of up to 100 mph. His friend's car went out of control and hit another car carrying a young couple. The innocent couple, and his two friends, aged sixteen and seventeen, all died. If this isn't enough, we have a sixteen-year-old who has been given twelve months' detention in a young offenders' holiday camp (sorry, institution). He killed a 27-year-old schoolteacher, who was walking to the school at which she taught. He had stolen a Sherpa van, lost control of it on a bend and pinned the young lady to the wall. She died instantly. The three-year driving ban he was also given means he will be back on the road by the time he is nineteen years of age. I think the father of the dead teacher summed it up when he said, 'The law should serve only one purpose, to open the eyes of other offenders. If it does not, then it has failed.' The sad thing is that he is echoing what 99.9% of the population are saying and know to be the truth. It is the 0.1% who have the power to make the punishment fit the crime, who never take heed. To restore the balance in the injustice tables, I am glad that the parents whose daughters died in the Hillsborough tragedy have lost their claim for compensation for alleged pain suffered in the moments immediately before death. Whilst one cannot begin to comprehend the suffering caused to the parents and the grief they have endured, no amount of compensation will bring their daughters back, and I feel it would set a precedent to be exploited by future generations as another excuse to cash in. I am not suggesting for one moment that that is Mr and Mrs Hicks' reasoning, but I cannot see what satisfaction, other than money, they could receive. Last May, an Appeal Court ruled that families of the victims were not entitled to damages for the shock of seeing the disaster on television. Over 150 claimants were awaiting the verdict that would have held West Yorkshire Police responsible for what happened. I am also glad that the Appeal Court ruled against further claims for damages for 'stress and shock', stating that the claims were 'too remote'. Those involved were to pay legal fees of £100,000. I find it tasteless and sordid that so many people should wish to capitalise financially out of such a grim situation as this.

It seems that it is not only the likes of Reebok and Nike who are destroying a child's formative years. Benetton and its ilk are continuing to target their marketing at very young children. It is sad the way greed has lowered the age of innocence and replaced it with competitive fashion and aggression. These companies have a lot to answer for.

You remember my comment about the Mid Southern Water Company, well I am not alone in water waste. I spoke to my father earlier, who has just received two letters, giving him details of a servicing offer by his local supplier, Sutton Water Company. The letters refer to an application form which should be filled in and returned – there were no application forms in either envelope. Two letters to one household is bad enough, neither of them being complete compounds the waste, but for both to be stamped first-class really takes the biscuit. Multiply the postage by the number of households and you have got a very strong case for raising water charges!

Only last month, Welsh Water, another of those recently privatised excuses for extracting indirect taxation, announced plans for their chairman and two senior managers to visit Australia and New Zealand. This three-week sortie is connected with a possible deal down under which is being contested by seven other British water companies. Welsh Water, apparently, has the highest water charges and disconnections in the country. Having priced up the trip, a figure in excess of £25,000 has been bandied about as the outlay required. I hope they don't come back empty-handed, they might just have some irate shareholders to answer to. After all, merely being a dissatisfied or disconnected consumer gives you no clout at all.

I have just been having a telephone conversation with R.F. I asked him if he had been busy this morning. He said, 'I have been out picking up the children from Terry's.' I had to stop and think, as the name 'Terry' didn't ring a bell with me. 'Oh,' said R.F., 'he hasn't got any children of his own, he is a paedophile!'

Now here is somebody the country could do without. In the *Daily Telegraph* appointments supplement, there is an article about a do-gooder called Sandy Buchan. He runs an organisation called 'RAP', a most unfortunate trio of letters for a start. It doesn't stand for Rent A Parasite, as I thought, but for Refugee Arrival Project, although... Not unnaturally, this little pot of gold is based at London Airport. It all fits in, doesn't it? The well-intentioned Mr B. used to be employed as a social worker for Hackney Council. He then travelled around Asia and later joined the 'Save the Children Fund'. He first dipped his interfering finger into the murky waters of immigration when he ran a reception centre in Osterley, Middlesex, for the nth thousand Vietnamese who eventually settled here. Obviously destined to wave the flag of welcome to all and sundry which puts so much pressure on our local councils and social services he moved to Brixton, South London, where he set up a general reception centre for 'refugees'.

In 1989 he gained funding from you and me via the Home

Office to set up his RAP organisation. This misguided cove was 'Concerned that refugees had nowhere to go for advice and help'. There are now eleven workers, paid by taxpayers and other concerns, who help these unfortunates to find a place to live, give them advice on money matters (that is hand-outs to you and me), health (free NHS facilities), and legal problems. Even Mr B. admits that most of those who arrive here needing his help do not come from Eastern Europe, but from Zaire, Iraq and the Horn of Africa. So it is more like Colonial Refugee Arrival Project – CRAP.

You can imagine how fast news of this honey-bucket spread. Must have been faster than the DHL advert. These tear-stained, hard-pressed arrivals must really believe they have arrived in soft-touch land – and they have. The *Daily Telegraph* article gives details of the job, or jobs, available at this centre. The salary is £20,000 a year, not bad, is it? Multiply that by the eleven-strong team presently in place, add on the usual costs and you have enough to re-open another children's ward in an NHS hospital. It is all a question of priorities, what is more important? Another immigrant who probably won't be contributing to the Pot, or the health of a child whose parents have worked hard to bring them up in a decent, cultured manner, despite all the inadequacies and injustices so very prominent in Britain today. It is a pity you cannot still send undesirables to Australia, because there are eleven of them working at London Airport.

Labour is ahead in the polls this morning, while allegations are being made against the Conservatives for accepting a £400,000 donation from the Polly Peck Group, which is now in receivership. They will probably remain ahead. It all seems a bit cloudy to me. I cannot see how it is legal for any company to donate monies to any political party. I think many factories should be forced to declare such information to consumers on its products. At least we would know where our money was going. It could help a company, as well. Food manufacturers often donate a percentage of their item price to environmental or animal welfare causes during a particular campaign. If we knew from the wrapping of a product that a company was donating, say, medical appliances to a particular hospital, the consumer, if sympathetic, could vote with their cash.

This government keeps telling us that market forces determine whether a company stays afloat or sinks. The Tory Party, however, rely on donations from companies where the end user has no say in the matter. If they are that concerned and have such moral fibre, why don't they rely on the party's membership to fund their organisation? Are we subsidising the Tories or are we subsidising the Tories?

I always question the need for stunts, spectacular or otherwise. They are organised for laymen with a view to raising money by the sponsorship of whatever activity is to be performed. Yesterday, out of thirteen parachute volunteers, twelve received injuries on landing, and the remaining member of the group copped out and stayed inside the plane. He or she was definitely the smartest on the day. Four of the injured suffered broken bones and whiplash, one landed on a factory roof and the other seven sported twists and sprains. Why can't these well-intentioned people involve themselves in an activity which could be seen to benefit or beautify an area? What is wrong in painting a building which needs smartening up, or digging over some old lady's garden, helping out as visitors at old people's homes. The ideas are endless and you do not endanger your own life or cost the NHS a small fortune in putting you back together again.

There's a funny one in the Hatch, Match and Despatch today, 'To Janey and Hugo, a daughter (Archie – Anne Rosie). Is it a misprint, or don't they know what it is?

Locally, we have lost another three landmarks, although two are in name only. The Staff Public House in Camberley has been closed and will remain that way for two months while the inside is gutted. It was a 'proper' pub, a traditional hostel with three bars. This, of course, will be changed. Game machines will be introduced and the Ind Coope spokesman said they would be looking to a greater profit – sorry, a younger clientele – on Friday and Saturday nights. So that is another place to avoid if you don't want to be involved in a late-night fracas. One golden rule I have is that if I am looking for a pub in which to imbibe, and I spot a sign which declares 'Open All Day, I know it is going to be full of riff-raff. If you do make the mistake of going in, by the time you have paid for your over-priced drink, someone will have fed the music machine and all hope of conversation will have disappeared.

The majority of 'open all hours' public houses are so uninviting and seedy, you wouldn't want to eat in them.

The second landmark concerns the renaming of the Royal Aircraft Establishment (RAE) in Farnborough. Someone with more power than sense has decreed that it now be called the DRA-Aerospace Division. It is still known, and will be for years, as the RAE, a name that summed up solidity, continuity, security. DRA means nothing more than the first three letters of the word 'drab'. The new sign is almost totally illegible. It is one of those stainless steel on – well, stainless steel. It is self-coloured, where you can only see the lettering if the sun's shadow is at the right angle. I cannot think why everything has to be changed. If asked, I imagine a spokesman for the ministry responsible would say the change was necessary to 'reflect the growing diversity of the division, within the parameter set by the competitive forces that currently prevail' – or some twaddle like that.

The third example is the Queens Hotel, situated by the side of an established roundabout, known to all and sundry as the 'Queens Hotel Roundabout', a name not totally unconnected with the aforementioned hostelry. It has now been renamed the 'Forte Crest Hotel'. Other than announcing its parentage, I do not find it is a very bright marketing ploy. It will still be known as the 'Queens' anyway.

We have booked up for a week's holiday in September. Mum and Dad have kindly offered to help us out and we initially looked at returning to Eire. The prices have, however, shot through the roof. A second enquiry with the travel agents concerning the Isle of Man brought the same reaction. 'If you are self-catering, it is cheaper to go to Spain,' he said. No, we definitely did not want to go there. Guernsey? Jersey? All too dear when you included the air fare. A lot of soul searching, well, actually map searching, and the destination of a lifetime was arrived at – Merthyr Tydfil. Actually, it is about six miles north, in the middle of nowhere, a converted granary, in fact. The area is beautiful, and being so close to South Wales, it is not really on the tourist circuit. Maureen is really looking forward to travelling on a narrow-gauge railway. I could take her on the nearby Brecon Mountain Railway, or the Talyllyn, or the Festiniog. Well, we will probably do all three, but don't let on. One place we will visit is the Ebbw Vale Garden Festival. I only hope that when it closes it doesn't end up like its predecessors. Many of us have seen photographs in newspapers and magazines of the various garden extravaganzas that have been held in Liverpool, Stoke and Glasgow. In the *Wales on Sunday* in December, they published an article with 'then' and 'now' photos of the Stoke and Glasgow offerings. In both cases the beauty of the event had been turned into wasteland awaiting redevelopment. So far, over £90 million has been spent on the aforementioned festivals. In the case of Liverpool's 125-acre site, the gardens have been closed for over three years because of politics, so once again, the public lose out. In fact, the only outcome from all the money invested is a total lack of a single area being retained as parkland or garden for public enjoyment. The Ebbw Vale committee have promised that at the end of the season, although houses and the inevitable business park are to be built, half of the site will remain as open space. This aspect of the 'final solution' is to be applauded, but then there is a large amount of countryside in that area, with a national park within a few miles. Glasgow, Stoke and Liverpool could all have benefited from beautifying, and what better than to have continued the good work that has been provided by the taxpayer.

It is over twenty years since Maureen has been to South Wales. The area is now a world apart from the industrial activity which provided the very life-blood for its inhabitants. From the heads of the valleys to the ports, it was coal, rail and smoke. When you think that even as recently as 1947 there were 214 pits employing 114,000 men. Now there are just three pits, supporting 944 workers. If industries such as coal mining, which appear 'unfashionable' and lacking in the need for direct computer involvement, are to be replaced with industries which can provide work for those made redundant, then so be it, but it is just not happening. Our exports are still decreasing and we are importing more and more cheap coal. I wonder how 'cheap' it really is. It would be nice to know what criteria is used to determine costs. Personally, I am more than a little surprised that lugging coal from the other side of the world is cheaper than mining our own. Is every seam either worn out or uneconomic? One wonders just what interference governments, and more importantly, banks have played in the question, don't you? Don't you? Oh, well, fair enough!

A couple of jokes now, don't you think. One slightly unsubtle, the other subtle, so you can tell already that it took me some time to understand it.

A woman visits the doctor's and asks if he can give her some advice on breast enlargement, adding that she has heard about silicone implants but is worried about the possibility of side effects. 'You don't have to resort to those measures,' the doctor replies. 'What I suggest you do is to take a few sheets of toilet paper and rub your breasts with them a couple of times a day.' 'Will that help them grow larger?' she enquires. 'Well,' says the doctor, 'you have been doing it to your arse for years and look at the size of that!'

I will give you a few seconds to calm down. Okay? Ready? Here we go.

Siamese twins visit their local travel agency. Facing the desk,

171

the one on the right says, 'My brother and I would like to book our holiday, please.' 'Don't tell me,' replies the agent, 'you are going to France again.' The twins both nod. 'Twenty-six years you have been coming into my agency and for twenty-six years you have gone to France, you must really love the place.' 'Can't stand it,' says the same twin. 'Really, it must be the French people you like, then,' retorts the surprised travel agent. 'Can't stand the arseholes,' comes the reply. The left-hand twin nods in agreement. The travel agent looks perplexed. 'Then, it must be the food,' he suggests. 'No, it is crap, we take our own, and don't ask if we go for the wine either, we are both teetotal,' the same twin replies. The T.A. looks very puzzled. 'Let's get this straight,' he says, 'you go to the same place for twenty-six years, you detest the country, you dislike the people, you won't eat the food and you don't drink alcohol. Why do you go?' 'Well,' said the other twin, 'it is the only time I get to drive a car.'

I have waited a few seconds because there are those among us who will still be deliberating as to the humorous content of that last little jape. You can't get the quality of readers these days, can you?

Well, Aldershot let in a goal less yesterday. They 'only' lost 4-1 at home to Northampton. The turnout was just 1,374 people. Still, that is another game nearer the end of the season or just nearer the end, who knows.

The latest NOP puts Labour ahead, and it still looks like a 9th April election.

If you want reassurance that the Commission for Racial Equality (60% of whose workers are black) is growing up and living in the real world, forget it. An independent report by the Department of Employment says that we have the most advanced measures and practices to combat any abuse of the race laws. We are ahead of our 'fellow' continentals in dealing with direct discrimination. We are the only EC country that gives what is known as the 'visible minority' voting rights. For 'visible minority' read non whites, the report says. Along with good old Holland, we have moved the furthest towards a multicultural approach to jobs. The sycophantic power-crazed, lefty-plebs at the CRE must be preening themselves reading that, but, hang on, what's this? The report goes on to say that 'British subjects cannot expect the same treatment and will face racial discrimination if they want to work in the EC'.

I haven't seen much mention of the recession of late, so we must be well on the way to full recovery – not that there was anything to recover from, in fact, the economy's really taking off...

Can you understand it, 'cos I'm buggered if I can? I was interested in a story reported in the *Daily Telegraph* concerning a chap who has just been released after spending fifteen months in a Japanese prison. Last week, a judge of the slit-eyed type threw out charges brought against the Brit and freed him. His accusations of beatings, mental and physical cruelty, solitary confinement and tiny cells where the lights stay on twenty-four hours a day, bring home just how little the Japanese mentality has altered over the years. A Japanese Justice Minister (or was it 'Injustice') said that complaints brought to their attention by the British teacher were unfounded. Given that 99 cases out of every 100 end in conviction, and that it is apparently normal for forced confessions to be made – a bit like here really – who would you believe? It does not matter how much they like playing golf, the leopard does not change its spots.

My views on a united Europe have not changed over the years, but they have hardened. Not, I would like to think, that I am anti for the sake of it, but because everything I feared would happen, *has* happened, or is about to happen. I may add that legislation passed and implemented, or still threshing their way through committees, were never considered in the equation when the populus was being sold the idea in those heady far-off days when a united Europe seemed a safe bet. I have no doubt that the threat of the Great Bear was lingering in the reckoning, but it was through the ease of transport and less paperwork that its 'ticket' was worked.

It is the 'control' by the EC of British subjects which I find most insulting. We are currently having our Sunday trading laws tested, and the might of the EC has been used by the big boys. We still have an elected government, albeit no more than a puppet committee. I heard John Major making a speech on industry recently, when he stated that he wanted to see jobs here, not Italy, Germany, etc. I thought he wanted to see a united Europe, wasn't he being somewhat biased towards the British workforce? Surely a true European would want work for all within the member nations. It must have been force of habit that made him state a preference for Britain, his country – if you can still call it that of origin. Smacks of favouritism to me!

EC proposals on transport include random breath-tests, which I am all in favour of, but we should not need outside influences to introduce such useful sections of legislation – even if it is belated.

They wish to increase the legal motoring speed to 80 mph, which will have the effect of upping the accepted limit to 90 mph before there is a sniff of police intervention. First aid courses for drivers as part of the L test will be introduced – more indirect taxation. Dipped headlights that turn on automatically when a car moves off, a peculiar practice I have never fully understood. This will increase the cost of a car when new, and will be another point on which to fail a car during its MOT – more indirect taxation. All cyclists will have to wear crash helmets and all bike wheel-trims are to be made reflective. Presumably all these safety measures at the cyclist's expense, will not stop him or her whizzing through shopping malls and arcades to the detriment of pedestrians. That is not important, think of the VAT. The fact that the death rate on our roads is under half that across the rest of the EC board will not be lost on the reader, but no doubt will be ignored in Europe.

You have only to think of the mess that agricultural reforms have made of our farming industry to question the ability of those on Euro committees. Mind you, when you look at John Gummer and consider some of the pussy-footing, namby-pamby comments he has come out with during his talks with the continentals, you realise how little we have in the way of ammunition to protect our corner against the absurd policies that are blatantly designed to protect the French. How can it be logical to pour away milk and be 'fined' for over-producing, when there are so many other outlets for one of the few natural basic foodstuffs. You are not allowed to let market forces determine price, you are not allowed to give it to hospitals or charities, but it can be thrown away quite happily. Only last December we were introduced to the F-word. The papers were full of it – 'Federalism' – a Jacques Delors special. Was this the face of Europe anticipated by the masses who voted 'Yes'? The general assumption was that it would mean less red tape at border crossings for imports and exports. How many people thought this joining at the hips would create so many jobs for administrators, officials, executives in this new club with unprecedented powers and financial muscle?

Their marketing men have certainly done a good job, I cannot see for the life of me why so many governments have been taken in. Greece, Portugal and Eire are understandable as they get out of the system more than they put in, which is a reassuring thought when a shop assistant tells you the price of an item and adds, 'It is plus VAT, of course.' Britain's ability to be conned and made suckers out of stems from the fact that we have no real leadership, no national pride at all. Those in power, regardless of party, have been sold the 'club' option as the only alternative, although I don't doubt that in their heart of hearts they know it its all a short-term sham. France and Germany are a different kettle of fish. Only recently have there been rumblings of discontent about the gross interference from Brussels. It has surprised me just how long it has taken the German and French people to wake up, but I expect the French have been sold the sop of agricultural 'brown envelopes' and the Germans have been too busy exporting and making money to really see the situation as it is. Germany has, of course, benefited from being top dog in the league of 'local authorities'. Other members finances surround the Deutschmark, so our Teutonic friends are bound to be a little slower at realising their loss of everyday control. We have yet to see any benefit from membership, and as our economy is bouncing along on the bottom and we are the least enthusiastic as well our continual misgivings will continue to come to the fore. Regional elections in Germany, France, Belgium and Italy have all seen an increase in the number of right-wing candidates, not enough to rock governments, certainly, but they must be aware of the growing trend. Ask any of these nations' people if they want large numbers of foreigners – even other EC 'foreigners' – foisted on them and the answer will be no. Still, every dog has its day.

One of the most worrying aspects of all the reams of Euro-legislation is the one concerning the abolition of border controls. Why is it that everybody except those in authority know the consequences? Terrorism, drug-running, illegal immigrants will doubtless be more difficult to detect. If these arseholes get their way, pets will be able to freely enter our country with an EC pet's passport. This effectively removes our quarantine laws, whch have protected these shores for generations. How can something as effective as this be described as draconian? The call seems to be one of jealousy. 'If *we* have rabies,then so should you.' Quarantine regulations of farm animals imported to Britain are already to be lifted this year. The Minister of Agriculture naturally denied that the risk of rabies spreading into Britain through infected livestock would increase. I am just wondering what excuse they will come up with when it does, because it is a 'when', not an 'if'.

In Greece, conservationists are concerned for the wellbeing of two endangered species of bird that live on marshland. The Greek government has laid out plans to divert the Acheloos River, or reasons which I won't bore you with. If that happens, the salinity of the marshes will increase and the area will be uninhabitable for these two species, the Dalmatian Pelican and the Slender-billed Curlew. The EC is funding the project to the tune of 35% of the costs, which total £360 million. The power of these people to allocate our involuntary donations to such schemes do not end at the borders of Europe. Since 1982, the EC have spent £143 million on a giant iron ore mine in the Amazonian jungle. The benefit to Europe is cheap ore for industry, the damage to the rain forest is immeasurable. What was I saying about financial priorities...

Even when an animal is dead, there is no respite. We have had lamb carcasses burned in France's very own Killing Fields, after lorries have been brought to a halt by marauding gaelic yobs, you couldn't call them farmers. Evidence has pointed, on several occasions, to their police acting with complete indifference to the unlawful deeds. What does John Gummer do? Well, he wants to see some protection for our boys. Is that it? Is that what this cameraderie is all about, lorry drivers suffering humiliation and the politicians eating humble pie and getting backache from the constant grovelling? The agricultural policy is designed around the French, but still they want more. The lightening of EC regulations has forced many of our smaller abattoirs to close. The consequence of this is that greater numbers of horses, cattle, pigs and fowl will be transported about when still alive. The animals are forced into such close proximity that bruising and injury easily occur. Knowing the views of many operators, both here and abroad, whose only concern is profit, can we really be certain that these animals get the refreshment stops they are legally entitled to? Of course not. No animal should have to travel to its death. It may sound over the top, but in the same way as many a domestic animal backs up when visiting the vet, farm animals know that death is imminent. It is no different than the transporting of Jews to Auschwitz, they still feel pain, they still suffer.

Its views on animal welfare seem contradictory to say the least. On one hand we hear of a plan to abolish the testing of cosmetic products on animals within a couple of years. On the other hand, British horses will be sold for food abroad, travelling as live meat to be slaughtered in abattoirs, the standards of which have not been seen in Britain since Victorian times. It is well known that animal welfare comes way down the list of priorities in those continental countries, the likes of whose families we wish to marry into.

A recent development is that 'Jacques the prat' Delors – I wonder if he has ever had a proper job – wants the community budget raised from 1.2 per cent to 1.37 per cent of its members' total gross domestic product over the next five years. So when taxes in the form of income tax and that Euro-swindle, VAT, are raised again, all 'local' governments have to do is point to a Euro-directive to stave off complaints from the populus. Your money and mine is going straight into some bottomless pit, to be regurgitated and spat out at the likes of Ireland who, as we know, receive thumping great wads of 'punts', while in Britain, we are still washing the landscape with milk.

I have just read the announcement that twins have been born to a family somewhere in these septic isles. A boy and girl have been deposited by a stork, the male version has been named William Peter. Nothing wrong with that, but the announcement adds 'Billy' afterwards. William is such a nice name, after all, we have one of our own, but Billy! I know of several council estates where he will grow up in not so good company. The pond life that frequents subsidised housing raises 'Billys', 'Tommys' and 'Garys' with boring regularity – who in turn breed...

Aldershot FC only lost 1-0 at Blackpool last night and they have appointed a new Chairman, and guess what? He is going to put together a survival package. He has been working on the salvage plan for three weeks apparently and was described as 'excited' in our worthy local paper. Oh, well.

The Budget's been and gone. I don't think it was positive – or negative – enough to sway voters one way or the other. With that sentence I seem to have taken on Paddy Ashdown's persona – well, I might have done but then again... It probably kept the Tories in with a shout, but not much more.

First, so that no-one thinks for one minute that I am biased for the sake of it – remember I am a Librian – I was pleased to see the outcome of a sex discrimination case finding in favour of the lady. If a sport can be fairly and equally participated in by either sex, then why can't females be allowed to join and play against men. Here we have the case of Miss Susan Thompson, who has repeatedly been refused admittance to the male-dominated professional circuit, purely because she is female. I don't know anything about pool, but she has apparently beaten some of the top males. Talk about sour grapes and egos, it will be interesting to see how she gets on. That is a point, isn't it, why do we never see any gals playing chaps at snooker at the Crucible?

Here's a sobering thought. Over the five-year period from 1983-1990, an average of 37,868 acres of land has been lost to development. Half of that figure was rural and agricultural.

You will be underwhelmed, and justifiably so, with the self-congratulatory, ingratiating bull that I have just read in our local rag. There is an advert by that unworthy organisation, Mid Southern Water Co., who announce as their heading 'Mid Southern Water voluntarily reduce water increase by 25%'. If you read that quickly, it comes across as a price reduction. I have no doubt that it is the intention when the word 'reduce' is used so blatantly. They go on to say that despite a maximum permitted increase of 14.3%, they are going to, without coercion, increase the price by 10.8% for 1992/3. Still double the rate of inflation. Surely they do not want congratulating. I find this type of advertising repugnant and unnecessary. Why can't they just say, 'We are going to have your legs up once again, and continue to rob you blind.' I wouldn't be any less happy, but at least they would have been honest. Their logo has the cliché 'Purely Yours' after their name and then they go on to tell you that they are a wholly owned subsidiary of SAUR Water Services PLC. I think it should be spelt SOUR – bastards!

The barmy army on Islington Council are planning to re-house, without any demonstration taking place, women who state that they have been subjected to sexual harassment by male neighbours. Not at the taxpayers' expense. It appears that a leer or a wolfwhistle, persistent requests for a date or the telling of 'risqué' jokes will suffice. Never a dull moment in North London is there.

Another loss for the Shots. 3-0 at home to Lincoln. Thirty-five games down, eleven to go.

Round one to the Tories in the election stakes, I see. Despite pleadings from the media, John Major has refused to kiss an infant on the first day of real campaigning. For the last six months the political coverage has been such that one could be forgiven for thinking that the named day was just a week away. Now, the race to get their fizzoggs through No. 10's orifice starts in earnest. The papers are full of equations. Would you be better off under the Tories or a Labour administration? I cannot believe that Labour have shown such an unnecessary hand, by plugging a shadow budget. I would have thought that the best ploy when in opposition would be to keep mum about anything that might be taken down and used in evidence. What an own-goal.

What happens the very first time the EC could actually be of use to this country? No notice is taken of their instructions whatsoever. The government's insatiable appetite for road building is still churning up vast tracts of previously unspoilt countryside, and very few are more damaging than Twyford Down near Winchester. A site of scientific interest means not a jot to the Department of Transport. As long as they can build their beloved extension. I have every sympathy with the protesters. It is a pity workmen cannot be as passionate about their work and refuse to tear down trees and destroy water meadows for ever, but in the real world there are no conscientious objectors in the building industry, only receivers of fat wads of greenbacks.

There are one or two good ones in the new arrivals column today. To Helen, who used to be a Prescott-Decie, and is now a Dennis-Smith, a daughter. This little lady is to be known as Charis Sophie, a sister for Mercy. Nice, that!

Here's another that has taken my fancy, and this young chap won't be found in an 'open all day' hostelry when he grows up. To Fiona and Charles, a son, Piers. The surname is Egerton-Warburton. Piers Egerton-Warburton, it does have a certain flow doesn't it. I have just looked at the announcement again. Fiona used to be a Bonham-Carter, you can't get away from them, can you. There doesn't happen to be one in the columns today but recently there have been one or two Ionas, a name I like very much, but you have to be careful with surnames. I mean, jollity would be had if your surname was Carr, Morris, Riley, Ford or Talbot. Away from cars you could be Iona Pond or Pool or Port. She could always be a Pratt – and she would be in the company of many who were prat by nature, which brings us on to animal names. She could be Iona Neagle – a subtle one that, as the grammar has to be correct. She could be the next generation in a family of Peacocks or Doves. What about Iona Katt or Iona Nightingale. She would spend her life with people saying, 'Do you?', after she had announced her name – and they would all think it was the first time that line had seen the light of day! Yes, it is a good day for arrivals today. There is also a Camilla India and a Jeremy Tarquin, who is going to be a companion for Benson. I am not sure whether he is a brother or a black labrador.

Well, another two polls have been conducted and they both point to Labour having a five-point lead – exciting, isn't it? Well, no, it isn't actually, but it still beats the hell out of waking up to 'regional fighting' around the globe. I am sick to death of having news foisted upon me concerning Serbs gunning down Croats, or vice versa. If it is not them, it is an Israeli attack on Palestinians or arse about farce again. Currently this round of boredom is only interrupted by voting in South Africa, and famine in just about everywhere you would rather not know about. I cannot accept

179

that an outbreak of sporadic machine-gun fire in a village no-one's ever heard of should warrant being headline news. Half the time Kate Adie isn't even there, so it can't be that important.

The old neurosis level of the racially 'over-aware' knows no bounds, does it. Even the native oak isn't safe. English Nature, a government agency, has decreed that as from now it must be known as – an oak tree. Our poor old humble representation of English forestry has been known as the 'native oak' since time immemorial, but some complete and utter arse has decided it causes offence to ethnic groups. I haven't seen hordes of black youths spreading graffiti calling for a ban on the title, have you? Who are these groups who will be offended? Whoever the said 'arse' is, he, or she, is probably waiting to be discovered by Michael Day, as they want to move from an area like conservation, which has little future under this government, to the race industry, where the sky and money seem limitless. Hold on, though, what's this I have found. There's an interested group, whose 'handle' as they say in certain circles, is the 'Black Environment Network'. This 'collective' champion ethnic concerns on green issues, apparently. They described the title 'native oak' as 'biological racism'. Well, I have looked at the date today and it is not 1st April. Surely a name such as the 'Black Environment Network' is racist in itself. Frankly, if you don't like the way we name our trees and you find it offensive – sod off. All that this change has done is to make the *native* population more angry about these little clubs who represent nobody of any consequence, but they wield so much power, and they cost so much money. They are usually assisted by the great white helper, usually a social worker with close-cropped hair and tasteless earrings. In English Nature's case, they are aided and abetted by an ecologist and urban programme co-ordinator, who describes the naming of such trees as xenophobic. The might of this quango is such that new leaflets sent to schools and local authorities will no longer use such words as 'native' or 'alien'. 'Native' used to describe a tree that was indigenous – oops – for the period of up to 1500 AD and 'alien' for any tree introduced since then.

Well, here's another one to be lined up against the wall. The news today gets worse. Terry Waite is to have his autobiography published by Hodder & Stoughton. It will cover his life from sprogg-dropping, through his 1,763 days abroad and finish with the free flight home and his waving to the crowds on arrival. Now we have got to wait for the pre-release signing sessions that will no doubt be awash with those eager to spout to friends, as they clutch their signed copy, 'He looks just like he does on the telly, only bigger', or 'He's such a nice chap, a lovely smile. He asked me my name and we shook hands.' I am just going to the toilet, I am making myself ill thinking about it. Presumably he got a tax rebate while he was away, or was the leave on full pay?

In Portland Hospital, Anna and Christopher Bunker have had a daughter, Minette – Minette Bunker! They don't get any better, do they. As Maureen said, she could have been called Nicole Bunker – or as my friend, John O'Pewsey, said, 'What's wrong with Four Minette Warning Bunker.' Ho, ho.

It is Thursday, 19th March and the Tories are now two points ahead according to a Gallup poll. The Labour party seem to be keeping Robin Cook under wraps, not an unwise move, which is probably why they are just behind the Tories. Another one they haven't wheeled out very much is Gerald Kaufmann. Have you noticed that it is the middle-aged faces like Brian Gould, and that up-and-coming starlet, Tony Blair, and Gordon Brown who have been very prominent on the box, along with Glenys K., of course. In fact, G.K., who the Labour party tend to think of as an asset, has been seen at little 'set pieces' which I have no doubt will escalate into full-blown orchestral gatherings as we move towards E-Day. As far as I can tell, her involvement is generally aimed at either schoolchildren who cannot vote, or the minority who will, and probably for Labour anyway. That, of course, reflects the level of support she will achieve for her troubles. Only yesterday, she was in Bradford visiting a mosque before moving on to an Indian Muslim Welfare Society Centre in Batley. Naturally, a primary school would not be forgotten. Playing with children, cuddling babies, sympathising with pensioners over their financial plight – Wonderglen's done it again! Meanwhile, not a sound has been uttered by Norma Peas Major. 3-0 to the Tories.

When it comes to sound common sense, then out of all the manifestos, the Monster Raving Loony Party leave the others standing. Their proposal to continue the Channel Tunnel through to Switzerland and leave out France altogether seems an eminently sensible idea. One that I think most voters, irrespective of party loyalties, would vote for tomorrow.

So, another royal marriage is on the rocks. Frankly, I couldn't give the proverbial toss for the Duchess of York. What I object to is the amount of public money that has been shelled out financing the building of that outsize council estate – Fergie Acres – in Sunninghill, along with £250,000 the pair of them get each year from the Civil List. It is all a bit much, actually it is bloody obscene.

I was pleased to see that a farmer arrested for allegedly head butting a thief he caught red-handed has been acquitted. The aspect of the case which I still cannot understand is how the would-be thief could have been given a conditional discharge, when he admitted visiting the farm with the intention to steal slates. The law gets softer and softer, and crime rises in proportion.

What is that, you wanted to know about my diet, as I hadn't mentioned it for some time? You know as well as I do that if something isn't mentioned, it is because it is not good news. Frankly, I can see how hard it is to give up smoking. I hate feeling hungry and, yes, I have put back on a couple of pounds, but we are going to make a renewed effort – honestly!

Well, Debbie's chances of passing her 'A' level English have diminished. She has just asked for my help with some homework. I reminded her of what happened last time she summoned my help, but she said she was desperate! When she was taking her GCSEs a couple of years ago, she confronted me with a question concerning Hitler's influence on pre-war Europe. We sat at the kitchen table for about four hours – I even missed highlights of football match – there's dedication, isn't it. Sorry, just the Welsh coming out again. To be fair to my daughter, she did point out that the avenue of theory I followed bore no relevance to what was being asked at all. I told her that the question was ambiguous and that a subtle approach was needed to glean what they were really asking of the pupil. Some weeks went by and I happened to be at home when she arrived back from school and said, 'Remind me never to ask you to help me with my homework again.' I was taken aback, I wasn't really, but it is the sort of thing you are expected to say. Anyway, she said her tutor had commented that she usually produced work of a high standard, and not only was the offering about fifteen minutes' worth of scribble (in his opinion) but no notice had been taken of the question at all – so much for ambiguity. She achieved the lowest marks in her class. I said the trouble was that different theories produce different answers, but she didn't buy it. Then again, to be fair, three marks out of a possible twenty doesn't look too clever, does it!

You won't believe this. Oh yes you will. Aldershot FC have just been wound up in the High Court, *but* there is another mystery backer waiting in the proverbial. So it is no longer the eleventh hour reprieve, but a possible 12.30 pm variation. The club have been given six days to rescind the order, and that means putting money on the table. This latest 'man in the closet' is very big in the leisure industry – gosh!

The computer suppliers must be creaming themselves. All those local authorities who bought new computer packages a few years ago are now finding that they are unable to cope with the demands being put on them. Rushmoor Council is having to spend another £17,000 just to collect the new council tax. That figure is, of course, only the local authority's share of the cost. The rest comes from central government in the form of grants. Take into account this action by local governments throughout the land and it shows just how far down the road to financial suicide we have travelled. It is so wasteful, but so very rewarding if you are producing or selling the bloody things.

Animal wrongs

I think it is time we took a look at animal welfare. Judging by the letters I received last time, a large number of people felt the same way as me – and none of them belonged to extreme groups, whose real hang-up is to play soldiers. So, if you are not into the one area of life where there is real inequality, and you don't give a toss about the most disadvantaged of the world's species, flip over the next few pages, and don't say you weren't warned.

Three years ago, when I was writing FWIS, stories would appear from different countries on a fairly regular basis. From each, its own. We suffered Japan, with its vast nets and the catch-all system of exploitation and we watched Africa lose its habitat to man's insatiable greed. If the loss of land didn't kill off herds of animals, the poachers would kill off the rest, and they did. The outlook was gloomy in the Amazon, whose forest fires continued unabated, denying many species of birds and animals the right to a home they had shared with native Indians for centuries. Virtually every country in the world had a cloud of death over its name, Britain included. Spain, positively lacked respect for animal welfare, and as far as I could see, must be of the opinion that animals do not suffer pain. Either that or they were totally uncaring, which is, of course, nearer the truth. Where are we now? Well, we are in basically the same position, except that there are less animals. At the end of the day, whether it is for it tusks, its body, or the space it is filling, it all comes down to money or more accurately, greed. Only last month a joint statement by the Royal Society in London and the US National Academy of Science in Washington warned that actions taken over the next twenty years will be crucial. The world population is currently 5.4 billion people. This figure is expected to rise to 10 billion, virtually double by the year 2050. Now I know we all read figures that can be debated until the cows come home – well all the ones without mad cow disease, that is. It is a long way off, past a lot of our lifetimes, and anything can happen. The one area that is never in dispute concerns the ever-decreasing number of animals. The vast majority of people in the world cannot actually do anything about it, sad as that may appear. One can lobby an MP, or present a petition. Donations can be made to the most worthy causes, but you cannot physically stop parents taking children to a circus, or leave the warmth and comfort of their semi-detached in Coulsdon to fly off to the jungle, in the vain hope of catching a poacher. As is usual, the power to determine the life, and continued existence for a whole host of species, lies in a very few hands, and these hands have the word 'profit' written all over them.

I have absolutely no wish to contribute or donate any of my hard-earned money to saving masses of people who have no compunction to help themselves. Being human, and part of the emotional, umbilical cord, they have a head start over their future, whereas the rhino, elephant and tiger do not.

You and I cannot be present at international conferences, chaired by heads of states, hoping to impress other world leaders, and more importantly, their own electorate. We cannot stop the export of live horses to the continent, a practice that will gather momentum the further we proceed down a federal road. As we have said before – actually I've said it – but I know you agree with me, European considerations for the animal's final hours of life are not on a par with ours, but no doubt we will have to lower the standards to take on our partners in crime. The report I mentioned earlier also states that 'if correct predictions of population growth proves accurate and patterns of human activity on the planet remain unchanged, science and technology may not be able to prevent either irreversible degradation of the environment or continued poverty, for much of the world.' Not to be underestimated is the fact that the earth's ability to sustain life has been damaged, and many species have already disappeared. This loss has never been matched in 65 million years. When put in these terms, you get an idea of just how far we have travelled down a no-through road. Stepping back and thinking about it, could I be right and that possibly, just possibly, the spread of Aids might be the definitive population destroyer, presented to us by Mother Nature as a balance restorer. The hype that accompanied its arrival in the annals (I was going to say bowels, but I thought better of it) of medical science, has largely been dismissed by the very players who take the biggest risk. The fact that you do not come out in spots within five minutes is a plus for Mother Nature. Not facing up to a death sentence because there are no immediate and visual or physical signs is a failing of human nature. Anyway, we can only hope that one way or another, the world population growth is stunted and that earth gets its revenge on man's greed. If the balance isn't restored, our children and their children will have an even bleaker future to look forward to.

There are, however, some things we can do to stop animal cruelty and once again, it concerns money. If people refuse to have their photograph taken, when on holiday in Spain, holding what appears to be a pet chimp, then the evil little bastard will go out of business. It would be nice to think that the same applies to bull-fighting, a practice common in southern France as well. The trouble here is that even if the British didn't go, the native population are sick enough to keep it alive financially. *The Mail on Sunday*, dated 21st April 1991, produced an article about the plight of Spain's monkeys. The poor little souls had been taken away as babies by poachers, who would almost certainly have killed the mother first. From the jungles they would have travelled to Spain, where beach photographers dress them up and make them wear shoes – some monkeys are now crippled. Apart from photography, bar owners use them to 'entertain' customers – again, usually British tourists who probably would care if they knew the full story. Life for a captive monkey is not good. Very often they are beaten daily, dosed up with drugs and they have their teeth pulled out – and all for money. Last April it looked like the beginning of the end, the authorities were starting to take notice of the complaints. A few lucky examples were saved and brought to the Monkey Rescue Centre in Wareham, Dorset. Only this week, *The People* has given over its lead story and two inside pages to the plight of the chimps. The irony is that the Spanish police have confiscated a number of chimps but have nowhere to put them. They are prepared to have them put down, but to the paper's credit, well-known animal conservationists and actors from *EastEnders* have joined forces to raise cash and bring them out alive. There are still a number of monkeys left on the streets and beaches, however, so if you are unfortunate enough to go to Spain on holiday – don't, please, have your photograph taken. Even better, cancel Spain and go to Cleethorpes, it will probably 'hiss' down all week, but you won't have a conscience.

Greyhounds are not having it too well at the moment either. What of their plight, you may ask – and well you might. Those that have finished their careers in Ireland can no longer be sent direct to Spain. They can, however, be sent via English ports to continue racing. Their treatment of course is similar to that meted out to the chimps. Having been encased in lorries for up to four days, they are dumped in small concrete shelters, where they spend up to twenty-three hours of the day, only being let out to make money (sorry, race) in very hot temperatures. They are apparently left in cages at the side of the track. These cages are so small that they are forced to stand the whole time. When they are injured or past it, they end up as a laboratory experiment or slaughtered and skinned to make cheap leather goods for all the visiting British plebs from Rainham, Billericay and Basingstoke.

Also last April came the news that the Cardiff-based Animal Protection Foundation had failed to dissuade Cardiff council from banning a circus from within its city's limits. Despite a petition signed by some 12,000 people, Cardiff obviously decided that the lure of the lolly was well worth an animal's suffering. I know not whether an animal is treated well or badly by its owners, but I can sympathise with the view that continually travelling around in lorries and being made to perform unnatural acts should be a thing of the past. By November, Cardiff's burghers had condoned more obscenities by allowing yet another circus to the city. It was not alone, just one of many towns, but the picture of the bear climbing onto frames cannot be excused, even by a certain Mr M.W. Lacey, Executive Director of Gerry Cottle's Circus, who, in a letter to *Wales on Sunday*, naturally ignored all the comments about the stress, frustration and boredom of a large mammal out of its natural environment, but circuses are there to make money, aren't they?

A circus does not have to travel, of course. In Blackpool, their Pleasure Beach is home to a 'Superdome', who include performing bears among the acts. Can you imagine being asked to bend over so your feet and hands touch each other, ten feet off the ground, on a contraption resembling something from a gymnasium. What? You have got one in your bedroom and you frequently bend over and touch your toes? Well, what you do in the privacy of your home is your own affair! I just hope you can make some money out of the videos! Anyway, while you are having fun and frolics, the poor old bear has to perform his or her act behind vertical bars, while an audience clap their hands at the 'comedy' of the animal's action. I am sorry if I sound a killjoy, but I just cannot see the pleasure to be derived from making an animal perform unnatural actions – women, yes, but not animals!!

If not visiting a circus means they cannot survive financially, then the same could be said for pet shops. For years they have sold rabbits, hamsters, gerbils and other furry, undomesticated creatures, under the all-embracing heading of 'pets'. Budgies, love-birds, cockatiels, etc. have also been very much in evidence, and probably demand, although I have never wavered from the view I adopted as a child, that no bird should be caged. We hear of more and more cases where exotic birds are brought into this country by the crateful, all of whom have suffered a distressing journey. Many of these are dead on arrival. From crate to cage to cage. Perhaps the luckiest are those who die first. Out of interest, the number of prosecutions against pet shops rose from 29 to 61 last year, over double the previous figure. So where is the British government, or the standard bearer of that 'brave new world' the EC? Nowhere, it would seem. Turtles, terrapins and snakes are sold without question, and have you noticed that the more exotic the bird or animal, the nearer to pond life becomes the mentality of the purchaser. So, just like the puppy who becomes an abandoned statistic on the twelfth day of Christmas, the turtle which should have had a lifespan of 40 years, is dumped unceremoniously in a lake where it will last a pitiful few months. But does that matter, all the financial interest has been accrued. What the 'end user' does is up to him. How is it that pet shops and the laws governing them are so lax? No doubt the cutbacks have affected staffing levels. It always seems ironic, but when restraint is needed in manpower, it is always those at the sharp end who are the first to go. The administrators, computer programmers and general office wallahs stay well clear of the flak, and in some cases increase their number to take account of the redundancies.

Another area where abuse can be perpetrated, and often is, relates to the fur industry. Not just wild animals abroad, but cats and dogs in this country and it is all perfectly legal. Britain has its own cat-skinning factory in Cheshire. The cat furs end up as waistcoats and handbags, the dogs' pelts become – surprise, surprise – gloves for Japanese golfers! They cannot get enough skins to satisfy the trade, so don't tell me that illegally caught moggies do not end up on the slab to aid the coffers. Last month in Tokyo a four-day extravaganza was held. One hundred and one furriers from all across the globe centred on Japan, that place again, to show off their latest exploitations. Japan imported £297 million worth of furs during 1990 which is up on the previous year's figure of £290 million. So their conscience shows no sign of... hmm... having a conscience.

Now I introduce a name that will not be familiar to anyone – unless you happen to be a bear, an extremely intelligent one to boot. The name, Shane Beary, will mean little to those with the power to issue merit points, or even better money, but it is a name that gives humanity a smidgin of hope. He is an Irishman who has worked for the SAS, been employed as an underwater explosives expert, and a guerilla fighter. He now concentrates on saving bears from the tables of restaurants in Thailand. Tourists, mainly Korean, sit in anticipation of their meal and watch a bear being beaten and tortured. The excuse for this barbarism lies in the belief, and no, I don't believe it, that the fear gets the adrenalin flowing and adds flavour to the meat. It is on a par with the excuse for cruelty perpetrated by fox hunters. Having witnessed this act of barbarity, they continue to sit and watch as the bear is suspended in a net and slowly lowered into a boiling hot cauldron of water and cooked alive. These complete arseholes pay £125 for a paw alone. The Thai government does not agree with the practice, but posseses neither the money nor the manpower to outlaw this disgusting and upsetting obscenity. No doubt, there are more than a few brown envelopes changing hands anyway. So, it is left to our Irish friend to save these creatures from a plate worse than instant death. He takes all those he can find to his own animal sanctuary. How can people be so cruel. Yes I know it is the money, but most of us couldn't be a witness to that for all the pandas in China.

With the Japanese still using their nets of death, the pollution of the seas is continuing unabated and John Gummer agrees with everything and does nothing, so the waters will continue to support only rotting bodies, discarded plastic and toxic waste. Around Britain's coasts, fishermen are bringing home their catch in such numbers that their greed will bring extinction and ruin ever nearer. The Scottish Office are buying two Cessna light aircraft purely to deal with illegal catches in Scottish waters. Apparently catches in excess of the legal limit are being landed in every seaport in Britain – another example of Mrs T.'s grabbing society. I, for one, cannot see the attraction of fish these days. Maureen served up some mackerel a couple of months ago and I just couldn't eat them. Since that day, I haven't even eaten fish and chips, let alone wet fish. I think it was the beach at Swanage that put me off. We all know that the majority of animals are injected with this and that (oh, and the other, of course) but at least we can buy what appears to have been organically grown vegetables, meat from animals which have been reared on organic land and free-range eggs – or am I being naïve again? With fish, however, all I can see is the glint of mercury, the inside of a toilet pan before flushing and a used condom.

It is not, of course, just our beaches that are tainted by greed. After some twenty years of constant hunting and the destruction of the Mediterranean coast for the tourist industry, only 350 Monk seals remain, and they reflect the decline generally. Canada is threatening to resume killing Harp seals and their pups. They are holding these animals as pawns in the power game with the EC over cod. They still managed to massacre 70,000 of the animals last year, now they are talking about upping the limit to half a million seals.

Back home in the rural backwaters of Somerset, thieves are stealing elvers that use the Bristol Channel to migrate up the Rivers Parrett and Tone. All the way from the Saragosa Sea they come, to end up as an eel. That is the way it has been for centuries. No, greed has now put its hand into action and some poachers are stopping them from completing the cycle by netting them as they arrive. They can earn up to £700 a night for their catch. Traders then buy them from the poacher and they are sold on again to Germany, France, Norway and, oh – Japan – fancy that!

Now we come to the animal which symbolises all the efforts being made by the conservationists, because, if the elephant goes, there will be no turning back. In the Selous Game Reserve in Tanzania, the population has dropped dramatically through poaching. Only two years ago there were 50,000 elephants. Now there are only 30,000. Virtually 30 examples are being killed each day. All this at a time when renewed pressure is being applied to governments to lift restrictions and start culling again. For the last three years elephants have had a fair measure of legal protection and the price of ivory has fallen seven times over. You and I both know that you can write what you like in a statute book, but making sure the laws are upheld is a different matter altogether.

The conference currently taking place in Japan (them again) will decide whether the killing of elephants can resume. Southern Rhodesia, I cannot bring myself to call it Zimbabwe, South Africa, Namibia and Malawi all want to resume killing. The Environment Minister has stated that the government will continue to back those wishing to retain the ban. Then again, this is the same government who said in 1979 that it had no plans to raise VAT. I think, in fairness, they meant they had no plans to raise VAT by a small amount, but to almost double it. I expect the computers are to blame. Meanwhile, back on the plains. Kenya at least seems to be sympathetic to the elephant's plight. Their total has dwindled from 130,000 in 1973 to around 20,000 at the present, so the last thing they need is renewed activity on the culling front, be it legal or poached. The EC is not exactly supportive as a united body of course, as individual countries see a quick buck being made as preferable to the long – or even short – term survival of such a wonderful animal. Germany, France and Portugal are all on our side. Spain and Belgium had said they would support a resumption in the ivory trade. The other six countries were undecided. How can anyone be undecided? Back to the brown envelopes, I suppose.

Zim-whatsit has also requested that they cut off the horns of Black Rhino so as to make the killing of the animal unattractive to poachers – this action was rejected. In twenty years, the Black Rhino population has dropped from 70,000 to just 3,500 specimens, a dangerously low figure. All this lack of concern at a time when globally the world's population is witnessing more fighting and unrest at any time since the Second World War. It is not just boring Yugoslavia either. There is the Zulu uprising (1992 version), internal fighting in Burma, the good old Mujahideen are gaining ground in Afghanistan, and we have street fighting in Newcastle.

This is where you start reading again if you don't give a bear's paw about animals. In the arrivals column today, a mother has just given birth to her sixth child. Six children in this day and age! To announce the birth in the *Daily Telegraph* indicates that they are not living on a council estate in Tottenham, so you would think they would have taken precautions, wouldn't you? They surely don't need the Child Allowance...

It gets worse. Aldershot FC lived to play another match last night, when they visited Ninian Park and lost 2-0 to Cardiff City. Five of the Hampshire team's side were on the youth training scheme, desperation is more than creeping in.

It seems a mish-mash of British law that makes it legal to sell and own radar detectors, but illegal even to be suspected of using one. Drivers caught in possession of one of these machines can be fined up to £2,000. If the police suspect you have used it, the detector can be confiscated. To my mind it would be easier just to make illegal the sale of this equipment. At £200 a throw, the only scroats who would buy one are the owners of Golf GTis, Peugeot 205 GTis and Escort XR3is. I can see the government's logic, however. If you ban the sale of these items, they lose the VAT content of the purchase price at the front end, and the ultimate fine at the other. These financial considerations are quite apart from the undoubted contribution any arrest and charge will make to the clear-up rate in crime statistics.

Well, you can always trust a newly privatised utility to fly in the face of public tolerance. British Gas has just announced that despite a lowering in profits for last year, good old Chairman Bob received a pay rise of 17.6%. In real money, that is about £1,252 a week extra. This rise brings his annual salary to £435,222. There is a photograph of him accompanying the article, and he certainly looks as if he is doing his best to look smarmy. Not for him a hint of embarrassment. Still, none of these lairds seem to be embarrassed about their charges, so thick skin must be mandatory. Over £430,000 per year, huh! Not bad for a state handout. Next year a Knighthood?

The self-interest in wage rises is catching. Guildford's councillors have voted to double their allowances for attending council meetings. The effect of this is that any borough councillor will now receive just over £1,000 for being there. If he or she is lucky enough to be the chairman of either the Policy or Planning Committees, then they get an extra £850. Chairmen of less important quangos get £625, still not bad, though. Even being top dog of your particular political party gains you another £400 per annum. The amounts paid out recede with the importance of the title down to that of oik ordinaire, of which there are very few. After all, titles are why half of them are there, finance being the other half. As residents of this brave new world we know as Guildford, we received through our letterbox – actually it was left in our porch as I had forgotten to ask the carpenter to cut a hole for the letterbox when he was hanging the door – a 32-page brochure. Could have told you that in a few words, really, but never mind. As it is Guildford Borough Council and not Aldershot, we will do it the posh way. One turns the front cover of this 'Citizen's Guide' to find an introduction selling one, sorry, telling one how cheap one's services are and welcoming any comments that one may have. This little piece is signed by one David Watts, the Chief Executive, alongside which is a photograph, just so as you know – I think that should be 'one knows' – he exists. I think I will revert to 'you'. As a friend of mine says, 'I can't be doing with it'.

Pages 2 and 3 centre on the historical beginnings and the town today. The fourth and fifth pages show the structure of the upper echelons of the council – more names and photos. Pages 6 and 7 concentrate on the 'decision-making process', accompanied by pictures. One is of a council meeting. This was obviously staged as every seat is full and they all appear to be alive. The other two photographs show the town crier and the mayor, both in full regalia. Pages 8 to 15 are a hoot. Someone, whose name will almost certainly have evaporated into the bowels of a committee, has been responsible for working out an A-Z of services provided by the council. Bear the word 'services' in mind, as you read on. Whoever collated the information either got in too deep or they have a sense of humour!

A is for Abattoir, Allotments, Abandoned vehicles, Annual Reports.
B is for Beautiful Borough, Bus passes, Bottle Banks.
C is for Car parks, Caring for the Elderly, Conservation, Cess pools and cemeteries.
D is for Drains, disabled, dog wardens – (listed in that order!).
E is for Elections, entertainment and the environment.
F is for Festivals and food hygiene.
G is for grants, Guildhall and guided walks.
H is for Help on hand, heritage, homelessness, housing.
I is for Information and inspection.
J is for Joint ventures – (they are obviously having trouble with J. The Joint Ventures they refer to concerns a statue sponsored by an insurance company and designed by a student, and according to the blurb, 'provides pleasure to many visitors' – then again, so would a massage parlour).
K is for Keep (Guildford Castle) and key – allowing 24 hour use of toilets by the disabled.
L is for Licensing, lido and litter.
M is for Mayor 'The first citizen of the borough, who acts as an ambassador – (is that the same as a prima donna? – for the Council at civic functions and chairs the meetings of the council. Last year the mayor attended nearly 800 functions – there's busy!).
N is for Nature trail.
O is for Orchestra – the Guildford Philharmonic. Don't know what they would have done for 'O' if they hadn't had them!
P is for Park and ride, planning applications, pollution control and public conveniences – thought the last two would have been combined.
Q is for Quality, no this is sycophantic. It is referring to the quality of services the Council strives to achieve and for answering 'questions' that you may have.
R is for Re-cycling, refuse, rebates, rent and a couple of others.
S is for safety, surfaced play areas, sports facilities, street naming and numbering – clutching straws here, and you will like this – 'Seventy four pence', which is, quote 'the community charge payer's contribution to the wide range

of services provided by the council – that is less than the price of a loaf of bread or two pints of milk'. I don't know where they get their bread, probably at a shop owned by a councillor, but Safeways in Aldershot charge 39p a throw.

T is for training, tourist information centre and TWINNING.

U is for understanding and caring. (This piece of ingratiating dross refers to the council always being on hand to help and listen.)

V is for Value for money (back to the equations again – £2.26 per week is the cost of all the many services provided, less than the cost of a book of 1st class stamps, apparently).

W is for Water and the weigh bridge.

X is for... ahh, they had more trouble with this one and cheated. Wait for it, X is for 'X'termination. Yes, that's their offering. It refers to pests, not a general culling of DSS claimants.

Y is for Youth (see above) – my words.

Z is for {I will repeat this one for you) Z is for Zebra. A licence is needed to keep certain animals under the Dangerous Wild Animals Act, 1976. As yet, no licence has been issued for a zebra – but there is a first time. Zest and commitment to excellence in the range of services that the council provide for the benefit of the community.

It makes it almost worthwhile living here, doesn't it? Pages 16 and 17 are devoted to a photographic Who's Who of the council, so not only can you find out where they live and what their telephone numbers are, just in case you have to ring for help about an influx of gypsies, but the captions also give you their titles, so you check on their allowances.

From the next page there is a directory of services and telephone numbers, interspersed with adverts. To be fair, it is a professional, easy-to-read guide. What the cost of production is, I would shudder to think, for the quality of the paper is not awful. Bearing in mind their comments about conservation, value for money, quality of services, I am surprised I cannot find any 'recycled paper' signs anywhere. Perhaps that is only for toilet rolls and not unnecessary extravagances paid for out of our 74p a day. Ah well, if it keeps them happy.

Meanwhile, in yet another unreal world, the polls are all over the place. One has them neck and neck, another gives Labour the lead, while a third insists that the Tories are ahead by a smidgin. I still think it will be a hung parliament, and as you know, if that is my prediction, look to an alternative for a more accurate conclusion!

It was heartening to see the 'before and after' photographs of an Old English Sheepdog that had been rescued by the RSPCA. The couple who previously 'owned' the dog, if 'owned' is the right word, were fined £50 each and ordered to pay £92 costs. They were banned from owning a dog for life. Ninety-two pounds is a paltry sum for such an obscenity. No wonder there was an 8% increase in complaints last year. If you had that mentality, a fine of that amount is not going to shake you into becoming a caring owner, bring back the birch.

So, the slit-eyed lot appear to be on the threshold of buying that beautiful landmark, County Hall, in London. There will probably be a mystery fire and a golf course will arise out of the ashes – for the Japs only, of course.

Argos are planning to open new stores, despite a worse than-expected result over Christmas. I have been to one of their shops twice. I found the whole operation cold and clinical. On both occasions, the object for purchase was selected and the obligatory code number jotted down on the form. I queued and then received, when it eventually came to my turn, the 'Sorry, it is out of stock' reply. Thinking about it, I suppose I am glad it happened. The last thing I wanted to admit was that my initial impression could have been anything other than wrong!

The days are drawing nearer and political tactics are becoming more desperate. From the 'let's keep it clean' image portrayed by all parties a few weeks ago, the clear waters of the campaign have become decidedly murky. Labour are homing in on health, with the emphasis on the length of time it takes to obtain an operation on the NHS. There is, of course, nothing to tug at the heartstrings like a suffering child, and Labour are squeezing out every last tear. Who is the child? Who are the parents? Is it the real case it is purported to be? All will no doubt be revealed, but it could so easily backfire. As Robin (weasel) Cook is involved, I hope it does. Could anyone seriously vote for a party that includes someone as shifty as Gerald Kaufmann or Robin C, owner of a face even his own mother would hate. It is not as if it is nature's fault. If he shaved off his beard, he might endear himself to the public a little more.

I won't be voting myself, I cannot see the point. Having read this, please do not say to yourself, 'It is your duty to vote, people died so that you may exercise your right.' Yes, they did die for my freedom, but does that not include the freedom to make up my own mind whether I wish to vote or not? Believe you me, I would rather vote, but what is the point in putting a cross for reasons that are negative? We are no longer in charge of our own destiny. If we had two major parties of opposite opinions and politicians who were clear in their idea, we might have a sporting chance. You might be able to side with the lesser of the evils at the very least. We have a third party, the Lib/Dem, who have no hope of real power at all. Actually, even if they were the main opposition party, Paddy Pantsdown would not get my vote. What a wonderful play on words that was. It was worth his little philandering just to read that headline. Having read their pamphlet which was delivered locally, in the hope that the voter will cast in favour of their candidate, Mrs Bucknell, I remain convinced that they have probably lost a few more votes. Under the title 'Full involvement in Europe', it states that 'Liberal Democrats believe in working towards a fully integrated, federal and democratic European community, sharing sovereignty and pooling power to achieve common goals for all.' The spiel then goes on to list the policies that the Lib/Dems will pursue in Europe. Nowhere does it offer the punter a choice. It all seems too cut and dried. Still, they are no different from the other two, when it comes to European rule.

What is there to choose between the two main parties? Labour will allow in more refugees and immigrants, but with an increase in tax would probably pay more attention to health. Neither party will take us out of the black hole of federalism. Neither will restore imperial measurements or L.s.d. Neither will fight EC regulations on punishment and reintroduce capital and corporal punishment, even if they wanted to. Neither will do away with minority quangoes, although I have no doubt that given a Labour government, more taxpayers' money would be devoted to unworthy causes, and that there would be increased discrimination in favour of any minority it could think of. If you are yellow, black, or whether you have got less arms or too many, Whether you are a lesbian or a homosexual, under Labour you will win, and win well. Being an unmarried mother will give you extra Brownie points with the social services, not to mention extra money. Remember folks, with Labour, the higher the number of bastardised sproggs you have got the more of the world's your mercury-filled oyster – paid for by those who do work, of course. Forget the smiley face of the moderates, the Labour party still sports its extremists and as we have seen from previous own-goals, many are in positions of power at grass roots level. Just over a year ago, nine council workers in South Tyneside were awarded compensation after they had been subjected to a 'bullying, vitriolic and vilifying attitude' by members of a union. All because they did not agree with their 'cause' and crossed the picket line. As is so often the case with the left-wing element, 'rights' are okay provided they are one-sided.

Our elected government has been told only today that by banning immigrants who have married purely to attain permits and passports, from living here, we are contravening EC directives regarding free movement. So who is in charge? It certainly isn't the elected British government, regardless of party politics and policies. We cannot even control Sunday opening, so the role of national government has been reduced to that of a local council. The real power lies in the hands of international banks and the multinationals.

Give me a party which encourages businesses to continue steady growth instead of imposing punitive taxation, i.e. the Unified Business Rate.

Give me a party who will reward effort and squeeze the wasters who take from the state and give nothing in return.

Give me a party who will not be frightened to use the full force of the law to break up strikes that threaten the rights of people to work if they wish, to confront hordes of travellers from polluting further acres of land, vandals who cost society so much and those who would harm animals for the hell of it. Make them suffer sufficiently that they would never be tempted again.

A party could do well by capping the borrowing on credit cards. They could impose legal price differentials on cash and credit customers. Why should someone paying cash subsidise those with plastic? The only winners are the financial institutes who are making obscene profits out of these all-too-invisible earnings.

What about a party who looked after the aggrieved rather than the ne'er-do-well. We can leave the likes of them to the 'Longford fraternity'. Legal Aid could be directed to those who genuinely need it, rather than those who are on the wrong side of the law to begin with.

The above is only a small list of everyday items, without getting into the moral issues of high interest rates, long-term security in employment, investment and the bloody Channel Tunnel.

Any party who had the balls to take on board a few of those

ideas, not new and supported by millions, would do very well in an election, but then you need balls, and vision.

Right, that is it. Enough of politics. I am going for a tom-tit now. It is, for me, the only sure way to lose weight – and I don't mean Terry (if only it were that simple)!

That Chairman of the Commission for Racial Equality is becoming intoxicated with the juices of positive discrimination. Last week we witnessed a senior police officer having his knuckles rapped for telling a racist joke at a dinner. Now we have the good, but misguided, Mr D. telling a conference at Bramshill Police College that jokes concerning ethnic minorities harm the recruitment drives aimed at bringing more non-whites into the police force. Okay, so you just shake your head in amazement and take no notice, but he adds that 'black and Asian' officers should be singled out for training to help them to compete for early promotion. If he cannot see that the action he advocates will only lead to greater distrust and resentment, then he is a bigger fool than I took him to be, for getting involved with those soulless wassocks in the beginning. These people probably think that a post of this nature enhances their standing and other people's respect for them. Sad, really.

Not far behind in the misguided person's stakes are the simplified spelling society. This offbeat education (or lack of it) lot could do worse than get themselves a proper job (and a dictionary). If they have other sources of income, they should spend their spare time more gainfully employed by working in an animal sanctuary or playing video games in some seedy arcade. Basically, their intention is to decimate the English language, yes, it can get worse. The main innovation of the scheme is to reduce the number of letters in a word. So 'write' becomes 'rit' and 'spelling' becomes 'spelng'. This body of odd-sods also maintain that as well as helping to make English easier – they said that about decimalisation and no-one I know has ever seen any increase in the standards of numeracy – there will be less wasting of paper. With signs and notices being condensed, less wood will be required for pulping, so the idea is environmentally friendly as well.

Once again, I looked to see if it was 1st April, but no.

What have we here, Pippa and Julian French are announcing the arrival of triplets. Maureen would have liked us having ours that way, all in one go. We had to do 'it' three times to achieve the same result, and over a much longer period!

A friend of mine said the other day that he was trying to find ways of making ends meet, so he had asked his wife if she would mind going out on the streets and earning a few bob. I said that knowing his wife, it would be a few bob. He didn't argue, in fact he apparently went on to tell her that Gurkhas are not that fussy and they will queue for about twenty minutes, even though they know that the lady of the night is a complete dog. So if you are passing a block of flats and you see a line of Orientals, sporting green jackets and standing to attention, you will know what I mean – then that is the place to avoid if you are a double-glazing or insurance salesman – unless you like dogs!

Britain has not arrived at the liberated stage yet, where prostitutes display signs advising you to 'get your Aids here'. I am reminded of a pre-decimal joke. 'My wife went out on the game last night and came back with 13s.4d.' 'Who gave her the four pence?' – 'They all did.'

A chap I know in the West Country picked me up – well, it was my lucky day – no, not really, he picked me up from the station actually, and on the way to his office, we were discussing various news items. He mentioned the case of a family where the husband had been forced to witness his wife being raped by burglars. He was sitting watching this news item with his wife and their sixteen-year-old daughter. After the report had ended, and the mum had tutted in disgust, the daughter said that if it had happened in their house, Dad would have asked if they could wait until he had managed to set up the video, as it would make a change for his wife to enjoy herself. Apparently, her sense of humour went down like a lead balloon with the mother, although my friend saw the funny side of it. They don't make daughters like they used to, do they.

So, it is all over. Aldershot FC are finished. A name from the past to many people already. The ignominy of having your name scratched from the Fourth Division records, even if you are bottom, is not one that has been encountered since Accrington Stanley's demise in 1962. Thirty years have elapsed since a league team failed to finish a season. It is sad when any team folds, but when the team in question have their own ground, albeit loaned, situated in a high street location, it is a double shame. The Recreation Ground is a friendly ground where one could turn up knowing one would see the same faces standing on the same steps, week after week. A former director is trying to salvage something from the mire by forming an Aldershot Town FC with the hope that it will be allowed into either the Beazer or the Diadora leagues. If they are successfully formed and are allowed to remain the 'Rec' then all the better. The last thing we need is for some 'bright young thing' in the development world offering large wads of money to redevelop the site.

Remember Mid Southern Water, whose motto is 'Purely Yours'? Well, they have just been fined £5,000 plus £290 costs for polluting the River Blackwater with oil. I think 'Impurely Yours' would be more appropriate, don't you?

Whenever I see a charity tin being rattled in a high street, I wonder about the amount which actually gets to the heart of the cause which is being supported. A case has just finished its run at the Old Bailey where a 30-year-old woman has been found guilty of stealing from the charity where she works. In her position as Deputy Director, she was in complete control of all its funds. Like many other charities where irregularities have occurred, the account had not been subject to proper audits. Over a period of two-and-a-half years, she stole £2.7 million, all of it has been spent – and more. Some of these charities have more money than professionalism.

Our unworthy Chancellor – the Man from Lamont – has not been seen very much during the election campaign – so far, anyway. I read that should a Tory government be re-elected, he could become an instant casualty, along with Kenneth Baker, one can understand why. The other Kenneth, Mr Arrogance himself, seems set to carry on with only praise from his peers. With children of one's own, there is obviously more than a passing interest in the future of state education. Maureen and I are no different from millions of other parents in wanting the best for our children. Despite all the debates about education, I fear for the future, should it lie in socialist hands, and look in despair at what twelve years of Tory administration has done to our schools. The main problem is what they are turning out at the age of sixteen. When you analyse it, primary schools seem to be places were, despite the odd misfit, most children enjoy themselves. Middle schools see increased numbers, but most pupils still seem controllable and content. The problems always tend to arise in the secondary schools where children can get lost in the crowd. The party whose policy states the emphasis should be on much smaller schools, where discipline can be effective, where bullying can be identified early on, and where competition should be encouraged but not taken as the be-all and end-all, will be the one to gain from most caring parents. We need schools where the numbers are no greater than 300 pupils, where uniform is mandatory, where emphasis is placed on the subjects connected to the real world and where party politics are kept firmly out of the curriculum.

Last December I read of a school that was being discriminated against because it 'opted out' – it resides within a Labour-controlled authority and headmasters at other schools still within the traditional structure were refusing to play this politically isolated school at sports events. If this isn't a recipe for antagonism between the various pupils, I don't know what is. While the heads and administrators vie for position of top dog, one wonders what the effect will be upon the children. All they will learn from this is that if you are ideological, arrogant and inflexible then one pursues a career in education. It was in the same month that our Ken published his ideas for a 'back to basics' teaching method with a formal 'whole class' approach, with single subjects being taught and the pupils sitting behind desks facing a blackboard. So where have twelve years been spent if this 'great leap forward' is all we have to show for it? What *has* happened in the intervening period? Very little, but it sounds good. We witness day in, day out, the pathetic efforts of a sixteen-year-old behind a checkout desk to come to terms with unlearned realities such as when a spanner has been put in the works by way of the customer offering a two penny piece, alongside the £5 note she has tendered, for goods totalling £3.02p. All they can see is a visual display stating £1.98 change. So where does this two penny piece come in then? Report after report, review after review, have failed to stem the decline. Teachers are to blame for contributing to a greater extent by their inflexibility and their 'copping out' when it comes to discipline. Only today we learn that, surprise, surprise, the National Vocational Qualification (NVQ) are of a lower standard than the old City & Guilds type exams. Well of course they are. Ask any employer. Lowering the standard for pass marks helps the statistics and heads off further complaints from parents, it also allows teachers to get away with poor performances as well. As it is, the biggest retard under the sun is entitled to a certificate these days. Just by sitting there they qualify, remember, no-one must fail, no-one must be a loser, it is unequal!

Looks good for the government though, all those statistics telling us of our 'bright young things' ' progress – and it is all such a farce. The NVQ assessments do not require pupils to put answers in written form. They can even answer oral questions by sketching or pointing (they didn't mention grunting, but I bet it is included), a slip maybe? The new NVQ course for building apprentices, sorry trainees – apprenticeship smacks of proper training and the prospects of a proper job – cannot hold a candle to that of the old C&G. Those exams covered eight separate aspects of arithmetic and geometry. The new NVQ covers just two aspects. According to the report, these should be considered acceptable questions for an eleven-year-old. All of the standards deemed passes here, are below the continental levels and would be considered failures. Isn't it short-term thinking for the certificate holder does not benefit, the employer does not benefit, and the country gains nothing, except the possibility, nay, probability, of another social security claimant. There is, of course, the view that, should you fail to obtain even the lowest of these 'fag-end' qualifications, you would at least have something in common with many ministers now in government.

Having read that there wasn't a recession, until they admitted we were coming out of one, was cause for a smile. To continually state that unemployment is always the last area to improve when the economy starts to recover is also a good one. The proof of the pudding, however, lies in the trade figures. When the gap starts to show a continuing narrowing then the public will accept that we could be turning the corner. Until then you might as well let the bearers of one of those worthless certificates have a go, because you could not possibly read anything more untrue from the statistics presented to you than from that lot in power, and they would certainly be cheaper to employ!

Another sign of a desire to be accepted was seen last night at Cardiff Airport, when Mr and Mrs Major were seen eating fish and chips out of a newspaper. The common touch, huh, if it all seems somewhat staged, at least it won't lose them votes. *The People* have just published an article entitled 'Ben meets Glen'. My most unfavourite, supposedly funny man, Ben Elton, talks to, and about, Glenys K. Not only is there a full colour picture of the pair of them on the front page of the supplement, but on the outside pages there are three more of G.K., one of G.K. sitting at a table with B.E., both preening for the cameras, and one of G.K. with, who's that? Oh, yes, the PM elect, so that should throw a few more votes to the Tories. Can you imagine anyone voting for a man whose wife has just been interviewed by Ben Elton?

Another chink in the armour surrounding our independence, or just another move towards harmonisation? The therm is to be displaced. The next bill to invade your home from those awfully smug people in the gas industry will be calculated in kilowatts. What I didn't realise was that the friendly Mr Therm fell victim to the Equal Opportunity lobby. So, rather than stand up and gain public support for a well-known advertising ploy, they laid down and put up their legs in submission. I do that at home, but what we get up to in the privacy of our bedroom is our own affair!

And now for something completely different, as they say. (Even though my wife says you shouldn't start a sentence with 'and'). We watched *Blockbusters* the other night whilst we were eating our Bubble and Squeak. Mr H., or Bob to his contestants, and probably his wife as well, asked, 'What "H" describes a bus service that starts at 6.30 am followed by another at 7.30 am?' The answer was not hallucination, as we guessed, but hourly, apparently.

I have just been looking at today's papers. The two murderers from Reading who killed the seventeen-year-old lad at the petrol station at Hartley Wintney have been jailed for life. The killing, for no good reason, of a youngster who did as he was told by lying on the floor, cannot have one ounce of justification. Why then are Britain's, sorry, Europe's, laws so lax? These two murderers should be hung. As it is, we know that life does not mean life but a few years until statistics pressure the authorities into requiring the beds for more murderers.

The Home Office is to introduce anonymous HIV testing for newcomers as part of a plan to discover the percentages of those carrying the virus. Having read the headline, or rather mis-read the headline, I thought the policy was to inject the new arrivals with Aids! Ah, well, and just when I thought I had found some good news.

The Turner-Powells have announced the arrival of a son (Francis St John), a brother for Pelham and Clementine. Nicky (who is mummy T.P.) used to be a Bruxner-Randall. Out of one double barrel and into another. Gosh, it's all right for some!

It is nice and quiet in the office at the moment. Glyn departed for the supermarket in good time for an 8.30 am start. Debbie is at college and William is at school. Maureen is working until 12 mid-day, so I have got the morning to myself. I shall scribe away.

It is three months now since Glyn left the fast food industry and he is really enjoying it. We have no idea what avenue Debbie will pursue after her 'A' levels. We can see her spending half her life studying. We shall probably still be keeping her as a mature student. She bought a dress yesterday, it was only £39.99, reduced from £65, so she had to have it. To be fair, she looks nice in it, actually, you get the impression she is modelling for the 1933 edition of the *Edwardian Lady's Diary*. The romances are still going strong. Glyn is still going out with his nice young girl from Guildford, while Deborah is going on holiday at Easter for a week. Not just with the boyfriend, however. This is a family holiday. There are nine of them going altogether, to a small resort in Cornwall. I haven't dared ask Debbie the name of the village, as you know geography is not her strong point, and I fear the whereabouts of Cornwall might tax her unduly, and we don't want her fretting that someone's stolen it, when she looks on a map and can't find it between Guildford and Farnham. To her, the most south-westerly tip of England could be Lands End or Lanzarotti. Still, no doubt she will recognise it when she sees the roadsign saying 'Cornwall'. Luckily, and not just for Deborah's sake either, roadsigns are reader-friendly and don't go in for joined-up writing, so that should help.

We are now into the final furlong. It is Monday, 6th April, three days to go before the non-event claims a victor. Mr Major seems to be beefing up the Conservatives' attack a little more now. We keep reading his views on the possible break-up of the United Kingdom, should the Tories lose more seats in Scotland. Today's front page photo shows the good J.M. smiling, waving with one arm, while the other is placed reassuringly on Norma's shoulder. They are surrounded by well-known athletes and personalities. Interestingly, among those shown clapping are many from the indigenous population, plus a token Caribbean and an Asian supporter. Still it shows that J.M. is a man of all our people.

Meanwhile, on Millbank, a jolly time was being had by the Labour party. Among their stars were Ian McKellan, Michael Cashman, Pam St Clement, Larry Adler and Bishop Trevor Huddleston. Just seeing that lot at a political do is enough to change your voting intentions. Kevin Whately, from *Auf Wiedersehen, Pet* and *Morse* was there, which is a pity, as I liked him. Anyway it gives you a few more bodies to put against the wall!

I am going to be a bit busy for the next couple of days so in fact the next time we meet will be on election day itself. I have, however, still got a few minutes left before I have to go out, just time to tell you about William's school's Open Evening. Yes, he is still with us. I know I said he was at school earlier, but you might have thought it was a boarding school or that we had moved and not told him. No, in fact we see him every day. Anyway, we attended the school Open Evening at the appointed time and sat looking at his work, while his teacher completed her chat with the previous appointed parents. At the end of each of his pieces of work, his teacher had written comments such as 'Well done', or 'Good Effort', etc. Against these, William had written

'Thank you', and had drawn a smiley face. At one point, quite recently in a book, his teacher had obviously been somewhat less than impressed. Against his work she had written, 'This work is half-finished', to which William had added 'I no' – with a miserable face next to it. Spelling is not one of his strong points. He is going on an overnight visit to a school education centre near Dorking in June. It sounds very good. They have to read maps, there is a need for teamwork, and hopefully, a bit of respect for the countryside. The village they are visiting has a church, which they will be taking a look at and making some notes about.

With the forthcoming visit in mind, homework was set asking the class to describe the activities of a church. William's offering was headed 'Homework. AAAAGGGG' (plus four miserable faces). You can see from this that his enthusiasm was not immense. Under the word 'churches' he listed the following, which is reproduced 'as it was rit'.

Churchers well pepple pray for god.
Pepple be burried
They get marrid
The get chrisand
Pepple go at Easter and Chrismas (actually a 'T' was inserted as an afterthought)
Theres a cross
Thears a tapple with candeldles
Organ

On the reverse of this 'effort' was written 'Homework dont touch okay or lose it or I am dead by teacher okay'.

We made him write it again – he wasn't best pleased.

Right, time's up. I am off and I will – see you on Thursday. Happy voting.

So here we are, Thursday, 9th April, when the only poll that counts is the real one. At a time when we have had the wringing out of every political cliché and the complete lack of photographic evidence to support the view that Gerald Kaufmann and Kenneth Baker are alive, let alone active, it is perhaps timely to note that in Germany the Right-wing Republican Party have 11% of the state vote in Baden-Württemberg. I have no doubt that this rise in popularity is not because everyone in the fatherland has become a closet Nazi – well, not everyone, but more to do with the fact that the electorate need to feel that their country is in control of its own future, to a larger rather than a very much lesser degree. This will become more prominent as the effect of the Maastricht Treaty takes shape. Where is Maastricht? It is like signing a declaration of war, or peace in Milton Keynes.

It is 11.30 pm. I have just got home having spent the evening at the Farnham Beer Festival. A very enjoyable time was had by me and all. The place was heaving with people, and some forty-five private breweries were represented. A jazz band played, refreshments were on hand throughout the proceedings and the interesting thing was that, as in previous years, there was a complete lack of drunken scroats trying to pick a fight. One or two chaps and chap-esses were merry, but nobody was obnoxious. I am convinced the main reason for this lies in the fact that there was no lager on sale, only real ale. Four of us shared a taxi home, and the driver commented that he had worked during beer festivals before and he had never encountered any trouble with his fares. I am now going to make some sarnies and then settle down to watch how the election and my predictions unfurl – on the BBC, of course!

Well, here we are, it is all over. The Tories have a working majority and I cannot wait to see the excuses that will be turfed out by the pollsters. No doubt the blame will lie with the electorate for being either fickle or just downright deceitful. Luckily for the Tories, they were re-elected just as we are coming out of the ever-so-slight recessionette!

Chris Patten, having lost Bath, looked like a nominee at an Oscar ceremony who had just lost out. I was sorry to see both Rosie Barnes and John Cartwright lose their seats. Mind you, having Shirley Williams campaigning on your behalf must be equal to the death wish. To be fair, of course, when your leader has called it a day suggesting that everyone votes Tory and effectively wraps up your party, you are on a pretty sticky wicket, as they say at Headingley. I am surprised the Tories were re-elected, and with such ease really, but as I said, don't bank on my predictions. I suppose it was worth having an election, if for no other reason than finding a good time to brush Kenneth Baker off of the Cabinet.

The farce did produce one or two good moments. The show-piece extravaganza when Labour fielded their replacement government, a second shot in the foot if ever there was one. A shot equal to that of the first effort when they announced their totally unnecessary shadow budget. Gordon Brown's post-election comment that 'The real message from the polls was that Labour was the only alternative government' caused my face to crack more than a tad, which is more than you can say for his. In fact, I would go so far as to say that I don't think I have ever seen the man smile at all. Is he just bland or has he had plastic surgery? Whatever the reason, the man is totally lacking in personality. I was surprised by the Shetland Pony managing to hang on to the Gladstone bag – or was it Disraeli's? It was also an election for personalities. Sebastian Coe, Glenda Jackson and Gyles Brandreth are all now awaiting their turn to become members of the inner sanctum.

Despite the raising of the deposit from £150 to £500 a throw, the also-rans were flocking back in droves. At least English eccentricity isn't dead, even if the rest of the country is. The 'Chauvinist Raving Alliance', 'Wake up Wokingham Campaign', 'Forward to Mars' and 'Justice from British Rail' were all perfect examples of our homeland individuality. Little understood abroad, indeed, little understood in parts of Guildford, come to think of it, but when we start to take politics seriously, then there is something wrong. The 'Monster Raving Loony Party' with Screaming Lord Sutch as its Prime Minister in waiting are both household names now. In fact, they have almost acquired the one thing they would hate – credibility. The new names I was taken with who also failed to generate enough votes for a major breakthrough were the 'Up the creek' party' and 'Let's Have a Party, Party'. Nice one that.

We now have to wait to see who will inherit the titles of Labour's new Batman and Robin. The overriding benefit from not having a Labour government is that the public will not have to suffer Glenys at No. 10. We can now return to our televisions knowing that the Palestinians and the Israelis will still be knocking seven barrels of shit out of each other, the Afghans will continue with their little fracas and while the Serbs and the Croats are shelling each other's cities, Norma will be in Downing Street shelling John's peas.

The hard hats have returned. City workers not wishing to miss out on a fast buck are prepared to risk life and mobile phone, it seems, to be the only one in the office who 'made it through to work'. A bomb which destroyed many offices in London's financial quarter – or an eighth as it is in these recessionary times – has been greeted in the press by pictures of these city slickers sporting headgear. I am just surprised it is not sponsored. Robert Dyas ran out of stock within a few minutes of opening. They had to ring the wholesalers for more. Still, it brings out the Dunkirk spirit, where powerhouses on two legs are made aware of other human beings and can be seen talking to the milkman, whereas they would normally ignore him, or more likely run him down. After all, they only have eyes for their mobile phones.

It was nice to see the judiciary working on behalf of the poor sod who pays for them. A high court judge ruled against two five-year-olds who tried to obtain council housing. The cases, brought through their parents, against Bexley and Oldham councils highlight the extent to which families will go to bypass the system, at someone else's expense.

Both councils had ruled that the two families in question had made themselves homeless, having left previous accommodation. There are, however, a couple of disturbing facts that have arisen from these actions. In the case of the Oldham family, having lost the case with the local council, they pursued their cause through one of these law centres, who took up the cudgels on their behalf. The law centre receives a £90,000 per annum grant from Oldham Council, who have had to pay costs running into thousands of pounds. Why? The family received Legal Aid – why?

I would like to know how they can be considered worthy of Legal Aid when many genuine hardship cases are denied access, and having lost the case, why the poll-tax payer should foot the bill. I hope the council reduce this law centre's grant, or even better, cuts it out altogether. The woman in this case, a young unmarried mother, was evicted by the council for getting into arrears with her rent. The court heard that her rent money was spent funding her boyfriend's drug habit – and she still gets support from the law centre.

The other family in Bexley, headed by a 'Ghanaian political refugee', had bought a home and then fell behind with the mortgage. They told the council they were homeless, yet still bring into this country three other children and a grandchild from Ghana. The council decided that a deliberate attempt had been made *not* to keep up payments, but they still have to pay costs as well. Why is this? Why were they allowed to bring in more relatives when they were in such a precarious position?

I don't know why I feel surprised that the cases were taken as far as they were. We all know that the law supports those who will not help themselves and seek to jump the queue.

You haven't seen my keys, have you?

British Telecom are trying to pull the wool over everybody's eyes (again) by offering a carrot in the shape of lower cost trunk calls. This piece of manipulation is balanced in their favour of course by the raising of rental charges by 35% to £25 per quarter. So, on the basis that you are free to dial where you want, but you cannot escape a rental fee, they have got you by the short and curlies again. BT have stated that their 'current results are depressed, partly in consequence of the new pricing rules, partly because of the recession and partly as a result of inroads by competition'. I would add 'partly because of the fees paid to personalities for advertising their products and partly because of the huge salary enjoyed by Ricky Valance.' At least Greedy Phone Bastards PLC are still making a handsome and obscene profit. Their attitude slays you, doesn't it?

So you lose your seat in the General Election and display all the signs of terminal misery. All of a sudden, it is Hong Kong calling and smiley face time. Chris Patten is being offered a five-year sentence and £140,000 per year tax free. Isn't awful is it? As long as you're a member of the right club. Some are golfers, some are masons, some are politicians – and many all three. Still, it increases the odds of coming up smelling of roses.

I find this a bit strange, or if you are reading this in the quiet of the Cotswolds – a bit rum, don't you know.

The National Trust is to be taken to court for selling items of clothing and plants on a Sunday from one of its many properties. Complaints (in the plural) have been received by Broadland District Council about Blickling Hall. To be fair, the council received complaints about sixteen other businesses that come under their authority, including supermarkets. Who would complain about the National Trust selling items when the money generated goes back into the pool to benefit everyone – including, no doubt, those who reported them. They could have found employment in France, working for the Germans about 50 years ago. Wouldn't they have enjoyed it?

209

Get this – there is another gem in the arrivals column. A little sprogg has been coughed up over the last couple of days. To Sally and Neil, a son, Maximilian Nicholas Haddock – Max Haddock, huh! Bet he will ask his chums to call him Nick. Whilst we are about it, the Osborne-Thomases, you must know them darling, have produced a sixth child. No time for equality here. Imogen, the latest, makes it girls 5-boys 1. Come on mummy, go for another 4 boys and bask in glory. What do you mean, you have a headache?

The march of dictatorship from Europe continues unabated, as does the club instinct, so endemic of these types. Big business will be very impressed by the mandarins who have decided that independent firms who produce car parts will be outlawed. They are planning to pass legislation allowing only car manufacturers to make and sell replacement panels, etc. Effectively, the manufacturers will have the monopoly, charging whatever they deem the 'free' market will stand, while us poor sods will pay more through lack of choice. The higher price paid for parts will lead to higher insurance as well. So, another piece of legislation that benefits big business and government coffers through VAT will, no doubt, be rubber-stamped and all the motorist can do is pay up.

There was a small chink in the armour the other day when an EC stalwart, one Leon Brittan, that Europhile of long standing said that if responsibility for certain matters was handed back to national government, the public would more readily back other regulations that needed community co-operation and blanket coverage. The chink is that he actually acknowledged there are people out there with views – a first, maybe? Now back to the Euros we know and dislike so much. The heading of this reported story started 'An enquiry...' which translated from Esperanto means 'Cover-up'. Anyway, 200 Euro MPs, along with their wives, partners, mistresses, boyfriends, who knows?, plus interpreters and other sycophants, were booked into a hotel for a week-long EC conference in the Dominican Republic. The £63-a-night 'stopover' is owned by one of the seventeen EC commissioners. 'Keep it in the family, nudge, nudge, wink, wink.' Naturally, the reservation has been described as a coincidence. Glad to see that we were paying for the others to go on the jolly. Part of their Equal Opportunity policy, I expect.

I have just been passed a note by William. He and I had a little set-to earlier, as is usual it built up over something and nothing and ended with him going to his room. The note reads as follows:

Again this is reproduced as 'it was rit'.

> To Dad – I am leving because I hate you, just like you hate me, so I am leving and you cant stop me so there (drawing of miserable face) and I shall not come back so ther! Rember you cant stop me I am leving on Saturday and I hate you like you hate me from William. AND YOU CANT STOP ME???????
> I love you but I am still going.

Not one for missing out on the emotional angle, is our William. We are currently packing his bags and collecting cardboard so that he can make a home for himself on the Embankment. I think it all went wrong the day they stopped sending them up chimneys. He does like to push you to the limit but in a subtle way. I don't know how many times he has walked into my office and taken some of my headed notepaper on which to draw, when he has scrap paper of his own. He is banned now from going into my desk drawer as the items he borrows are never returned – pens, pencils, rubbers, stapler, *Playboy*... Notwithstanding all the dire threats I have uttered should I find my expensive paper being misused, I come home to find a sheet on which he has written lying on my desk, as if to taunt. He has drawn a man and a woman, apparently Maureen and I. The female is wearing a wedding dress and it is his interpretation of our wedding. The drawing is headed 'To mum and dad from William'. At the bottom of this defaced sheet he has added, 'Dont tell me of' and underneath, 'To Dad I am sorry I used your paper, sorry Dad'. See what I mean?

I have just looked at our calendar. In fact all the calendars in the house have 10th June clearly circled, as that is the night William is spending in Dorking with the school. I wonder just what Dorking has done to deserve him? Ah, well.

Here is another form of indirect taxation which begs further questioning. A couple in Farnborough have had their wheelie bin stolen. Rushmoor Borough Council, who you must know by now control Farnbrough, passed a decision in January through their Health Committee, that passes the financial onus (as opposed to anus) on lost or damaged bins to the houseowner, or tenant. No-one asked for these bloody eyesores in the beginning. The cost to one borough must be phenomenal, imagine the cost country-wide – and all out of our money. Guildford Borough Council collect the rubbish in black (or non-white) plastic bags, what's wrong with that? This Farnborough couple are being told that they must fork out £40 for a replacement bin. The council also mentioned that last year bins cost them £26,700 and that although their new money-spinning policy was designed to charge the majority of poll-tax payers there were exceptions. Yup. You've guessed, it is those on low incomes and those receiving benefits, usually both at once. So those of them who did not pay for them in the beginning get free replacements if they lose them. Yes, I see. Just think of what better usage that £26,000 could have been put to. Town twinning, mayoral car washes, bedding plants for a roundabout which is just about to be churned up for repairs...

So, California has at last cleared every hurdle in the execution stakes. It is to end the life of a convicted murderer. Glad to say they didn't listen to Mother Teresa who pleaded for mercy – why was she sticking her oar in? It would have been more productive had she visited the relatives of the two sixteen-year-old boys he killed in cold blood. If the execution goes ahead without any hiccups, the precedent will be set in the state that apparently leads the rest, where change is concerned. One of America's civil wrongs leaders said that this decision will open the floodgates and accelerate the marches to the death chamber. So it is not all bad news then, is it?

We are in tonight and it is feet-up time and a wallow in nostalgia. Three-and-a-half hours of TV Heaven, one of the few good reasons for having a fourth channel. Tonight's offerings include *Oh Boy, The Bob Monkhouse Show* and *Double Your Money*. These are followed by *Robin Hood* and *Dial 999* with Robert Beatty, who died earlier this year. The only problem is the adverts. A friend of mine said in all seriousness that he now records all ITV and Channel 4 programmes and skips through the breaks on Visual Search. Anything he wants to watch live is viewed on either of the BBC channels. There is little enough to watch as it is. At least London Weekend Television and Independent Television were acceptable names. Carlton, one of the new franchises, sounds like a third-rate hotel in Bayswater. The only known fact about the new companies is that profit will be the only motive, despite all the guidelines and provision for a quality service. If a programme does not knock a competitor off the ratings list in six easy episodes, there will not be a second series. Everything will be geared to short-term returns. Programmes known to be aimed at minority audiences will continue to suffer. Drama will be cut back even further and don't look to the BBC for solace. There never appears to be any money left after paying Terry Wogan's salary.

As if this decline isn't bad enough, both the Beeb and Thames Television are to launch a new joint channel on the Astra satellite in a few months' time. *Dad's Army* and *Steptoe and Son* have already been mooted as examples of the classics to be repeated. Initially to be free to more than 1.2 million homes equipped with satellite and cable connections, a fee will be charged when everyone has been hooked. Of course you have got to buy a dish to begin with, and you know my views on them! So what it boils down to is the fact that many of the good programmes shown on BBC will be available only for those who buy a licence and then pay again – and again – in indirect taxation. The question begged, of course, is that how, and with what, do the TV companies replace the space currently taken up with repeats, not *Keynotes*, *You Bet* and *Challenge Anneka*, surely. The last-mentioned has to be one of the most ingratiating programmes ever dreamed up. Well, along with *This Is Your Life*, *That's Life* and *Surprise, Surprise*. Do the producers not realise that the majority of the public are actually aware of the extent to which the generosity and goodwill ends and the toadying begins? If you and I said we wanted to rebuild a kids' playground and asked for labour and equipment, we would be told to 'bugger off', but the thought of a fizzogg on the box, and it is 'Yes, Anneka, no Anneka, three bags full Anneka.' It doesn't even look spontaneous. On the assumption that you have to watch something before you make your mind up, I did sit through one manic episode, there were phones going, people being swelled into action, and as in *Treasure Hunt* the task was completed with just a few seconds to go. Where was the spontaneity of it all? The lorries, loaded to the gunwhales, are hidden out of sight. Two thousand scouts are waiting in a cupboard for the signal to jump, the carrot being that they don't meet Miss Rice. All and sundry are giving away fortunes in goods and services just to see their names come up as sponsors, or to be given the chance to tell the directors that their six-year-old daughter is a really brilliant dancer and 'is Wayne Sleep making another series of the *Hot Shoe Show*' (sycophants).

I have just got time to mention the result of a harrowing saga which lasted five years. I remember reading about it in 1989 and commenting upon it in *FWIS*. A couple in Kingston upon-Thames, Surrey, fostered a child twenty-six years ago. When in their care for a short period an accident occurred and the child scalded one of her feet. She was taken to the doctor's for treatment. Shortly afterwards the child was sent to a new home where the foot became infected and some of her toes had to be amputated. The family in Kingston knew nothing of this until 1987, when the girl concerned, now twenty-two years of age, sued the couple and Kingston Council. An article appeared in the

Mail on Sunday during May last year, highlighting their plight and making the point that although the girl had lost her case in both the High Court and an appeal court, she was going to the House of Lords in order to seek compensation. She is getting Legal Aid for this, whilst the couple are faced with a bill for nearly £100,000. We move forward to the present, and Mr and Mrs Hughes, the foster parents have finally won the battle, for the Lords have refused the girl's petition for compensation. Five years of agony this couple have gone through. All local authorities have now reviewed their insurance policies governing fostering. As Mr Hughes said last year, 'The Legal Aid system is a bottomless pit if you are in the right financial bracket.' How can they be left out of pocket, though? It isn't fair at all. Yes, justice was seen to win through, but at what price?

It seemed ironic that on the same day, literally, that the *Mail on Sunday* was giving news space last year to the above story, the *Sunday People* was showing in glorious colour pictures of a mum who had fostered just under 600 children over a 28-year period. She has four grown-up children of her own, eight grandchildren and two adopted eleven-year-olds. All the good work put in by people like these could have been lost if the decision in the House of Lords had gone against the Hughes.

Right! I'm off. There is a massive curry awaiting me, so the bedroom windows will have to be wide open tonight! It is okay, I have got a bit of a head, anyway.

It is Sunday morning. The curry went down a treat and I am just looking at the stock book to see how many cars we've sold so far this month. Just six. Three Escorts, a Cavalier, an Astra and a Fiat 126. It doesn't seem to get any better. The situation is not helped, of course, by continually being at the top of an overdraft limit. Purchases which could be had, where an advert in the paper would probably result in a quick sale, still require money being tied up even for a short period. If I go over the limit by even one pound, the interest rate rises out of all proportion. Still, it is nice to know I am helping the third world debt.

Some good news regarding circuses. Cardiff City Council will be saying 'goodbye' to the Big Top for the last time next Saturday. There are to be no more acts which include animals within the city limits. There is a long way to go, but it is a step in the right direction.

I didn't tell you yesterday, but I have lost a set of car keys (again). Luckily it is the first car in the drive, which is a relief. Keys and me do not have a relationship of any quality, I am afraid – you haven't seen a set of Mini keys, have you. If you could check your pockets I would be most grateful. Some years ago, when I first worked for Hertz Rent-a-Car, in Victoria, I had a brief encounter with Sod's Law. Having been recently promoted to Deputy Manager, I was determined to show how clever and organised I was. The counter receptionists were all female and knew much more than me, but being 21 and ambitious, I had to make my mark.

I redesigned the delivery board and insisted on everyone changing a perfectly good system because... About 3 pm on this particular afternoon, the manager came through and said he had received a complaint that a delivery to Wimbledon, due half an hour before, had not arrived. He enquired as to who was delivering the car, and at what time the driver had left. I hastened over to my wall-mounted brainchild and stood red-faced amongst the tittering lasses (and some of them were very tittering!) My fail-safe method had failed. Not to lose face I told my manager, who was looking decidedly angry, that I would not subject a receptionist to any possible abuse and would deliver the car myself. This would increase my credibility factor, I thought. Off I went heading through the wild plains of West London in the 1600E Cortina. I crossed Putney Bridge and raced ever-onwards towards my goal. The customer was waiting for me on his door step. He was not best pleased. A few words were exchanged, actually I apologised profusely. I put my hands up and admitted my failure to read a delivery sheet properly. To be fair, he calmed down and accepted my apology. I asked him to sign the pre-prepared paperwork. He offered me a lift to the station but I said I could see a bus coming and ran across the road to catch the old-style RT bus, still sadly missed in transport circles. Back at the office I explained with almost arrogant confidence – which is something you would not expect of me – the way I diffused a potentially explosive situation and brought the man back from the brink of writing to the chairman, by my honesty and integrity. I sensed that the girls appeared to be holding back slightly more than a smile. Had someone farted, I thought? The manager informed me that the customer had rung just after I had left him, to explain just how my honesty had stopped him from writing a letter of complaint, but that he now felt compelled to do so as I had run across to catch the bus still clutching the Cortina's keys! The manager, having listened to my pompous assessment smirked slightly and held out his hand. I delved into my pocket. Lo and behold, there were the keys for the Cortina. The staff, by this time, were rolling around in a manner reminiscent of the Cadbury Smash characters of a few years ago. It was not a good day.

Well, it is not a good start to the week for British comedy either. Both Frankie Howerd and Benny Hill are dead. Is this the only way we are to see repeats of their shows? Turning the pages to find other stories isn't too promising, either. There is a picture of that weather teller, Sian Lloyd, sporting a thatched hat. I didn't read why she is wearing it, but I assume there wasn't a very good reason. The main news today concerns Freddie Mercury's commemorative gig. BBC2 devoted three hours and thirty-five minutes to the event. I nearly tuned in by mistake but made amends quickly and managed to avoid a face-to-vision confrontation with punters anxious to shell out fortunes that will benefit those who have 'queue jumped' the charity bandwagon. Still, when you have got a leader as charismatic as Elizabeth Taylor to urge you on, and a veritable plethora of stars willing to miss *Coronation Street* and *Thunderball*, just so that you can say you were there, the NSPCC and RSPCA, you know, real charities, do seem a bit dull.

Good old Californ-I.A. stood their ground against the do-gooders and executed Robert Haines, the convicted murderer I mentioned a few pages ago. Despite stays of execution and last-minute lobbying by the 'mis-led', it could be all systems go for the state's 328 death row inmates. On the basis that whatever happens in America usually happens in Britain within a few years, we live in hopes. You don't hear so much from Lord Longford now, do you?

Ah, a modicum of sanity has returned, I am glad to say. From 1st May, sanitary towel adverts are to be shown from 9 pm only. There has been 'significant adverse public reaction' to the Vespre ads that have been running since January, according to the Independent Television Commission. Having said that, a Ms Shuttle, she would be a Ms, condemned the decision as ludicrous, saying, 'It was worth offending a few people to give teenagers the chance to bring the debate on sexuality forward.' The last thing I need is for the TV companies to find another excuse to push Claire Rayner in front of me, especially holding a sanitary towel which has been used by a member of the Royal Family. It is blue blood they are showing, isn't it?

Right. You really find out how your children feel about you when they are pushed into a corner. I think I mentioned, in fact I know I did, that Debbie was going away for a week at Easter, with her boyfriend and his family. She was going to take her car over to his house and leave it there for the week. My suggestion was that, as she would soon be in need of an MOT for her car, it would be better for her to leave it at home and for me to drop her and the mountain of luggage off at their house. I could see that my suggestion had only been accepted with reservation. At the appointed hour we set off and arrived in the road where their house is situated, some twenty minutes later. I slowed because I did not know the exact location. 'Over here,' said Debbie pointing. 'Park over here.' I countered by saying that she had previously told me that their house was on the right-hand side. 'No, it is okay, you can drop me off here.' 'Nonsense,' I replied, 'we can stop in their drive so that you can unload your cases.' She seemed agitated. 'Okay,' she said, 'but if they ask you in, say that you are in a hurry.' What confidence, huh. I said I would only exchange pleasantries and Debbie said, 'Yes, but I know how many subjects you can get through in two minutes, and they are a very nice family.' Her prayers were not answered, both parents came outside as I unloaded the car with a year's, sorry, a week's, luggage. Handshakes were enacted and the offer of a cup of tea and a chance to look at the ordnance survey maps was taken up. About an hour later I departed. I expressed no controversial opinions and even Debbie admitted later that I had behaved myself. As to the holiday, they all seemed to enjoy themselves, the weather was acceptable and I think we only suffered ten reels of film, at thirty-six pictures each. Debbie and her boyfriend seem to take photographs that are so similar that when you place them in order and flick through, you have almost got a complete cartoon.

One of the biggest hoots this month concerned a telex received by the BBC from the Libyan director of foreign information administration. The complaint related to our one and, thankfully, only Kate Adie. It read, 'Each time she is in Libya, she is causing us more and more troubles, as if we have nothing to do, except Kate Adie. She never hesitates in insulting or scolding our representatives as if they were her personal slaves, while they are trying to give her facilities. We don't appreciate her presence among us. We are demanding never ever send Kate Adie to Libya, whatever the reasons are.' There was a bit more but that was the general idea. You would never have thought, would you, that the British public could have so much in common with the Libyan authorities.

I see that once again we are kow-towing to the minorities. This time it is footwear in Leicester and Peterborough. Shops in these towns have been selling slippers imported from Italy which apparently bear a quotation from the Koran. The Muslim view is that shoes are considered dirty and although finding writing taken from the Koran is bad enough, to actually wear them as well is extremely offensive. However, instead of allowing other people to make up their own minds, one of the shops selling these shoes has been destroyed by arson. The police are now being asked to protect shops which are still selling the so-called offensive items. So the taxpayer is once again forced to pay for more unnecessary police involvement, when their time could be better spent fabricating evidence, copying signatures, etc. The simple answer is, if you don't like freedom of choice, sod off!!

We have a new speaker for the House of Commons, I see. A lady, Miss Betty Boothroyd, will be the first female speaker the country has seen, and there is nothing wrong with that. In fact, I hope she is more successful than some of her forebears in keeping the noise down low enough for the radio listener to hear the speech being made, without the yobbish chants we have to endure. What I find disappointing is her refusal to wear a wig, it is part of the tradition. She is quite happy to wear the robe and buckled shoes – but no wig. No-one else has refused to wear one, so why should she? I am not sure whether it's pig-headedness, vanity or a cry to be different, but I feel it is a shame. As far as I am concerned, if you do not feel able to take on the whole persona, then don't bother. It might be a step forward for feminism according to those ideological sections of society, but it is another nail in the coffin of eccentricity.

Now I like this story. There is a chap in Yorkshire who has tried for 36 years to pass his driving test. At last he passed and bought a small hatchback. One Sunday he walked to his local pub for a lunchtime drink, having supped a few ales he walked back home and found the temptation to drive overbearing. In he got, started her up – cars are still females – and drove off, erratically. A neighbour noticed this and rang the police. Yesterday, he was banned for one year and fined £350 plus £25 costs for driving with excess alcohol and no insurance. Thirty-six years waiting and then banned for twelve months. One to tell the grandchildren, though.

I was encouraged to read that Mr Major has stated that the long awaited economic recovery is finally under way. No-one else can quite see the upturn, except the computer industry, who continue to supply the hardware and programmes regardless. If the country's economy is on the up, then we need more computers for the growth in business. If there is a trough we still need the damn things to sort out benefits, invent statistics and continue to be an excuse for why this and that cannot be sorted out.

Post Office Counters Ltd are to issue two million pounds worth of uniforms to their staff. It appears that their 'corporate profile' needs upgrading. The range of career wear will include saris for Asian female employees. Only one photograph appears to accompany the article in the *Daily Telegraph*. No, it is not the uniform to be worn by the majority of the Post Office employees, but a young lady in a sari. The article spends most of its space telling us about the new uniform and then shows the ethnic minority variation. I am not against it at all, but why not show both styles? Is it another sop to placate somebody who might complain about racial bias?

One of today's announcements in the births column informs us that a young lad called 'Tucker' has just arrived on the scene. Tucker – poor sod. I relaxed when I espied that the insertion was from one of our American cousins. You can imagined what his peers would have called him in Hackney or Homerton. In Washington DC he may well fare a little better.

The Young Farmers Federation has lost a few brownie points and will have to clean up its act and certainly vet its members in future. This organisation, where you don't have to be a farmer or even live in the country, arranged for its annual convention to be held at Butlins, Minehead. The 'do' was even opened by Princess Anne. Having drunk the place dry and becoming obnoxious and abusive, they upset hotels and restaurants with their mouthy obscenities. Stripping off and throwing food around were other activities in which they indulged. Customers naturally decided to leave and public places were forced to close early. There were even allegations of animal cruelty, including the beheading of pigeons and the killing of ducks. You know, all the usual country pursuits. As some local chap said, 'They are nothing more than a bunch of upper-class lager louts with more money than sense.' Remember what I said about beer festivals – no lager! The photographs accompanying the article showed scenes reminiscent of a First Division (now Premier League) football match, caps back to front, long garish shorts with trays of alcoholic drinks. Still, as long as they can bugger up someone else's holiday or night out it is okay I suppose.

I have just read that B Sky B was on the brink of closure just over a few years ago when its chairman visited America and asked Rupert Murdoch for 200 million pounds over two years. He agreed, and B Sky B has just announced its first operating profit. That close to liquidation, huh. Bloody Australians.

Here we go again, more ethnic moans. The Society of Black

Lawyers – isn't that racial inequality already – are claiming that black defendants are being coerced into pleading guilty to crimes for which they are not responsible. The report by this legal concern states that too many deals are being made between prosecution and defence counsels which end in a plea of guilty with a 'discount' on their sentences. It goes on to say that black defendants are often given a misrepresented picture of the legal issues involved and therefore plead guilty. I am damned if I would plead guilty if I wasn't. There is, however, no mention of this happening to white or Asian defendants. This interminable report goes on to say that some of the worst miscarriages of justice involve black defendants, well they would, adding that since 1980 sixty black people have died in custody or after arrest. Again, so have whites and Asians but these statistics obviously do not count. They want changes in the law to stop uncorroborated evidence being used as the basis for convictions, as the present law leads to abuse by the police. This implies that false confessions are limited to the black population. I thought there were plenty of cases recently where white people had been found to be victims of injustice? Again, being white, they won't count in the equation.

Any credibility these people may have had goes out of the window when you learn that they want all judges to discontinue the age-old tradition of wearing a wig and to follow Betty Boothroyd's example. Defendants, they say, should be allowed to sit with their lawyers in case they get lonely and 'stressed out' in that nasty box. Again, they make the point that clear bias has been shown by judges in the past, leading the jury towards a conviction. Not content with this, the society wants the rights of defendants to bar up to three prospective jurors from taking part. This, they say, will help black defendants service their fundamental human rights to a multiracial jury. What a load of balls, and what a bloody cheek! What they are really saying is that the more respectable a juror looks, especially if he is white, the more chances are that the case will go against them. If we have someone who is either young or rough looking, preferably both and non-white, we have a much better chance. Isn't that a lot more like the truth? If I am ever called for jury service, I shall dress in old jeans, buy press-on-tattoos and not shave for a few days. If I am still on the jury after these people have had their say, which I should be, as I am sure I would be what they are looking for, I will appear the following day in smart casual wear and stick two invisible fingers up at their sort and think 'Now let me decide the case on its merits and not on a colour – although they're probably guilty!'

In the announcements column today, having given the name of their new arrival, there follows the additional note, 'Thanks to all friends and relatives for their help.' Didn't he know what to do, or did they invite a few friends round on conception night?

I wouldn't be very happy if I lived in Brighton as a poll-tax payer. The twenty-sixth Brighton Festival opened yesterday and the Labour-controlled council have given £5,000 to lesbian and homosexual events. This includes lesbian abseiling and a 'Queer on the Pier' Day. This fringe activity, free from censorship by the Festival Committee, comes under the heading 'Pink Parasol Festival'. This little do will last for three weeks and the umbrella people will finish with a procession of more than 2,000 lesbians and homosexuals parading through the streets, and with a bit of luck, straight into the sea!

Having suffered the demise of real money in the early seventies, two coins survived, the shilling and the florin. The former succumbed a couple of years ago to be replaced by that most awful of metal discs, the five-penny piece. Just who this benefited is beyond me. Nobody likes it, but it is cheap to produce and it falls into the category of standard Euro crap. In the meantime, the five and twenty pound notes have been redesigned, naturally made smaller – cost cutting again – with the end result being that the two notes look so similar it is easy to become confused by then size and colour. Still, once again I am sure they know what they are doing. After all, they are experts. The Chancellor, still surprisingly our beleaguered Shetland Pony, has today announced the demise of the florin, or 10 pence piece. A new, smaller coin, the size of the old shilling, will replace our last tangible link with Britain's traditional coinage. There is a new ten pound note on its way, as well, which will no doubt lead to even greater confusion leaving only the £50 note as an example of real paper money.

Talking of money, it is not only the newly privatised utilities which offer their top dogs out-of-all-proportion salary rises. Some chap called David McCall, the Chief Executive of Anglia TV, has received a £178,811 pay increase. From £152,000 to £330,811 in a year, not bad, is it? Their staff are still negotiating their pay rise. No doubt this will be nearer 7% than the 117% their good chief has been awarded. The Chairman of Tesco's gets £1.08 million a year, closely followed by Sir Paul Girolami, head of Glaxo, who weighs in at a comfortable £1.06 million every twelve months. Top dog at Kingfisher grosses £724,000, whilst Sir John Quinton takes an embarrassingly low £356,357. No wonder they are all smiling in their photographs.

It was nice to see that a bull got its own back recently. One of those bullfighter's assistants was gored to death, unfortunately his is the first fatality in four years, but it may stop someone else from entering this sordid little job.

On that tack some people's priorities really make you think about their ability to be in positions of power. A woman in Binfield, Berkshire, has for the last three years taken in, and looked after, unwanted pets. She has now been told that she must either have her house reclassified as a pet shop or a sanctuary – or the animals will have to go. If this is the case, many will doubtless have to be put down. This lady appears to be one of the few in her area who care about the wildlife. Binfield is situated between Wokingham and Bracknell, where development has been devastating and the village has been virtually gobbled up by both towns. If you drive around the area there is hardly a field which has been left intact and still the rape goes on. All these council servants can do is to push through more red tape concerning those who wish to help someone or something – bastards.

We have entered a new era, or should it be error, within the equine world. I wasn't aware of this fact, but twins are not produced naturally in the horse, remember the word 'naturally'. Four years ago a pair of twin foals were artificially created. The hope is that this will benefit the racing industry – not sport, take note. The principal veterinary research officer of the Thoroughbred Breeders Association Equine Fertility Unit, has already 'created' three sets of identical twin ponies. Apparently they inseminate mares with semen from the Association's own stallion. When the mare ovulates they flush out the uterus and recover the embryo. This is cut in half and each portion is transferred to two mares who then carry the little one until birth. Next year they are hoping for six pairs of identical twins to be born. They say the work is necessary for research purposes. This includes looking at bones and joints, and damage suffered, cartilage problems, etc. They listed other so-called benefits but the technicalities were lost on me, I am afraid. One part I did understand, although I remain unconvinced, is where it says that the value of creating identical twins is that they are genetically the same and are perfect subjects for research, as one foal can be used as a 'control' to measure against the other. It sounds like a Frankenstein experiment. If twins are not a natural occurrence there must be a reason for this. I would suggest these births have little to do with helping the horse and more to do with certain people helping themselves to money. At the end of the day the only reason for tampering with nature is for the single purpose of acquiring money more easily.

There is a most peculiar article in the *Telegraph* today. It is written by a chap called John Carey, and accompanied by a picture of 'Hero... Freddie Mercury'. It is about death. Mr Carey writes about the effect that three deaths have had upon his son Jack who is six years old. When Jack was two, his grandfather died. At age four, his hamster passed away and now at six, he has witnessed the demise of Freddie Mercury. On Easter Monday Mr Carey and Jack went to the memorial concert at Wembley and at the end the young lad apparently said, 'That was my best day.' Jack started listening to Queen when he was three, on a personal stereo as the family drove through France – so I now have a question mark over the father for a start! Fancy going for a drive through France. Jack joined the official fan club when he was four and collected vast numbers of videos and tapes. They watched 'as a family' Queen receiving an award at the 1990 Brits do. Young Jack allegedly 'repeatedly asked if he was going to die' as F.M. did not look one hundred per cent then. Rumours had spread by that time and Mr Carey says that he couldn't ignore his son's questions. They started to 'prepare' him for what would happen. He goes on to say that come last November, when he did die, Jack watched and read all the tributes and 'we watched, read and cried with him'. I can't write any more of this, I have got to get a bucket. I keep looking at the top of the page, don't I, to see if it is April 1st, but it is not so I will continue. The parents then take this poor kid to see a wax model of him at Rock Circus in Piccadilly. I thought it would have been more appropriate if the wax model had been situated in the public lavatories. Still, ever onwards. This family continue their quest and end up at his house in West London. At this point young Jack scrawls a message on the gate (vandal), saying I am your best fan, love Jack. xxxxxx. I hope his parents made him wash his hands afterwards. The next three paragraphs are concerned with a psychiatrist's views on telling children about death, and how they felt having come home from that Wembley concert. I would be surprised if this kid does not grow up with a rather confused and conditioned view of life. The father says that F.M.'s death affected his son more than the death of his hamster, but to be fair, the hamster didn't record *Bohemian Rhapsody*! He also says that F.M.'s death affected Jack more than his grandfather's death, and being fair once again, the grandfather did not record *Bohemian Rhapsody* either! To be serious though, the boy was only two at the time. I think the father expects an awful lot from a child, and I find the obsession with good old Freddie somewhat unhealthy to say the least.

There is a chap called Steve Williams who has thought up the idea of building Europe's first Aero Homeway – a private estate where every resident has their own hangar. This idea came to mind when he was playing golf at Gleneagles. If this is what happens when he goes there, I hope it is his last visit. Wrekin District Council are now being asked to give planning permission to a consortium of developers who want to build this environmental eyesore. There will be a ten million pound airfield, sixty-five houses with hangars, a country club and a 37-acre communal woodland. All this is to be built near Telford, Shropshire. Quite what Shropshire has ever done to deserve Telford, I will never know, let alone this latest monument to money. The consortium claim that business travellers from Europe and the Far East will be able to use the 1,000-yard runway. The houses are designed to give a 'flavour of America', it gets worse, doesn't it. It looks as if Wrekin DC are keen on the idea and that if this project is a winner then more estates will be built throughout Britain. That really is all we need. Light aircraft buzzing around at all hours and more concrete and tarmac. The next generation will no doubt be built with the runway to the side of the golf course, so that our slit-eyed friends can get straight off a plane and start whacking their balls all over the place. I would like to whack a few balls all over the place, but apparently it is illegal. Actually, these oriental coves are causing a strain on English water supplies with their love of golf. The Council for the Protection of Rural England has stated that the Japanese demand for golf courses close to London is putting increased and unnecessary pressure on underground water supplies. Japanese money is being used to quench the thirst of their golf-loving natives' penchant for artificial lakes on these courses. At the same time as residents in Berkshire are being asked to mend leaking taps to save water and money, the River Lambourn, which is only flowing at half its normal level, will be used to supply 84,467 gallons of water a day for an artificial lake. This golf course is being built on ancient water meadows by She Tenoji International. Naturally it is a private course, which is good news for the locals. A Buddhist sect has just won permission to extract 3 million gallons from the same river for their golf course.

In Kent and Surrey applications for golf courses are coming in at three a month, many are for the exclusive use of the

Japanese. It seems very unfair that locals are suffering from a hosepipe ban, yet you can easily get permission to build an artificial lake. I don't think it will be too long before water becomes a very important topic in this country and then the shrugged shoulders and acceptance of Japanese traits will start to get ugly. Until then water companies will buy and sell their water for profit. Councils will pass applications, thinking only of the short-term financial gain, whilst another 100,000 natives of this country will receive summonses for non-payment of those obscenely high water charges – bastards.

Here is a joke which I heard many years ago and it is still one of my favourites. I will set the scene. We are on a Dan Air flight from Majorca to Gatwick, the plane is flying over the mainland of Europe and the captain turns on the tannoy. 'This is Captain Stewart speaking, welcoming you aboard Flight 123, ladies and gentlemen. We are flying at 16,000 feet, the weather is clear and if you look out of your windows you can see the Pyrenees. The weather in England is good and we should be landing in approximately 50 minutes.' He then forgets to switch off the tannoy. 'What are you going to do when we land, Skip,' says the co-pilot. 'Well the first thing I am going to do is have a bloody good clear-out. That Spanish food goes straight to my 'arris, then, I am going to get hold of that new blonde stewardess, take her to the hotel and hand out the biggest portion of helmet that she has seen for a long time.' Everyone in the plane hears this. The stewardess flushes in embarrassment and runs full pelt down the aisle, tripping over an old lady's handbag. As she pulls herself up off the carpet, the old lady looks at her and says, 'I wouldn't 'urry love, he is going to have a shit first!'

Another? Oh, go on then. I am feeling frisky today. Have you heard about George the Sheepshearer? If so, move on to another page. If not, stick with it.

A chap walks into a country pub, catches the attention of an old man sitting alone and says, 'Hallo, George, can I buy you a drink?' 'Yes,' replies George, 'I will take a drink with anyone who calls me by my right name.' The other chap enquires as to why George is more than a little off-hand. 'Well you tell me this,' says George, 'who won the Devizes furrowing contest, who won the Wiltshire furrowing contest, who won the all-counties furrowing championships with the straightest furrows ever witnessed. Who was carried shoulder high and became the local hero?' 'Well, you George,' says the friend. 'Exactly,' says George, 'but they don't call me George the furrower, do they? Who was it who won the local sheepshearing competition, who was it that went on to win the south of England all-comers section and represented his country in Australia, and who won the world sheepshearing competition, huh? But they don't call me George the sheepshearer – yet I shag a sheep just once...'

So, having suffered from the EC sticking its intrusive and unwanted nose into every facet of our very breathing, the Scottish Law Commission have recommended that smacking a child with the hand will be the only physical form of punishment still legal. The time-honoured 'clip around the ear' is to be allowed as well. This Commission, again you never hear the name of those involved, as it provides a cover to hide behind, has sat for eighteen months studying all forms of corporal punishment seeking advice and opinions from dozens of organisations and experts. They also sought advice from psychologists, social workers and the church. Why them? I suppose if you want a totally biased view then they are the ones to go for. It does not mention whether they spoke to parents, you know, those who actually look after the little sods.

Hard on the hooves of biologically created foals we now learn of the super pig, as exhibited at the Café Royal, London. This new hybrid is part Chinese Meishan and part British. It is here, of course, because it will save money for the farmer, if that is what you call these food engineers still. This allows him and the rest of the food chain a greater profit margin. The idea behind this latest merger is that you need less sows to breed the same number of piglets, as these newly engineered souls produce up to 30 extra piglets a year. It is not right, though, is it? I have no doubt that like the horse twinning we will witness side effects because we are buggering about with Mother Nature, once again – remember Mad Cow Disease?

You will be glad to know that we, well, Glyn, found the keys for the Mini. They mysteriously re-appeared in the kitchen and were found on the Welsh dresser, so who knows? We have put it down to Andrew. He is the mythical character we blame when something goes missing, something gets broken, or things get moved without any apparent reason or logic. Personally, I think that 99% of the mysteries can probably be explained by William. The problem is, catching the little toad in the act, because he does a very good impression of someone surprised and hurt when being considered the suspect. Meant to tell you the other day, but it slipped my mind, that episode of TV Heaven was extremely enjoyable. Most of the programmes shown in that, and other episodes, were obviously set-based, black and white and lacking in modern technology, but that pales into insignificance when you compare them to some recent offerings. What I find frustrating is the dipping the toe attitude of the producers. Why not start at the beginning, using all remaining footage of programmes like *Oh Boy*, *Six Five Special*, *Ready, Steady, Go* and *Top of the Pops*? It would not only be of immense interest for those with a nostalgic bent, but would provide a suitable platform for discovering the progress of popular music over the last 40 years. It seems such an untapped market. A little while ago they had a series introduced by Dave Lee Travis, looking at different years in the pop world. This effort, alas, was little more than another toe-dipping exercise. There never seems to be a commitment to cover a subject fully.

The Bob Monkhouse Show was, on the whole, a disappointment with too many long sketches. Mr Monkhouse, however, as well as being without doubt our most professional game-show host, is one of our finest comedians. His delivery and patter are very American in timing and I have long felt that the topicality of his jokes could be better put to the old-fashioned variety scene. As we have said before, though, variety is seen as old-fashioned.

A friend of mine has a son who has spent a few years on the circuit as a dancer. He has never made the big time but was, a couple of years ago, in the chorus line at the Royal Variety Show. Now to dance at the Palladium and mingle with all the big names must have been a dream come true, but he said that afterwards virtually every 'star' ignored the dancers and backing singers, with the exception of Bob Monkhouse, who popped his head round the door more than once to offer words of encouragement, and telling them to enjoy themselves and relax. Nice that.

The *Double Your Money* episode shown was the very first of the line apparently. Now I did find that interesting. So much has changed in quiz shows, not to mention the subjects you could ask questions on. It was all very parochial and lovely. For instance, there were three separate categories for the armed forces, RAF, Royal Navy and Army, but Hughie Green came over as being dreadfully patronising.

Take Your Pick, the other quiz show shown, was enjoyable because of the humility and innocence of the contestants. Little concern was shown for the material gain, but great store was set on just being there. Having seen the revamped version with Des O'Connor and his female assistant, I can honestly say I would prefer to watch the re-run of the original and genuine.

The episode of *Robin Hood*, with Richard Greene, brought

back memories of a childhood spent watching that nasty Alan Wheatley, playing the Sheriff of Nottingham. Many a supporting actor seen in a British thriller passed through Sherwood Forest during the early years of children's television. I used to like *Dan Tempest* and *the Buccaneers*, starring Robert Shaw and *Sir Lancelot* with William Russell, who is currently about to take Rita up the aisle in *Coronation Street*.

Without doubt, *Dial 999* was a joy to watch. Robert Beattie teamed up with British policemen to beat crime on the streets of London. You just needed to forget the storyline for a moment, the sheer social history which was shown in this half-hour episode was reward in itself. Rows of small shops in a high street, local garages, RT buses, ancient taxis and British-made road vehicles. Smoke and smog abounded, river barges sounded their horns in the background and engines shunted in sidings, be it day or night. Muted violence, no bad language and acting that was not awful, either.

They showed an episode of the psychiatrist series with Herbert Lom as well. Very well scripted and still fresh. Why don't they show more of these series? I cannot believe that they would not be popular. Anyway, we have to be thankful that some of the tapes were not destroyed and just hope for a more positive attitude by those in charge.

They started it, they invaded Poland

It is funny how the growing up of a child is never reflected in their parents' – or grandparents' – appraisal of any situation. Debbie has just started working a couple of evenings a week in a new pizza parlour take-away. Part of her work involves deliveries of pizzas by car to customers. Every time I speak to my mother, she asks me if our daughter is still delivering and couldn't she make the pizzas or go on the cash till full-time. My mother actually asked if two girls went together, just in case. At the end of the day, if you thought like that then no-one would go out at all. I think it is best if you tell parents, and grandparents especially, as little as possible.

A friend of mine who's in his fifties, had his mother ring him up one day a couple of winters ago, to check if he was wearing a vest to work as it had been very chilly that particular morning! I cannot imagine what his wife would have thought – or said.

Another classic is the 'ring three times to let me know you are home' tagging system. My parents have employed this since I left home 24 years ago, and still occasionally ask me to ring if the weather is rough and there is a possibility we might be swept away by unknown forces during the 35-mile journey from deepest Wallington down the A3 to Ash Vale.

Having said that, I use the same tactics with Deborah. Not for her the quiet life of independence. My concern is, however, tempered by my desire to stay at home and not have to go out looking for her. As she works until 11pm and a little later on Saturdays, we assume she is coming home when the work is completed. Little girls, however, grow up. We now assume that she is gassing with the other staff until we hear three rings and I know that she is on her way. If she has not arrived a quarter of an hour from that call, then I would go looking for a broken-down Mini. I am glad to say that it hasn't happened so far. I consider this system as eminently sensible, because it does not stop her from coming home at midnight, or later, but it does mean (a) I know where she is, and (b) she is not out in the car, broken down somewhere.

Last year I remember getting out of bed in the early hours of the morning, getting dressed, unbolting the front door, going to my car and forgetting the keys. Back inside the house to search for them. Ten minutes or so later, I returned to the car and found that they were still sitting in the ignition. Vehicle security has never been high on our list of priorities. We do, however, now lock the house when we go out, so there has been some improvement! Anyway, into the car I got, reversed out of the drive and, with more than a little apprehension, I scooted up the road, turned into the main road and proceeded towards Aldershot. Towards me, bobbing along the road, is Deborah in the Mini. She recognises the car and waves. I pass her, turn around and head back home, arriving to find her making coffee. 'Where were you going?' she asked me nonchalantly. 'I was looking for you,' I replied. 'It is late and we were in bed.' 'Oh,' she answered, 'we have been chatting outside in the car park at work.' She sounded irritated. I told her that it was 12.30 am. I had rung the night porter who had told me that all the staff had cleared up and cleared out about half an hour before. Now munching toast, she interrupted her fodder time to state that there were about ten of them sitting and standing by their cars, talking and that time has just gone on (a bit like their chatting, really).

That night convinced me that a better system should be instigated, so the traditional three rings came into play.

One of my sisters-in-law drives home after visiting her parents in Putney – which isn't common because Jilly Cooper once lived nearby! She (sis-in-law) also has to give three rings. The difference here is that Deborah is 19 and sis-in-law is 39 – a big girl now. The other day she forgot to ring, and was in the bathroom at the time when her parents thought she should have been at home. This being the case, she didn't hear the telephone ringing to ask if she had arrived. Her father, panicking like mad, as usual, decided to go over to Southfields to investigate. You will like this bit. Most fathers, owning a car, would take the car with them, wouldn't they? Not her dad. Being a busy road, chock-a-block with parked cars during the day, he did not want to lose his parking space, so he walked to the bus stop and jumped on a bus. He arrived at her flat, just as she was getting into bed. So while he waited, she got dressed again and took him back to Putney in her car. Having dropped him off, she then set off for home, for a second time, and remembered to ring three times as soon as she got through the door. The last thing you need is to travel to Putney for a third time in one evening.

This sister-in-law has had a couple of funny experiences when driving, one with her father and one by herself. Starting at the nearest destination, Reading, our heroine is on her ownsome heading for a hotel in the town centre, where she is to meet a friend. Having circumnavigated the ring road and surrounding offshoots twice, she finds herself outside the railway station. With the engine of her Escort ticking over, she asks a likely looking fellow if he wants a good time. Sorry, she asks him if he knows the way to this particular hotel! Seeing which way her car is pointed, he indicates that she has to turn left, left again and follow the road to the next lights, etc. Off she goes, does what she *thinks* she has been told and is very concerned by the inconsiderate driving of motorists coming in the opposite direction. On reaching a roundabout and feeling that somehow this is not right, she pulls the car around and heads back down the same road. A siren sounds behind her, a police car pulls alongside and flashes lights for her to stop. She thinks that he wants to get by (after all, she isn't doing a thing wrong!). She pulls over, slowing down for the police car to overtake. As they pull in, she pulls away. Just in time, the policeman climbs out of the car and stops her from continuing her great escape. 'Are you lost?' he asks. 'How did you know that? I am looking for the George Hotel,' says the Southfields Girl. 'Well, driving in the wrong direction up a one-way street tends to give us a clue,' replies friendly copper, adding, 'Didn't it occur to you that people were coming towards you on both sides of the road? Anyway, do you own this vehicle?' 'Yes,' replied S.G.

The policeman's companion has, in the meantime, made a note of the registration number and checked with the computer – they then confer. Mr Plod returns to the window of the Escort and says, 'You are... and you live at... ?' 'Yes, that is right. How did you know? That really is awfully clever of you,' says our girl, amazed at the efficiency and not thinking that they had checked on a computer. It is wonderful how naïve you can be, isn't it. So, having told her how to get to the hotel they pull off and the Escort follows tentatively down the street, until a set of traffic lights appear where the police car is held up. Out gets the policeman again, walks back to the Escort and asks if she is happy about the directions, a question to which she comes over as somewhat lacking in confidence in her reply. 'Okay,' said the policeman, 'follow us and we will take you there.' Aren't our policemen lovely – even the West Midlands Crime Squad. The policeman then walks back to his car, stops in his tracks and says, 'You are only visiting Reading, aren't you? You are not thinking of moving here?' 'No,' says S.G. He was then heard mumbling, 'Thank Christ for that', as he walked back to his car. They drove off and he pointed to the hotel before roaring away in a cloud of hero's exhaust.

The trip to Oxford was in the company of her father, as I said earlier. Getting into the town centre of this university city is a fraught affair, with the added hazard of bikes and people everywhere. Here they are, the traffic is building up, two lanes of traffic and them not knowing where they are, except that the centre should not be far away. Now Dad always gets panicky when driving and doesn't like the thought of the unknown. In this case the unknown is a possible right-hand turn that could lead anywhere. And here his true pessimism shows. Phrases like 'You'll never get back on the right road now', or 'Well, we will have to go for miles to turn around', spring forth from his lips.

Our luckless heroes have found themselves in the outside lane of two. The inside lane is nose-to-tail, the further they travel, the nearer that intrepid set of lights becomes. 'We'll have to pull over into the nearside lane,' says Dad, who is the front seat passenger. His daughter indicates, but no-one will let her in. She keeps indicating, driving slower and slower as she passes the now stationary line of cars. Suffering abuse from drivers in the nearside lane and the flashing lights of drivers behind, backing up their frustration at her lack of progress by hooting as well, the situation was becoming fraught. Dad opens the window and sticks out an arse (oops, sorry arm), to emphasise the indicator's lack of success. A window on the car alongside theirs is lowered and a man accuses them of being selfish, inconsiderate and lacking in manners. 'We only want to go straight on to the town centre,' says Dad, 'we don't want to have to turn right just because we have got in the wrong lane.' The man leans over and says, 'You are in the right lane. It is the only lane. This is the queue for the petrol station. Don't you know there is a petrol strike and everybody is trying to fill up while they can.' So that was it. That was why everybody was so determined and would not let them in. The funny thing is that Dad is the last person to ever try to push in anywhere. It is not in his nature. Incidentally, there was no right-hand turn for a mile and within another few yards the garage would have come into sight and the queue of cars would have disappeared. Still, it was worth a few palpitations just to have been told the story.

I see that robotic policemen have just joined West Mercia police force. Armed with a radar gun, the precursor of this new mechanised organisation has been named 'Sam', short for Speed and Aggression Moderator. He comes complete with uniform and stands a modest 5' 7½". The head is made of papier maché and it moves sideways, being powered by a battery-charged motor. So having had cardboard policemen making absolutely no name for themselves whatsoever, we now have Sam. Doubtless this prototype model will be followed by even more detailed followers, what is the betting that it won't be long before the real police find one of these life-like characters demotored and the powerhouse stolen to run somebody's lawnmower. The batteries will no doubt have been stolen to keep a vibrator vibrating, and the uniform and hat will be used by some perverted chap to stop and abduct some unsuspecting female. All this in an effort to stop someone who is speeding. No doubt future productions of Sam will have to come in black and Asian as well, mustn't upset anyone.

They don't stop, do they? The EC is proposing an idea to take away a producer's ownership on film rights. The effect of this, should they be stupid enough to pursue this line of thought, and let's face it they are stupid enough, will be to allow even the most menial extra a cut for every repeat showing. As someone said, 'What about films like *Gandhi*?' Again, the cost of administering such a scheme would be absurd, but then administration is where these people began their grey, unnecessary lives, and administration is where it will end, preferably in the signing of their own death warrant!

David Puttnam said that if this idea were to be implemented, then he will be making all his films in America. Other European countries feel the same and the nett result will be that Europe will lose its film industry. But they just cannot see it.

Well, the book *Diana, Her Own Story* by Andrew Morton seems to be doing well in both the conversation and controversy stakes, not to mention its sales. The picture of her on the cover of Vogue could confuse readers. I think she looks more like Selina Scott, than herself – they haven't swapped places, have they? More than once during the television programme *A Prince Among Islands*. I could have sworn I was watching Prince Charles walking with his wife, before realising it was the S.S.

Very rarely do I find myself in agreement with anyone connected to a religious persuasion, but I have been impressed with one or two of Dr Carey's comments. The Archbishop of Canterbury said yesterday at a service in Derby that it was 'wrong to make money for its own sake', adding that industry suffered when shareholders and executives appeared to be unfairly rewarded.

He also commented on those same people appearing to enjoy the fruits of success at the expense of others, and the massive individual pay rises during a recession do not encourage public support for wealth creation. Now *you* know and *I* know that this is a logical and well-supported comment. The Director General of the Institute of Directors said afterwards, 'The Archbishop's remarks appear to demonstrate a fundamental misunderstanding of the dynamism of the market economy and reflect the general unease the church demonstrates in its dealings with the question of wealth creation, profit incentives and success.' Yes, I read it twice, as well. You can see which side of the office he hangs his hat. That sort of arrogance is half the cause of the breakdown of respect between workers and management. Can you imagine having someone like him involved in your pay negotiations. Pompous sod!

Talking of sods, the Badminton three-day event, which seems to attract every upper-class twit and double-barrel, fell into disrepute yesterday. Three horses had to be put down after falling. One broke a foreleg, one crushed two vertebrae and a third broke its neck. There is a picture of the latter horse during its final gasps of breath, descending almost vertically into a lake. His rider was thrown off. Asked to comment, the RSPCA inspector, who has been at Badminton for ten years, said it was sad that horses had died but there were risks in any sport – so he showed genuine concern. The spokesman, or spoke, as she is a Ms, from Animal Aid, gave what most people would consider the honest comment. She said, 'I don't know how these people call themselves animal lovers. They're more interested in money than the welfare of the horses.' Hear, hear.

Do you remember earlier – no let us be positive, you do remember earlier – when I mentioned town centres being ripped apart. Well, an interesting article has appeared in the *Telegraph* today. It makes soulful reading but it illustrates exactly what is happening to our towns and cities and all in the name of progress. The accompanying picture shows Carmarthen's new Cambrian Centre, brick built with glass mall, the first shop on view is Etam. This development has swept away the traditional high street, full of small shops of differing height and design. Again, gone is the individuality and in its place the clinical, covered areas, locked at night and with no-one living 'over the top'. In this small country town a pharmacist aged 91, and his brother, are the last people in the area to live above their shop, and the aged gentleman has just been beaten up by burglars. Until recently, nearby lived another old person, a lady whose home was above a grocery shop. She moved, having been attacked twice in two years. The town centre has witnessed three fires in the past twelve months alone. One of these fires was responsible for one million pounds worth of damage. The writer of the article, one Byron Rogers, throws the ball firmly into the planners' court. It is they, he contends, who are as guilty of the assaults carried out in people's houses, as the attackers themselves.

Councillors, planning staff and businessmen, Mr Rogers contends, have altered the heart of the town and destiny of its people. The same repercussions have been suffered there as in any town – Aldershot is no different. Pedestrianised areas, large supermarkets and arcades lead to the closure of small shops, the equation is continuous. You move people out of a town centre at the end of a day's work and you are left with drunks and drug-taking yobs congregating in the vicinity, making it a no-go area for decent people. Mr Rogers goes on to describe the more detailed changes that have happened to the town. I last went to Carmarthen in 1982 and it obviously has altered tremendously since then. It looks like, well, anywhere and still they cannot see it. Over the last few weeks I picked up another couple of cases. These concern individual buildings. The first example is in South Wales. Blaenavon Workmen's Hall is a wonderful building. Ninety-eight years old and constructed from contributions given by miners over a ten-year period. Until recently it has been host to unemployed youths who would otherwise be out on the streets, and pensioners whose fathers paid towards its erection. It is now in excellent condition, having recently benefited from a one million pound restoration project. It houses an 80-seater theatre, meeting rooms, bar and pool facilities, yet it has got to be closed otherwise the local council may be charge-capped. So, the future looks pretty bleak – and what a waste of money if it does go the way of many fine Victorian edifices. Out of interest, even in the 1950s there were 300 or so welfare halls. There are now just 60, most of those which closed have now been demolished. A few lie derelict.

The second case is particularly sad as it highlights the stubborn arrogance and intransigence shown by those with the power of demolition at their fingertips. Having suffered the destruction by British Railways years ago of the substantial Tudor-style station it was once proud of, you would think Kidderminster's ruling authority would think twice about erasing yet another monument. This time it is the town's Victorian 100-year-old library.

It does not look beautiful, but it is described as 'having been judged of special architectural or historical merit by the DOE'. They wanted it listed as a Grade 2 building. The slight technical hitch is that a certificate of immunity has been issued, so that it cannot be listed until September 9th, 1993. I know not why this should be. Conservationists have described the proposed demolition as being on a par with that of Kensington Town Hall and the Firestone building, both demolished in haste and regretted ever since. But that is money talking.

Hereford and Worcester County Council, playing the part of the big ogre rather well, have received representations from SAVE, the Victorian Society and the Ancient Monument Society. What is the response from the gnome-infested ivory tower? 'There is no reprieve. When we get vacant possession we are going to knock down the building and put up a super de-luxe library, but first the site will be a car park!' These are the prophetic words of a Hereford & Worcester spokesoik, one Alec Mackie. The very words smack of arrogance. Still, car parking charges will bring in more revenue than library book fines, so it is okay then. I hate to say it but I think the word Bastard is applicable again!

I have just seen on the News that the Corn Exchange in Newbury, Berkshire, is to be refurbished as an arts and community centre, so that won't see much use then, will it.

Back on the subject of towns, Aldershot's replacement arcade is nearly completed. Again, clean, clinical and all the blandness of any other mall. The builders obviously think that a modicum of filigree ironwork and mock Victorian lamps make it a passable Victorian replica. They could put all the money in the world into this project, but they will never replace the shops with their wooden lower halves, sturdy supports and traditional mix of products. Not one estate agent, not one photocopying shop. There was a cheap-jack's who sold everything, a hairdresser's, greengrocer's – there's rare – lingerie shop, jeweller's and a lovely toy shop staffed by an old couple, who actually enjoyed serving you. This new glass concoction won't be entertaining the likes of these independents. They couldn't afford the rent if they wanted to. National and multinationals are bound to be in situ amongst the empty shops. It is just a question of how many building societies there will be.

This is odd, there is a councillor in Rushmoor who seems to be able to understand the realities of life. Councillor John Hiscock has said that Aldershot's town centre has been ruined by road closures and building sites over the last twenty-five years, and that the heart has been ripped out of the town. He put forward a motion that development on the outskirts of Aldershot should be appropriate to the 'historic gateway'. This motion was thrown out amid cries of 'Cobblers' by a fellow councillor – actually, Councillor Wally Grantham, who is the father of Leslie Grantham, ex-*EastEnders* and the *Paradise Club*. You would probably know that if you lived locally, but not necessarily if you are a native of Poulton-le-Fylde, Lancs., or Cockermouth, Cumbria. At least one's lack of faith isn't greatly tested when you read such comments from the baying tribes of the inner sanctum. The cheek of it, someone daring to comment on their great planning and rebuilding objectives – did someone mention twinning with Kurdistan?

Following on from that, the demolition of the King's Head Public House was completed very quickly and within days, all the trees and shrubs had been cleared. Lots of concrete had been laid and another conglomeration of brickwork had started to sprout up. The end product is an overbearing structure which sits uneasily on the corner of the main road. Neat fencing has replaced the shrubbery and asphalt has been laid in front of and around the building. Lacking imagination and oozing blandness out of every pore, the development prettily named 'The Poplars' is a poor substitute for the former Victorian house, but think of all that poll tax.

As if by magic, Maureen has just brought in the local paper, and what are the headlines – 'Great Plan for Store Complex'. This time it is ex-Ministry of Defence land which has recently been sold to a developer. The site in question was formerly the Royal Aerospace Establishment playing fields, you know, grass. The area surrounding the site is being devastated as I write in order that the Blackwater Relief Road can make its way from the M3 to the Hog's Back and cut a few minutes' travelling time off the journey of those with no local connection. We all know that the roads it will bypass will continue to bear the brunt of local traffic but it does give weight to companies like this West Midlands based company who are involved with the playing fields, when it comes to their planning application. After all, it is only another infill. The plan they have here is to build five superstores and three smaller ones, all non-food. This isn't a surprise as we already have one of the largest Tesco's and Marks & Spencer's about a mile away. In between those last two and the proposed development site Sainsbury's open their new store next month. There are already numerous DIY stores, none of which sell a wide range of emulsion, but they are all very big on white and magnolia. 'Toys R Us' (bloody stupid name) are after one of the large sites and the others will be electrical and DIY. If the electrical company is anything like one of the multiple stores in Aldershot, they will only try to sell you products on which a promotion is being held, and if you pick a particular item which is listed but not on show, you have really shown yourself to be an awkward customer. We made the mistake of attempting to buy an electrical item from this particular store a couple of years ago. Having stood like dummies, we eventually collared one of the assistants, who was making a gallant attempt not to be seen by any prospective punter. Of course, the tumble drier we wanted was out of stock. Undeterred, we chose another. Delivery, yes, about seven days. It was that pained expression which tells you that the assistant hasn't got a pen and will have to find one. I have to say that this total lack of service was a repeat of the situation we found ourselves in the only other time we shopped there some years ago. Off we went, without ordering, finding ourselves a small independent shop only yards away. Yes, they had the drier in stock, our original first choice. It was delivered within 48 hours, fitted and then they rang to see how we were getting on with it a week later. That was service. I have just read on, there is going to be a McDonalds as well. Isn't that all you need. Access will be via the main Farnborough Road, which is continually jammed with traffic, and the new Blackwater Relief Road. See what I mean? Build a road and before it is even open they are cashing in on the land around, until you can build another road, and then the process starts all over again.

Some court cases have to be read to be believed. It comes to something when a lady who owns chickens is taken to court by the local council because some 'person' has complained that the cockerel wakes him up too early with his crowing. Cockerels crow. It is a well-known fact. They tend to do it early in the morning. That is another well-known fact. The resident who complained actually managed to get a Noise Abatement Order issued because the cock interrupted his sleep. We are not talking about a suburb in London, but a very small hamlet in Devon. That is right, the countryside, where chickens and cockerels live. Sixty villagers yesterday cheered as the order was overturned on appeal. The lady who owns the cock has kept chickens since 1975. The neighbour who complained has lived next door since 1980, so they were there when he moved in. The poor soul who complained said that he and his wife had suffered stress (I wondered when that was coming into play, because that is always a good line). Either that or a bad heart, anyway. Have you noticed that these stress and heart problems always get better when either the case is won or you have mustered enough support. The solicitor for the cock owner said that Mr Ritchings, the neighbour and complainant, was over-sensitive and a natural complainer who whinges until something is done. Now a judge has got to decide the bird's future as this chap Ritchings has been granted an interim injunction of course. The bird has been bannished to the greenhouse. This same story is also being run in the *Daily Mail*, where a photograph of Mr Ritchings is included in glorious colour. He is balding, with a beard, and the paper adds the information that he is a personnel manager. So there we are, that is three reasons why we don't like him. Oh, and he as also got one of those ingratiating smiles that gives rise to the view that he has just received a whopping salary increase.

Here is a little snippet to confirm, if confirmation were needed of the course legislation has taken us down over recent years Maureen went to a cooking demonstration put on by British Gas at a local hall. Various dishes were made and apparently looked very appetising. The demonstrator apologised for not offering to raffle any of the resultant masterpieces, as 'We are not allowed to give away food cooked tonight, due to possible legal action should someone become ill through food poisoning and sue the Gas Board'. Again, a case of a few grabbers and stirrers spoiling it for everyone else.

When I was writing *FWIS* I remember commenting on what I considered the unnatural childhood suffered/endured/enjoyed by Ruth Lawrence, the maths prodigy who graduated at the age of thirteen, to become this country's youngest-ever graduate. She got First Class Honours, to boot. Three years ago, when she was eighteen, again with her father by her side, she upped and left for Harvard University. Her father, who is estranged from Ruth's mother, was very instrumental in her early devotion to maths. That was the reason for my comment in the first place. I find it strange that a father should guide his daughter almost in quest-like fashion to the total disregard for any other form of enjoyment or appreciation of outside life. I may be wrong, but that is what it seemed like. Now, at the age of 20, she will be 21 in August, they – father and daughter – have returned briefly to Britain, Warwick University to be precise. She is spending a month carrying out work at the Mathematics Research Centre. Next month she will be off to Trinity College, Oxford, for eight weeks. Where is her father? Well, he is here as well. Apparently, he gave up his full-time job as a computer consultant so that he could devote all of his time to Ruth's education. Remember, she obtained the top grade in 'A' level maths at the age of nine!

Whilst at Warwick, they share the same office and extension phone number. When at Oxford Mr Lawrence used to go with his daughter to every tutorial and student debate, she was there for seven years. Going to America hasn't separated them either. He is well known in the Maths Department there as well. I don't mean this in an unkind way (perhaps I do) but it does seem cloistered and unhealthy not to give a young lady of nearly 21 years of age the opportunity to test life. I mean, to give up your job so as to spend the majority of your time riding on a tandem bicycle and discussing Pythagoras's theorem, does sound a tad obsessive, I wonder how her mum feels.

Glad I wasn't in Coventry earlier this month. Actually I am glad I am never in Coventry, but the mob violence culminating in looting and arson just shows how ineffective our policing and judicial systems are. We all know of the high numbers of scum who reoffend when still on bail, so that is no deterrent. I had to smile the other day when reading about the little sods who were ripping tiles and guttering off the roof of a so-called modern prison, where bonhomie has replaced out-of-fashion discipline. Being nice to these oiks does not do any good, they just throw it in your face and come back with even bigger club hammers.

It is strange, isn't it, how ideas and opinions follow a circular course. As I have said before, there is no such thing as old-fashioned, something is either 'in' or 'out' at any given time. Dear old Nicholas Ridley resigned from government after making a speech about Germany, stating that their might and authority could overshadow, indeed override, Europe. The Eurocrats all stood back in amazement, upset and annoyed that this talk could undo all the so-called good Euro work that was being put in by the blind and faithful. Ironic, really, but the only opinion he gave in public, that the masses felt affinity with and understood, should be the one to bring him down. No-one I know disagrees with his view, but then you must not say anything nasty about Europe. Today's headlines concerning Mrs Thatcher's latest salvo in the *Daily Telegraph* reads, 'The problem of Germany's power'. The article goes quite a way to spell out just where Germany stands in Europe at the moment and where it could stand if America were to pull out. Strange, now that she is not No. 1 any more, how the anti-view rears its head. Yes, she has always been sceptical of

Europe, even though she never did anything except utter threats to relieve this country of its Euro burden, but she appears more aggressive, more assertive and more convinced of her ground now, and she is right, of course. Why did she not let the British public vote on Europe during her eleven years' reign? I suppose it is because the truth not only hurts but is usually found to be embarrassing to a government hell-bent on taking an opposite view.

So there is a second spacewoman who has been walking around in the solar system. One Kathryn Thornton has been out and about busily doing – well, whatever they do out there. I hope she wasn't too disappointed not to find any of those 'little shops one just discovers' or a 'little coffee shop which sells that over-rate crappucino varity' where you can stay all day talking over old times with a girlfriend and slagging off some face-lifted old dog who sat across the way. Can you imagine letting two women out on a moon walk. They would spend the whole day gassing, swearing that they had seen the kids waving whilst trying to outdo each other with the colour of their new outfit. I suppose space would then be witness to comments like 'Just a little something I threw on' or 'If only I had had more time to prepare'. No, I don't suppose three years in a simulated shuttle was ever going to be enough. I wonder if I can put Kate Adie's name down for a trip?

What a welcome relief it is to hear an archbishop actually address the basic raw problem – population control – or rather the lack of it. He made the point that when he asked UN officials why population control was not on the agenda of the forthcoming summit, there was an uncomfortable silence. Again, we suffer those who want to party, to be involved but not at the expense of anything controversial like Catholicism and its ruling on birth control and the misery it brings to millions of its faithful – and they would have to be! If someone wants to follow the Catholic faith, then fine, but the church's power over individual rights is affecting all of us, a point not lost on Dr Carey. At least if we have to suffer the Church of England poking its nose into all and sundry and being given an inflated share of the media's attention, it might as well make the occasional intelligent, if simplistic, point. Of some concern to me is the fact that Dr Carey has given more than a couple of logical contributions over the past couple of months, so that could be the kiss of death. At the same time the world bank has published what is deemed a 'major study' of world development. It says that education of third world women is the key to the future. I would have thought that it would have been sterilisation or contraception, preferably the former in large bucketfuls.

How is this for naïvety? The Cambridgeshire police attempt to break up an acid house party, which by the very nature of the affair is going to contain a number of people who are more than a little past their best when it comes to useable brain cells. Over 200 of these zonked-out yobs attacked the police and the local force's deputy chief constable says he is 'Shocked and saddened by the level of violence used against his officers'. Where *has* he been?

Here is an unusual one in the Hatch, Match and Despatch. To Lindsey and Barry, a daughter, Keziah Rose Blake-Mizen. Nice, that.

Remember me saying some time ago that the local parish council were still considering the possible sale of Carrington Recreation Ground, well they are still talking about it, until midnight it seems. The local paper tells us that they have decided to hold a postal vote conducted by the electoral reform society. Prior to this an exhibition showing the various course of options will be displayed – I think we have all been here before. We await developments with intense interest, or maybe not so intense, if you live in Biggleswade, and I am assured that some people do!

The ludicrous case of the crowing cockerel forced into a greenhouse because of a neighbour's complaint goes on. With the stakes being extremely high, i.e. does the cockerel get its oats or not, the for's and against were debated long and hard by both solicitors. The end result was that the injunction forcing the bird into the greenhouse was not to be lifted, but that this proud and randy male can join the fourteen hens he used to live with between 8 am and 10 pm Mondays to Thursdays, and from 3 pm until 10 pm at weekends. It didn't mention Fridays. Get this, the weekend visiting times have been worked out to take into account Mrs Ritchings' (wife of the moaner, sorry, complainant) night work as a nurse. The bird's owner has still got to wait to see if the cock can return full-time to the henhouse. As Mrs Johns, the owner, said, 'My father and grandfather, who were both countrymen, would be turning in their graves to think I was being dragged through courts for keeping chickens.' She is right, isn't she.

So, Ian Woosnam has just received his MBE at Buck Pal. The Queen asked him how he had been playing. He said, 'Not too well.' She said, 'Things go up and down.' Fairly predictable stuff, really. Pity she did not discuss with him the slit-eyed brigade with their exclusive membership who are turning on the taps for themselves while the rest of us pay through the nose – a continually dripping nose!

The news we had expected has just arrived. No, it is not a Page 3 girl offering to come on down and give me a good time. That news would, to be honest, have been unexpected. It is football on TV or rather it won't be unless you have got a bloody aerial. B Sky B will be showing live football while the BBC picks up the scraps to be shuffled into highlights for *Match of the Day*. Isn't it funny how people see things in different lights. B Sky B itself admits that although the first year's viewing will be free, fans will have to pay in excess of £12 per month, probably from August 1993. David Hill, their head of sport, described their 'ownership' of soccer as the 'biggest advance in TV football since the invention of the camera'. How does he come to that conclusion without a strong sense of bias? As far as I am concerned, the ordinary man has been sidestepped in the quest for profit, and having paid his licence for years, is now relegated to Second Division – now First Division – viewing. The only 'advance' I can see is the complete abandonment of non-commercial television within the not-too-distant future.

Here we go again. A lorry driver loses concentration when he tunes in his CB radio and in a few seconds, five people are dead. No, he didn't mean it, no, he wasn't drunk or driving dangerously, but five people still died because he was not looking ahead. What sentence does he get? Two hundred hours Community Service and a three-year ban. No wonder the relatives feel let down. As one of them commented, 'You get that sentence for theft.' Enough said.

Did you read the story about the shark in Oxford, a glass fibre shark, actually. Built six years ago and mounted on the roof of a terraced house in Headington, the owner has been battling with planners who say it should be taken down because he was never given permission. Now, after all this time, the Department of Environment Secretary has ruled that the fish can stay. There was a picture of the house accompanying the article. It has been built to look as if the shark has crashed through the roof, so you cannot see its head, but the body, fins and tail are all there in glorious technicolour, well, a greyish colour anyway. It is the size of the structure which takes some getting used to, about two-thirds of the size of the house I would say. It is fairly noticeable. Again, it is strange how diverse people's opinions can be. While Michael Howard the Secretary of State, said that it can remain as 'a symbol of rebellion against the drab uniformity', the Chairman of Oxford's

Planning Committee declared the decision 'a victory for anarchy'. Personally, I can see both points of view, well, I would do being a Librian! I contend that it is nice to see a little bit of innovation and imagination, so long as it is not near me!

The cock-crowing episode has turned out to be the thin end of the wedge. In deepest Sussex, in the village of Fletching, it seems that the smell of muck-spreading has become so unbearable for ex-townies that they have had to complain to the council. The result, incredibly, is that the farmer concerned has been banned from spreading manure over his land on all but fifteen days year. Those fifteen days cannot include weekends and Bank Holidays. The farm has been there over 200 years, the estate backing onto the farm, just twenty-five. One of the complainants has only lived in the 'affected' area for two years. They should be so lucky. If it were noxious gases from a chemical plant or a local PCB recycling system I could understand, but here we are again. 'Now we have moved into the country, we want things our way at the expense of someone else's livelihood and tradition.' It is that sort of view that appears to be getting the townies everywhere. Presumably there cannot be too many other local affairs for them to gossip about. At least the farmer's spreading manure and not chit-chat.

In the Hatch, Match and Despatch today, Jennifer Staunton has just sprog-coughed a little lad, to be known as Oliver Sebastian Boucher Staunton. He is a brother for Gregory, Camilla, Barnaby and India-Jane – as opposed to Indiana Jones! Bet that lot will be fun in McDonalds!

As far as I am concerned, Friday 22nd May belongs to Mr and Mrs Owens from Sittingbourne in Kent. Today, they can hopefully start to rebuild their lives after almost three years of misery. Their son, Darren, was killed in the high street by a lorry driven by Kevin Taylor, a man accused of being violent and completely without remorse for the loss of their son. One can quite imagine how the various facts and attitudes could make you want to seek revenge. Mr Owens acquired a sawn-off shotgun and confronted Taylor and his common-law wife, and fired at him. There was only one verdict that the jury should have given, and thankfully they made it, by acquitting him of all charges. To see the killer of your son, who had never held a driving licence, driving around the area after the accident, would be grounds enough for most people anyway. Without doubt, part of the reason Mr Owens took the action he did was due to the lenient sentence handed out to Taylor. He was given eighteen months' imprisonment, only to be let out six months early. He had killed someone with his whole life ahead of him. He should never have been let out of prison again. Do the lawmakers not understand the frustration of being let down by the system? It will get worse, as I have said before. More and more people will take the law into their own hands, not because they are macho and want to be powerful, but because the legal system and the judgements made are all biased towards the aggressor.

So, Freddie Mercury's £8 million will has just been disclosed. The bulk of it goes to a girl he 'always loved', his sister, parents, assistant, chef and a male lover who has copped a half million. None for Aids Research though. That is a relief. At least the family and friends might spend the money on important things, like a holiday in Majorca, or a new oven, or the complete works of Queen...

I suppose I should have considered myself lucky not to have heard or read about that misguided and arrogant fool, Bruce Kent. We have managed to get a fair way through the book without him bringing a new low to the proceedings! Now he pops up aided and abetted by one hundred and fifty other like-minded oddities and a wooden cut-out dove. The aim is to insult the fifty-five thousand chaps who fought for the likes of them. The statue they are complaining about will hopefully be unveiled by the Queen Mother next Saturday without any of the spoiling tactics from these left-wing has-beens from another age, and probably planet. The reason Sir Arthur 'Bomber' Harris organised the attacks on German cities was because they started it. Can't *they* understand that? Fools!

Talking of the misguided, there is a letter in our local paper from a Sandhurst resident who announces in the Letters Column that he has been to Waterloo eighteen times – no, not our one, the Flemish one where you can't train spot. To have visited Belgium eighteen times must, in itself, be some kind of record, because nowhere in his letter does he mention that he was forced to go, or that he received payment for it. On one of his recent sorties in March 1991, he was approached by the Burgomeister of Waterloo Commune, well, it is legal now, and the suggestion was made that Sandhurst should twin with Waterloo. As it is recorded that twelve former Sandhurst cadets died at Waterloo in 1815 during that 'brief encounter', the writer suggests that this is good enough reason to exchange pleasantries, and anything else that satisfied the Euro culture, I imagine. He adds that they had a fine band and sports facilities. So probably does Crawley in Sussex, but then it is not 'over there'. Our man finishes in stirring form by adding that this act would be 'in the interests of lasting peace and a better knowledge of an EC fellow member'. Yuk!!

By the time you read this the name Castle Morton, nestling in the Malvern Hills, will not mean much to most people. If it does, it probably means that the good villagers are still having problems with drop-outs and scroungers. The term 'New Age Traveller' indicates an intelligent oik who has turned his or her back on society, which is acceptable if you completely break the ties. As I write, some 20,000 of these NATs, plus the hangers-on, druggies, those in work but seeking a weekend away from it all, are camped on Castle Morton Common and are basically buggering up the countryside – and probably a few sheep as well. Throughout the Bank Holiday weekend, local people have been unable to leave their homes. There has been criticism of the police for not doing more. To be fair, how do you muster enough of our boys in blue to deal with 20,000 of the sods? Surely this is a case for army lads, with Ulster experience, to be deployed. Yesterday, Bank Holiday Monday, saw a surveillance helicopter being fired on with flares. The police are continuing enquiries to identify those responsible. To be subjected to one night of rowdy behaviour and noise is bad enough, but for this situation to be allowed to continue for three days is disgraceful. A lovely beauty spot is being spoiled by human excrement, used needles, and broken glass, while fencing and small trees are being used for firewood – and still we stand by and keep an eye on things. The local police farce – must stop using that word – have set up a 24-hour lukewarm line to deal with residents' problems, so that should sort them out. Surely the fact that the children of these oiks and oikesses do not attend school should be grounds for social services to be involved. I would like to see the children taken away and fostered or adopted, preferably in another country. It is okay living off the land if that is what happens, but it is all a cop-out at the taxpayer's expense. The wide open road that they travel goes all the way to the social security office, where the scrounging hordes – the word horde described in Websters University Dictionary as a large predatory band – gather their giros. Then there is the allowance for their common-law wives, although even that title seems too conventional, and the benefit for their illegitimate sproggs. I mean, how else do you buy food, petrol, cigarettes, alcohol, road fund tax, magic mushrooms, needles...

I am staying with this story because we have moved on another day, and despite police protection for the locals, the fourth night of hostilities has been marked by phones being cut off after telephone posts were cut down for firewood and a car was burned out. There are several carcasses of dead sheep lying around which have been killed by the marauding hounds which travel with these arseholes. An article in the *Telegraph* has centred on one of the female specie travelling in the convoy. She has been on the road for nine years and has six children, aged between four years and twenty-two. The latter has now graduated to running his own lorry. The other five stay with mum in her bus. A confirmed drop-out, she comes from the quintessential middle-class background, being born in Singapore and educated at a convent in Norfolk. This lass, called Lin, ran away from home when she was sixteen and never went back. Life on the road and the needs of her children are provided for by the selling of yarn and food when they stop for a while. This two-fingered alternative lifestyle is, of course supplemented by that bottomless pit of conventional finance, social security and child benefit, to the tune of £110 per week, you know what I mean, money that could be better spent on a hospital bed or the real education of her children. She appears to think that the taxpayer is under-funding her and we have got her cheap. So for all her own education, she is basically no different from all the other drop-outs who snub society and want to find themselves, the financial ties can never be broken because they still need the system. It is the kids who I feel sorry for.

It was sad to see that Joan Sanderson has died. I never saw her in a duff comedy, as far as I can remember. I recall her roles in *Please Sir*, the deaf guest in *Fawlty Towers*, the grandmother in *After Henry*, and playing the same part in *My Girl and Me*. She had the sort of presence that you felt would go on for ever. I didn't realise that she was 79 years of age.

Have you seen that a new video called *The Gay Man's Guide to Safer Sex* has just escaped. Naturally, the Terrence Higgins Trust have been involved with its production, and probably with some of its participants as well. The British Board of Film Classification have deemed that it be given an 18 certificate. I would have thought it should have been given a concrete boot and deposited over Brighton Pier with the Pink Parasol Set. Of course, if it had been a lesbian example, it could have been buried at the Devils Dyke – I have just thought of that and it is only 8.30 am. There is, apparently, a concern that men are becoming bored with safe sex and the discipline that goes with it. Well, there are always sheep, aren't there, and it would provide some variety. Remember, you have to read this with a lisp, whilst holding your wrist slightly limp – I said your wrist!

To be fair, regardless of one's views on homosexuality, it is difficult not to believe that this bit of film isn't pornography dressed down. It includes graphic scenes and coarse language – why? You can watch five set pieces which take place in various settings, one of which is a cellar job with chains and a cage. Surely the safest way to avoid disease is to distance yourself from your friend when he is bending down – or have I got it wrong? The last word goes to the chief executive of the Terrence Higgins Trust, who states that this work of arse (sorry, art) is not pornography but an erotic life-saver – can you see that flying pig? I am buggered (sorry again) if I can. Naturally, it will be available through Virgin stores as well as by male order. I have done it again, I meant to say mail order! Still think it should be disorder.

It is a shame that such an old-established family-run business should call in the receiver. Belling, the cooker people, have announced that in their 80th year of trading, the Bell has finally tolled. At our last home we bought a Belling because it was not a badged model from one of the multinational companies. We also felt at the time that we had scored a first by finding a British product. It gave great service, with no problems, over a five-year period, and as far as I know is still going strong.

On the subject of private companies, the brewery merger and takeover situation shows no sign of abating. Again, the only loser in these scenarios are the drinkers who are left with even fewer choices and ever-increasing prices. In the case of Morland Brewery the aggressor comes in the shape of Greene King, the East Anglian brewers. The final pint that you and I buy seems to be the last thing on the agenda, doesn't it? Whitbreads have just sold their 28½% share to Greene King. Morlands would like to stay independent but look to be in a very vulnerable position. The end result is always the same. The brewery that is bought out either loses its brewing capacity immediately, thus ending another family of brand names and jobs, or the site is retained as a distribution depot with a few jobs saved pro tem. This course of action is invariably short-term and any pledges about the buildings and employment last only until the next upturn in the housing market. Once again, the product comes a very poor second to asset-stripping and profit.

The Abingdon-based brewery we have just discussed – I say we, because I am sitting here by myself and I get lonely – is fairly close geographically to our next village of call. This is the turn of Turville to make a name for itself. Nestling in the Chilterns, with a population of around 60 people with no shops and one pub, there is dissent within its camp. On one side there are the 20 or so parishioners who are in favour of turning the old village school into a field study centre, on the other side against the idea, are approximately the same number again. In the middle not knowing which way to turn, or more likely who is going to be the least offended, are the remaining third. The idea of a field study centre is in itself not much of a problem. The stumbling block appears in the form of a 'community centre' to be used during the summer months for under-privileged children from inner cities. The flagship of the 'fors' appears to be the writer and barrister, John Mortimer, a local resident. I understand and sympathise with the 'againsts' myself. It is sheer naïvety to expect these so-called underprivileged oiks to come to a 'nice place' and for them to fall in with the lack of demand ten days in the country would place on their braincell. No one-armed bandits, no passing cars to play chicken with, no-one to buy drugs from. And with such a small population, there is always the possibility of getting caught when you are committing a burglary. Let's be honest, even the 'fors' will be locking everything up, even if they don't admit it. Our young townie friends will also have a problem in the lack of choice if they are thinking of rape. That is assuming that the female percentage of the population is half. This gives you about 30 possible targets, unless of course you are AC/DC, in which case your prospective list has doubled again! Armed with your gay video, you may even be lucky and stumble across a dungeon, or two. Seriously though, I cannot think of an easier shot in the foot since the Labour party publicly started congratulating itself as the next government two weeks prior to the election. Who in their right mind would want to invite children of dubious parentage to the blissful peace of our countryside? It is bad enough having them forced on you, but to offer them a hand is beyond reason.

Another little tear in the fabric, I feel. The Science Museum in London has done away with the astronomy exhibits and replaced the display with a replica supermarket check-out area featuring tills and hamburgers. The previous incumbents of this space have been relegated to storage in Olympia. A spokesman has stated that the astronomy exhibits can still be seen by appointment, which is not much use to anyone. The spoke also said that the supermarket shown, my words, plays an important role in bringing across the relevance of science to everyday life and makes important scientific points. No, I don't believe that either. I do believe, however, that Sainsbury's sponsorship of this little mini acreage is far more important. No doubt this kind of invisible selling will become the norm. We could have fossils from only one country being on display, alongside holiday advertisements and brochures for that particular place. We could well witness the 'history of computing' being sponsored by one of the multinationals who wish to extend their products into more government-funded bodies. This list is endless, and frightening.

Despite the protests from the misguided of England and the mayor of Cologne, the Queen Mother has unveiled the statue of 'Bomber Harris'. It was bad enough reading that there was to be a protest in the first place, but to hear those insulting fools shouting 'Harris was a mass murderer' in our own country, must be disheartening and upsetting to say the least. Not content with protesting in a peaceful way, the yobs then had the audacity to interrupt the Queen Mother's speech. Ironic, really, that Bomber Command should help towards preserving the free speech that this scum tried to deny the Queen Mother. One of their loathsome number was arrested for spraying red paint over the crowd. Just what he thought he would achieve is beyond me. There was among the crowd a chap called Nigel Lewis, whose name appears to be the only normal thing about him. He represented the 'No Statues for Murderers Group' which is allegedly supported by the Communist Party, which, coming from them, would really be rich. Then there was another lot called the 'Peace Pledge Union', about 150 strong. Where do these misfits go when they are not protesting? You can bet your bottom dollar they don't go home to a conventional husband or wife and children with names they won't be embarrassed to own. You can also put money on their not working at Boots or Sainsbury's – that is if they do work. No, we probably paid for their bus fare enabling them to protest in the first place. It is bad enough when Cologne's mayor says the statue 'idealises a man partly responsible for the deaths of tens of thousands of civilians'. Coming from a kraut, that really takes the biscuit! It is interesting to note where those arrested for breach of peace, being equipped to cause criminal damage and actual criminal damage come from. Four of them are students, all from places you would rather not visit – Rotherhithe, Hackney, Tottenham and Camden. Another three of unstated employment hail from Hackney. The only female among this tribe is a facilities manager, whatever that is. She has come all the way from

Kensington, while the last to appear is a preacher, there had to be one. If they are not homosexuals they are pacifists – usually both, as long as they have got their rights...

The Industrial Relations Services have recently organised a survey concerning sexual harassment at work. We all know that the main reason for this waste of paper is not concern for those who have suffered as much as a wink from a member of the opposite sex, more a desire to see complaints pour in so as to justify their own continued employment. Needless to say, all went well, for according to the statistics, 55% of the 132 companies canvassed admitted that staff had complained of harassment. Nine out of every ten complaints had been upheld with at least one sacking taking place. No doubt the Industrial Relations Services will hope to see an improvement to 100% of all cases being upheld, and the pitifully low number of sackings increased to at least double figures. I mean, fancy saying 'hello' to a workmate of the opposite sex and not receiving a Final Warning.

Poor old Hertfordshire County Council is in the frying pan, according to Graham Day and his racial quango. They stand accused of discriminating against Asian pupils when it comes to the allocation of secondary school places. The council asked parents to send in written applications. These irritating plebs from the Commission for Racial Equality have deemed this unlawful and unfair to the poor immigrant souls who speak poor English or are unfamiliar with the English school system. Frankly, I am now at the stage when the fun is being taken out of writing about this lot, and I am getting pee'd off. Just how far do we have to go to accommodate the wishes, desires, rights, etc. of every minority. Hertfordshire just used to be such a nice place.

Question marks are often placed over judges with regard to their being out of touch with the handling of cases and their lack of sensitivity when faced with the victims' families who want to see justice done. We can now add another name to the growing list of judges who could benefit from being in the victim's shoes for once. Judge Tumin, the Chief Inspector of Prisons, has castigated Dartmoor, calling it a dustbin and recommending that it should close within the next eighteen months. That is, unless it can be converted into a community prison, whatever that might be when it is behind bars! The very name 'community' prison smacks of a cushy life, with snooker tables, cable TV and long breaks in town to see loved ones. Judge Tumin is also recommending that its security status should be downgraded. He comments that he was appalled to see prisoners scrubbing dishes with the same brushes that they used to scrub lavatories. Okay, give them some new brushes if that is going to keep him happy. Peculiar, I thought, that our learned friend should mention that no prison has had a more melancholy or chequered history, or that it is located more remotely from the homes of the prisoners it holds. I have got it right, haven't I? The prison is there to stop prisoners from carrying on their illegal practices at the public's expense? It is there for our convenience, not that of their families? Apparently not. I appear to be wrong. The very reputation of this prison, according to the judge, offers the prisoner very little! The Home Office are spending £25 million on refurbishing Dartmoor, money doctors in many hospitals across the country could make far better use of, and generally with a better class of recipient. Our fine inspector goes on to say how the installation of a lavatory in every cell is two years behind schedule – so? It is only two months since one of our multi-million pound new-style prisons was the scene of unrest, with its inmates throwing guttering and roof embellishments onto the ground wrecking cars. Windows below the rooftop demonstration were smashed by levering guttering upon them. Thousands of pounds worth of damage was done. And for what? There is no respect, however much one pours in money and goodwill. In the majority of cases, if there was a modicum of respect in the first place, many of the crimes would not have been committed. We are only throwing good money after bad, and sweeping changes that benefit only the ne'er-do-well and his visiting kin are an insult to the rest of us.

Another sign of the times now. Have you seen that British Rail have found a new way to make money? No don't be silly, it is not running services which are cheap, popular and on time, but crèches. The first two, costing the punter-ess between £75 and £100 per week will cater for children aged between three months and five years, and are situated at Wimbledon and Oxford stations. Eight more of these sops to the feminists will open this year. A BR spoke says that his employers are not seen as carer-friendly and thinks that these 'missions' for caterwauling kids, as I see them, will improve the quality of new recruits, reduce absenteeism and improve staff efficiency. Almost half of the 50 places for the little loves will be available to passengers, the rest going to staff. BR will not be running this little sideline themselves, but will contract out the operation to a company specialising in this field, which would probably be the best place for the little sods. It just remains for us to look forward to the first case of a lost or abducted child, and BR blaming the late running of the 3.25 pm Ballynowhere to Auchwereclosed service and promising an immediate investigation. Frankly, because I am Frank, I still feel that contrary to EC, Equal Rights, CAB, and everybody else's dictate, who leans to the left of centre, that this move is only in the interest of BR's profit and the parents' greed. Once again, the only loser will be the child of three months of age, who actually does need his or her mum.

Our esteemed Treasury Department is now firmly entrenched in a battle royal with the EC over future VAT ratings. That bottomless pit with absolutely no accountability to those who didn't elect it in the first place, are now expected to pay VAT on an even wider range of products and services. If VAT is levied on food, children's clothes, books, newspapers, domestic gas, electricity and rents, the cost of living will increase enormously, and presumably knock all attempts to stifle inflation.

And what are we left with? EC officials are of the opinion that if Britain will not accept the imposition of Brussels' most insidious taxation, then they will test the legality of Britain's zero-rated items. Does this not smack of Big Brother tactics? If only this country would wake up to the monstrous bulk of officialdom.

Denmark's name will be firmly and warmly implanted on many Euro sceptics' brains for a long time to come. Governments only usually have the guts to offer a referendum when the outcome is set to go their way. How refreshing for the electorate to buck the set piece and bugger up the Maastricht Treaty. Not by many, I grant you, but 0.7% of the population's vote is still the majority vote, and that is what counts. It is amusing, if not unexpected, to see the Euro puppets running around as if their income has been cut off. The papers are full of 'what ifs' and 'what abouts'. I shall savour this expression of doubt that exists in most countries within this dictatorial bloc – with the exception of Ireland. They are to have a vote but that result is a foregone conclusion. With their ability to win six pounds for every one they put in, the Irish are no fools, and they certainly know which side of their bread is spread with Kerry Gold. France is considering a vote, but Britain is keeping aloof from all this sort of thing, as it smacks of democracy, not to mention the fact that it might just go against the Europhiles (which is probably on a par with being a paedophile!) At least the child molester can receive treatment, but the channel tunnel vision of a perfect Europe is far more entrenched an ideal.

The good news is that Gerald Kaufmann will not be standing

again for a place in the Shadow Cabinet. Always worth a few votes from the Tories, it will at least be one less weasel to suffer on TV.

Meanwhile, in the Arrivals Column, the Beebees, that is Sarah and Robert, are celebrating a little wonder – a brother for Joshua and Sebastian – Benedict Beebee (or Ben Beebee, for short perhaps). Poor sod!

It was last month that a young girl wearing a T-shirt with the wording 'Somerville's got enough balls' across the breast caught my eye. To be fair, I was initially more interested in the size of them than the wording, which I considered as an afterthought! The issue isn't about the end of a financial year and the government finding themselves embarrassed by an excess of balls, oh no. This is about Somerville College, Oxford, an all-female bastion of learning and their students' desire to keep it that way. Now, some three weeks later the decision has been made to accept male students from late next year. Over the last twenty years, 23 all-male and 3 all-female colleges have relinquished their traditions and become mixed. It seems a pity that we cannot leave alone anything which lacks so-called equality. What is so wrong in retaining all female and all male colleges.

Come back Rutland, all is forgiven

What was I saying about things going in circles? Actually, what *was* I saying, oh yes. It could be good news for those living in Rutland, Cumberland and parts of North Yorkshire and Lincolnshire. The name game looks like going full circle and the detested crop – or is it crap – of designer authorities like Humberside, Cleveland and Avon, seem destined to fade away. No-one wanted them in the first place, but it gave some grey soul employment, I suppose. With the proposed return of the Welsh counties of Cardigan, Pembroke, Montgomery, etc. the map of Britain might start to resemble something of its former glory. I shall await with bated breath to see if the Soke of Peterborough is to be reinstated. As a child seeing the map of England and Wales, I was always fascinated by the anomalies of our county system. How some could have shire after their names, whilst others did not, continued to perplex me. Then again, I was easily perplexed, as easily as I was amused. Others would just call me retarded – but I digress. It was in 1965 that my parents bought me a copy of the Complete Atlas of the British Isles, published by Readers Digest. This fascinating tome should have been used by schools as a basis for virtually all forms of education. Geographical, historical, social, it covered all aspects of our daily lives, aspects that are not even mentioned in the course of learning today. It was, however, the structure of the counties which held my attention, when I wasn't train spotting. Looking back today, I have the Atlas here, sitting on my desk, open at page 22, which is headed 'The Counties of the British Isles', only Eire and Ulster remain in the same form as they did in those heady Beatle-ridden days, when we all giggled about a famous pop singer and a Mars bar. Oh, the excess of youth!

Funny, really, before I started the last paragraph I asked Debbie if she had seen the atlas so that I could delve further into my nostalgia. It is in my room by the bed, she told me. Upstairs I went, and yes, it was where she said I would find it. Back in the kitchen, where she was microwaving chips, I stated that Glyn before her, and hopefully William after her, had all found the book interesting. She broke off from munching a banana sandwich, long enough to inform me that 'I should be careful not to hold the book at a particular angle, as her pressed flowers would fall out'. 'Is that it', I asked. 'Is that the only use you and your new love have found for my treasured artefact?' 'Well', she said, 'it is heavy and keeps them nice and flat!' She offered this explanation without even a hint of an apology. I was going to say that she deflowered my book, but she had actually enflowered it. So, here we are, on page 22 in 1965. The southern half of England was always easy to follow. Nothing messy, and each one metaphorically ticked off as having had my foot, nay feet, tread upon its earth. In fact the only dotted lines denoted East and West Sussex. Middlesex had sadly gone prior to this, but its ghost still lingers on. In some ways far more tangible than that of other counties after 27 years. Let's be posh again. One still addresses one's post to Twickenham, Middlesex, after all, it is, I believe, still an accepted Royal Mail postal address. How many people address letters to the Isle of Ely, or Huntingdonshire? Actually, that part of the country suffered quite badly at the hands of the county-crats. Cambridgeshire swallowed up the Soke of Peterborough, the Isle of Ely and Huntingdonshire, whilst Leicestershire absorbed Rutland. Its county town, Okeham, being about the only place people could name as being within that county's boundary. Today there are whole herds of pond life who have not got a clue what a county is. It just happens to be some letters on the DSS book.

Moving up the East Coast, Lincolnshire was an interesting case, divided as it was between Lindsey, Kesteven and Holland. Yorkshire, with its three Ridings was always romantic and to me became the gateway to uncharted seas. The four most northerly counties of Westmorland, Cumberland, Durham and Northumberland stood solid testament to Britain's history and tradition. All that was swept aside by the unwarranted interlopers in the form of Teeside, Tyneside, Humberside and Cleveland, known mostly for its social workers. With their appearance came the demise of Westmorland, whilst the other two 'lands' became 'brias'. There was no such thing as a metropolitan borough in those days, either. Manchester was in Lancashire, Stockport resided in Cheshire and Birmingham lay in Warwickshire. I believe if my memory serves me correctly, that a section of Worcestershire was divorced from the main mass, but I stand corrected, as I often do. Certainly Flintshire in Wales was, in fact, made up of three separate lands. There was Flintshire, bordering the River Dee, part of Flint, an arm that dared to stretch into Shropshire, or Salop, and a third, tiny segment that lay fully within Denbighshire. Oh, for the times when things were not prepacked and little eccentricities could be tolerated. I doubt if we will see that part of Flint returned, but this news is certainly a step in the right direction.

Joni and Adam Zetter have just announced the unleashing of a little lad who will travel under the handle of 'Zachary Ross' He will be a brother for Alex and Jake, how rural. Oh, it is all right, they live in Santa Barbara, California, phew! I don't think I could have stood a Zachary Zetter in Guildford. The repercussion on house prices would have been felt for miles around. Questions would have been asked in Esher and Claygate.

I have just seen a Sit. Vac. which asks if you can answer 'yes' to three questions. I can answer two, so I should be in with a chance surely. Yes, I live in the Thames area, yes, I am interested in earning 25 k, even if I prefer the figure to be printed as £25,000 instead of the use of computer-speak. The question I fall down on is that I do not have much experience of hospital laboratory diagnostics. The ad is headed 'Could you sell clinical freagants?' Knowing what a freagant was would help. No, I have to give this one a miss. Someone else here is looking for an adventurous sail-training skipper. There are another two positions for medical reps, one is in critical care, whatever that is. I think it is just outside Derby. I have read on, it means intensive care products. Things such as catheters, I am pushing my knees together as I am writing, and electronic technology. Actually, it is surprising just how many medical sales jobs are going begging. Glaxo, Wellcome, Smith & Nephew Ltd are all actively seeking employees. It would seem that there is a lot of brass to be made out of somebody's misfortune.

Tomas Cook, that romantic founder of the travel agency business, has been sold by the Midland Bank to the Sauerkrauts. One hundred and fifty one years old and now in German hands then again, for how much longer will the Midland Bank be a British establishment?

Talking of tour companies, I am reminded of a friend's assessment of the Maxwell affair. His theory is that whilst standing by the yacht's railings, he was approached by one of his crew who asked him how much it had cost to get to the Canaries. Maxwell replied, '2s. 6d. with Lunn Poly.' The crew member exclaimed 'Get away' and the railing, along with Maxwell, disappeared over the side. Simple wasn't it? I still have my doubts, though. This same friend of mine seriously thinks he will reappear alive and well in South America. Stranger things have happened. I mean, Jeremy Bates, Britain's number one tennis player, is actually ranked within the top 200 worldwide, a British player so near the top, now that is strange.

Isn't it funny how different values and morals are placed on issues where a sense of conformity should prevail. Over the past year 21,286 homes have had their water cut off. Gone are the days when the last resort was to turn off the tap. One home in every thousand is disconnected, the percentage increase being 177% on last year's figures. The water industry watchdog, Ofwat, consider these figures very worrying. The strange thing is that Mr Byatt, Ofwat's director, says that he will not permit companies to raise their charges to cover bad debts. This, he says, would not be fair on those who have paid. Well, no it wouldn't, but that logical line of thought flies straight in the face of the poll tax, where there is a built-in figure for every authority to cover their losses. One of the newly privatised water companies, Anglia Water, have announced pre-tax profits of 171 million pounds, that is a 12% rise over last year's figures. Their chairman, one Bernard Henderson, announced plans to raise prices by 9.4%, and admitted that, 'Customers are becoming more concerned about the increases in their water bills.' Does he really find that so surprising?

What a mucky business religion is. I see that a Belfast couple have travelled to Virginia, USA to get married. The bride is Presbyterian and the groom a Catholic. They come from Lurgan and were afraid that the controversy might spoil their day. The couple chose Charleston, Virginia, as that was the home of the husband's grandfather. He visited Ulster in 1942 as a GI and married a local girl. The townsfolk of Charleston laid on a cake, champagne, all the accoutrements and musicians. The mayor even proposed a toast. Those entrenched in their religious bigotry should take note. How clean I feel not being involved with any of these god-bothering circuses.

I have just been looking through the local paper's property news. It is a pull-out section. Builders' interpretations of the truth show little signs of abating. A new development in Camberley, Surrey, is shown on a half-page advertisement, called Tall Trees, the main picture shows eleven houses built on top of each other, around a car-free, and person-free road. In fact the only thing that is tall is the lamp-post. How do they have the gall to call it Tall Trees, when there is bugger-all left. There is another development here called Grantleigh Meadow, in Hook, Hampshire. This is another extension site. You can see their logic. Every few houses built brings them that much closer to another raped area, so you are now left with only an infill area, and that will be a doddle with the local planning department.

It is all so buyer-friendly, and all so false. In Yateley, you can buy one of the new houses being offered for £65,950 in Church View. Yateley has become almost a dormitory town of its own. The usual story, of course, you widen the roads, put in roundabouts and telegraph the signal for developers to start again. To get to Church View you enter through Stable View, Village Way and The Croft. Well, there is no village, the developers have seen to that, The Croft is romantic but that is about all, and as for the Stables, they might still be there, but if they are, don't blink, for sure as eggs are salmonella-friendly, the stable won't be there for long.

Bovis are good at the name game. Only twelve years ago I worked at a small garage, the site of which is now covered by Safeways. At least it is a high street shop. Marks & Spencer's and Tesco came, conquered and concreted the nearby area and produced The Meadows. Acres of these meadows were destroyed but the name lives on. A bypass followed and development has continued so that the road from Camberley north to Wokingham is now one continual clatter of traffic passing estate after estate, with very few undisturbed fields left, and even fewer trees. Bovis, however, pander to the romantic, and probably succeed. There is nothing like a good address to impress relatives, or even yourself, so in the over-congested jungle of modern affordables we have 'Shepherds Lea' and 'Meadow Brook'. In Crookham Village, near Fleet, another ex-nice place which is being submerged by greed, you can buy a house in 'Mayfields'. Croudace proudly announce the last two remaining three-bed semi-detacheds in 'Watchetts Green', Camberley, although, of course, there is no green. Here is another one. 'Reserve a superb first-class Bryant home at Kings Oak, Great Sheldons Coppice, Hook, Hants. I don't know this site, but if they have arrived at the Coppice and it is still there, don't hold out much hope for its future. Laing Homes are offering new houses at the Hedgerows, Fleet, while the sprawling urban development at Ancells Farm, Fleet, is still going on. This devastation had started when I wrote *From Where I Sit*, and has just about ruined the whole east end of Fleet, but still they drive ever onward in their quest to lay barren whole acres of rich countryside. This development was particularly sad as it contained meadows and woodland which lay totally unspoilt.

There were hedgerows, wooden rustic fencing and tired gates that sprung out of the natural growth in a picture-book setting, but alas, no more.

The lengths to which the various builders are going to sell their houses show just how deep we are in recession, or should it be depression? You know the one. Mr Whiplash himself is still announcing that we are coming out of it. Charles Church meanwhile are inviting you to look at the quality of their work and ask about their payment protection plan. Woolwich Property Services are sending out invitations to their garden party, to be held on Saturday, 27th June, for an afternoon of tea and nostalgia, with vintage cabaret from the roaring twenties – oh, and by the way, would you like to buy a flat? Admiral Homes would like you to contact Lyn or Sue now and they will help you with legal fees, a part-exchange scheme and mortgage protection. Crest Homes are erring on the side of basics and offering you value for money and affordability. Wimpey, with their welcome home slogan, are offering to pay your deposit, while Bryant Homes are extolling the virtues of a duty-free house – provided you buy before the deadline date of 18th August, when stamp duty will return to haunt us. Now here is a novel scheme. If you reserve an apartment at Lakeside Court, Fleet, during June, you will get a season ticket to Waterloo absolutely free. Well that makes it all worthwhile, doesn't it? (Especially if you work in Andover!) It just goes to show just how desperate things are getting. Talking of names, we have friends who live in the Chilterns. They moved about ten years ago to a small village where local people were referred to by friendly, if somewhat eccentric, names. They have since moved to one of the more picturesque towns which nestles quietly on the metropolitan line. Living in the High Street, a conservation area, they hoped to find that their newly-acquired home would be more than just a number. The wife spent ages in the records office of Buckingham County Council, searching through the annals of time, but alas, no Lacemaker's Cottage, or Drayman's Roost for them. They have to be content with two brass numbers on their door. Much as they like the place, they are concerned that the council estate nearby offers panoramic views of listed buildings and the local church. The husband advocates high brick walls to keep their view to a minimum, as much as to help those in private accommodation from suffering heart failure, should they chance upon this monument to Socialism, and more importantly, the common classes. They will, in fact, drive miles out of their way just to avoid any contact with High Wycombe or Frogmore, both areas now heavy with the consequence of our multiracial policy. We were sitting in their front room last Saturday, looking out onto the conserved High Street, awaiting the arrival of their other guests, before commencing the usual gastronomic delights, when I spotted a man across the street. I mentioned to Maureen that he looked drunk. He was swaying slightly, head down with cigarette between fingers and not making much headway. The husband came through from the kitchen. He called his wife. 'Look at that,' he explained, 'he must have come from the pub that has a Happy Hour.' He looked at us. 'New management, you see.' He looked back across the road. 'We don't know him, he is not a local, must be from High Wycombe.' We were in fits of laughter. Our host stayed by the window, motioning the man away from our view, adding, 'We have got visitors, quickly, away, away.' I think that if we had not been there, he would have had to have a shower just to rid this creature from another culture, not to mention another town, from the system.

The Dissolution Honours list has just been announced. I don't think there is a political animal from either side of the House of Commons arena that hasn't received something. Life peerages have been handed out like clocks on *Every Second Counts*. There are some privy councillors and Knights Bachelors, while an Order of the British Empire goes to Baroness Serota of Hampstead. I expect they all received signed photographs of Terry Waite and a sheet of tokens enabling them to obtain a cheap Sky aerial.

Having seen Ricky Valance fronting television ads for BT I propose that a ban should be imposed on ads with a high ingrate level at mealtimes. It was, however, pleasing to see that the industry's regulator has said that phone charges must come down. Only a couple of months ago, I read that in East Anglia the Maureen Lipman character of Beattie had been shelved and that a new caring advert has replaced the mini-soap. Since 1984, when British Telecom was privatised, around 50 million pounds has been spent on advertising. The average household apparently spends only £35 per quarter on telephone calls. Naturally, BT want to increase that sum. Their advertising director, Robert Bean, says we compare badly with the Americans and we do not like using the phone. I find that rather odd. How many people do you know who don't like using it? Talking into answerphone machines is another thing, but by then, the phone call has been made and BT has rung up another donation to its coffers. Still, as they say in their spiel, it is them we answer to.

Just when I thought it was safe to open the paper again –

more bloody honours! Lord Jeffrey Archer – yes, he will like that little accolade, won't he? Andrew Lloyd Webber receives a knighthood, which really will be useful. Michael Caine and Prunella Scales become CBEs and Maurice Denham an OBE. Cricketers David Gower and Ian Botham both receive the same title, as does our first astronaut-ess. I cannot believe this one, though. Suzy Lamplugh's mother gets an OBE. Ah, here we are, this is more traditional. Mr Roy Watts (who?), the chairman of Thames Water, receives a knighthood, whereas he should have received a ducking stool and straps. Prof. Anthony Kenny, a philosopher, also receives a knighthood, so that's one up for the unemployed, while the lady 'what does the make up', and names Princess Di and Norma Major amongst those she has advised, is the recipient of an OBE, and will no doubt be the target for a gag on *Have I Got News For You*. Martin Bell, the news presenter, who has spent a lot of time in Yugoslavia, takes home an OBE. I cannot quite see why, other people have been to Yugoslavia, and just sat on a beach for a fortnight without the slightest thought being given to the possibility of a prezzie. To be fair, Mr Bell, when he went looking for shells on the beach, wasn't too interested in the little opaque coloured fellows, which crunch underfoot. He was, however, only doing a job for which he is paid, like millions of other poor sods who never get a mention. Glad that's over with for another few months.

Only a woman could be this petty. That well-known campaigner against abortion, Victoria Gillick, is to stop listening to *The Archers*. All because a storyline did not end in the way she suggests it should, which is miserable ever after with an unwanted gift of a child benefit book. People like her make me truly sick. Having been a devoted fan for 40 years, she is going to cut her nose to spite her face. This is all because Elizabeth Archer has decided not to cough up the sprogg. I am concerned about people like her, no, not Elizabeth Archer, but Mrs G. This is not because of what they believe in, but because of the influence they have on their own offspring. Not for them the chance to weigh up the pros and cons of an argument and think for themselves. She actually said that 'When our children listened to the programme, and Elizabeth said she was keeping the baby no matter what, they all cheered.' Well, something is wrong, if listening to a soap instils that kind of obsession, then it is time to question the wisdom of the woman. Let's face it, she has had ten children of her own, so she doesn't give a bugger about the rest of us. If we all followed her example, Wisbech, which is where she lives, would be touching King's Lynn at one end and Peterborough at the other! As it is, one hopes that sense will prevail in the children and that the realisation dawns about the pressure everyone suffers from decisions like those of their mother. It cost the state a lot to support that many children. Mrs G.'s comments would not usually be worth putting pen to paper for, as the last thing she stands for is freedom of choice, but I feel the suffocated, oppressed frustration she shows in her views are necessary to record, just to illustrate to others how the single-minded desires of one person can inflict themselves on those around them. Lucky her name's Gillick and not Killit.

Did you know that Britain's last Button A and B payphone has just been taken out of use? I thought they had all gone long ago. So don't shut the book, before restoring it to pride of place next to your other favourite author's works, and tell yourself that you haven't learned anything. If, of course, you are returning it to the library, or even worse a friend, then I don't wish to sound bitchy, but I hope your car won't start!!!

Very often it is not only the names which I find fascinating when reading the 'Announcements', but the comments that are written afterwards. I shudder when I read 'To so and so, a beautiful baby girl', or 'gorgeous son called...'. In this particular case the gorgeous son had been named Moses, born to Lupin – I think Loopy would be more appropriate. Fancy calling your offspring Moses, or Moe. Don't they like him? I must confess a liking for a recent addition to the Catmur Family. To Deedle, née Clarabut, and Philip, a son, Henry Stucley Carabut, brother for Fergus. Who says imagination is dead? If they haven't over-worded the introduction, the reader falls for the sucker-punch after the naming ceremony. Having announced its name, they carry on with 'Another little helper for daddy', or 'An accomplice for', etc. One of the worst entries was found in March, when Laura and Alistair Subba-Row, you know, the cricketing Subba-Rows, were fairly chuffed with their daughter, Emily. The announcement continued, '9 lb. 3 oz., a perfect maiden delivery'.

Well, England has taken the European Championship by slight breeze. It really is great news that we have not lost to Denmark, the side that got in by virtue of the little fracas currently being chewed over in Yugoslavia. I note that the Germans are the only side to have booked in for the full two weeks. Our fans also did well. They actually managed to stay out of trouble until the first match was over. You don't see that kind of restraint at Leeds or Birmingham. Even if their hearts and heads were a little misguided, their boots seemed to be more on target when kicking foreign bodies than England's official team were with the ball. To be fair, President Bush was more positive about the Earth Summit than England's footballers were in the opening game.

Our local Citizens' Advice Bureau has just held its AGM in the local church hall. It was open to the public, and afterwards there was a slide show, presented by local author and historian, Mrs Sally Jenkinson. She recently produced a book on Ash and Ash Vale, entitled *Ash and Ash Vale*,and you cannot get much more descriptive than that! In conjunction with the local camera club, she took the audience through the history of the area, picking out characters from times past, who were known to several members of the gathered throng. Even some of the recent views show just how much the area has changed, even in the twenty years we have been here. At the end of the show Maureen and I walked outside, to be confronted by a massive chauffeur-driven Daimler trying to negotiate the car park. The Mayoress sat in the back, weighed down in braid and gold, smiling and waving as she passed. Was she being driven home to cook hubby's tea, or was she about to be whisked away for a night on the tiles? We may never care!

It did cross my mind as we walked home that the CAB prides itself on impartiality and its policy of equal rights for every cackhanded bugger there is, plus, of course, a mandatory racial code that we all love so dearly. So in that case, why was it that as we walked across the car park on the way in, three chairs had been placed restricting two 'normal' size cars, or one Daimler, from parking? This large space was, in fact, the last space, so regardless of timing, the poor sod who actually got there before the mayor, couldn't park anyway, so he would have had to reverse back into the side-street. How can 'Reserved for Mayor' signs be placed anywhere, when the organisation she is visiting extols the virtues of equality? Perhaps it is akin to Animal Farm, where some pigs are more equal than others! Daimlers are not cheap to run or to repair. It would be interesting to know just how much it costs the taxpayers to keep this expensive tradition alive. Still, she is the first lady of Guildford – it said so in the throw-out – sorry, hand-out.

We have had a couple of circulars dropped into the porch recently. So before I bin them, I will bore you stiff with a couple of comments. The first piece of fairly useless information is a folded sheet of thick paper, issued by British Gas, Southern, telling us about their new head office in Basingstoke – not something I would have thought worth shouting about, and certainly not a move designed to raise the morale of one's workforce. They give us a new telephone number and add, 'We are now closer to you.' Well, yes. If you live in Old Basing, you will be, is that it? No, the cover shows three people in different photographs. Male – female – male, so that is lacking in equality for a start. The male on the left and the lady in the centre are white, they are talking on a white phone. The chap on the right is black, and he is seen exchanging pleasantries on a black phone. Isn't this taking things a bit far? They certainly seem to be happy with the donation they are making to the Ricky Valance fund, so they have obviously misdialled and cannot believe their ears. After all, they didn't expect to get through to the Terrence Higgins Trust and learn about Aids and how to catch it. Overleaf a map, showing the area served by the new office, and a note (plus photo) of the District's General Manager, Owen Gigg. He poses the question, 'Why the change?' He then answers it by saying that it is all part of BG Southern's commitment to customer policy. There is an invitation to peel off the stickers containing their new numbers, along with suggestions about where to stick them! They do not mention that most customers would prefer to see a reduction in the price of gas, or whether the paper is recyclable, so I presume it isn't. What a waste. It could all have been sent with the gas bills but I suppose that was too simple. They have probably done a deal with the Post Office whereby they buy x amount of stamps if the Post Office buy the same amount of gas.

The rear page of this 'giant step for gas-man' wallows in self-congratulatory praise and shows you the O/S/F – that's off side front for those of you not in the motor trade – wing and door of a BG Southern van. Surely once you have seen one van you have seen them all. A second photograph is of two women in a gas showroom, who appear to be demonstrating the versatility of a hob's knobs to a mere male, who looks most uncomfortable. The very last photo shows equal numbers of men and women – four of each. One lady is Asian, one of the men is black. Nice and tidy. Graham Day will be pleased. None of the men shown have beards so it doesn't look as though there is a pervert amongst them! My only criticism, and you know I am not one to criticise but I have to say it. The coloured lad could do better than sport one of those 5" off-the-head hairstyles, with nothing at the sides. He looks like a Grace Jones impressionist, I mean, it is all a matter of opinion, and taste.

Our next waste of paper to be delivered was the 'Parents

Charter'. This tome is worrying, because it sets out to achieve improvements that were an accepted part of our life when we were at school. I am also concerned about the phenomenal waste of money, because a large proportion of parents could not be bothered less about their child's welfare. Inside this booklet is a pre-paid card – why? By filling in the boxes, you can obtain, free of charge, the same booklet in eight other languages – Bengali, Gurarati, Hindi, Punjabi, Urdu, Chinese, Greek and Turkish. Tick some more boxes and you can receive (free again, naturally) booklets on the options available to sixteen-year-olds, or advice on grant maintained schools. Would you like to know about the national curriculum or how to become a school governor? Just send off for more free brochures. The major problem with these freepost cards is that besides all these boxes you have to laboriously tick, your name and address also have to be inserted. I know what I would like to insert, but that's another story. Anyway, help is at hand, don't bother to write, simply pick up the phone and ring 0800, etc. and order umpteen copies free. Now surely, if you were an interested parent you wouldn't mind forking out for a couple of stamps. It seems such a waste of taxpayers' money. Perhaps the DOE has done a deal with the Post Office as well.

Well, we have moved on another four days and struggled over one more hurdle in our quest to be European Champions. Yes, I know we drew 0-0 with France, and that makes 180 minutes we have played without scoring a goal, but Mr Taylor says he is very pleased with our performance. He made the point himself that we are playing some of the top teams in Europe, and yes, we did manage to subdue the French goalgetting Mr Papin. Of course, if it had not been for injuries to Wright and Barnes, the story would have been the same. I don't know why he places so much store on Barnes. In all the international matches I have seen him play in, he has never performed anything like the standard he achieves at times for Liverpool. I am just sorry that he is not playing, as that would have taken away 95% of the excuse for England's failure. We are not out of the competition yet and there is everything to play for. Mr T. always said it would be tight and go to the last game, and I am sure he is right.

All the time our lads are away, letting England down – both the fans and the team – Charles and Di are presumably meeting occasionally to discuss their future. A photograph of the Royal family watching the Trooping of the Colour was interesting. Whilst the Princess was looking straight ahead, the camera captured Prince Charles giving her a sideways glance, which is just about all he could give her bearing in mind the Queen and Queen Mother were standing in front of them. Anyway, should that photo be used on *Have I Got News For You*, in the caption section, I wouldn't mind betting that someone will come up with Charles saying, 'If only you were Selina Scott.' I do think this new book is a bit of a rum do. The Princess of Wales is being made the subject of a very nasty piece of journalism, so far removed from my own offerings on the world and its live-in lover. No-one thinks about the effect that talk of attempted suicides will have on the children. They may have everything materially, but their feelings are no different from that of people in council homes – except that they don't have to be embarrassed about the stone cladding, theirs is real!

I see that the feminist magazine *Spare Rib* has just celebrated 20 years of publication. What never ceases to amaze me is how these independent women are never named Daphne or Tracey. They are always Roz or Petra, Nula or Vesna. Were they really born with these names, or did they adopt something 'new', something 'aggressive'. I would imagine it would help them to put their point over, along with the short-cropped hair and long dangly earrings, of course. The two who started this little extension of the literary cause were Wisty Hoyland and Rosie Boycott – see what I mean.

What was I saying about the waste of taxpayers' money. One hundred and thirty-three million pounds was spent last year on publicity by the government. The Department of Education got through £8.8 million, whilst the DSS shelled out £16.8 million, reaching people who would have claimed anyway, once they had got their 30-year-old bus out of the winding lanes around Castle Morton and down into the nearest town to cash their ill-gotten gains. Believe me, the general rule of thumb is that if someone says 'they are entitled' it usually means they shouldn't be. The Health Department more than doubled its spending to £24.4 million. All that money could have been put to so much better use within the health service. Probably the most offensive use of our money was on the Citizens Charter. That little timewaster cost around £1 million, £812,000 going on newspaper advertisements alone. At least they could claim back the VAT.

As expected, those members of GPB (Greatly Privatised Bastards PLC) did extraordinarily well, bearing in mind we are still coming out of recession – allegedly. East Midlands Electricity have announced pre-tax profits of £150 million, that is 41% up on last year. Power Gen stated their pre-tax profits to be 32% higher at £359 million, so they are okay. National Power are presumably fairly embarrassed at their hike being only 18% with pre-tax profits reaching £514 million. Norweb homed in at £138 million – a cool 96% rise. I think the Chairmen concerned should be given a round of applause and a pay rise, myself.

Now here is a case I take issue with, which is something you wouldn't associate with one so shy and retiring as me. A pair of lesbians have won the first stage of a high court battle in their attempt to adopt an eight-month-old girl. The 'real' mother of the girl 'gave her' to this pair, after having given birth in their house. So presumably, the next time a holidaymaker drops a sprogg two months ahead of schedule, while holidaying at a B & B in Skegness, the landlady will be deemed the next of kin. These two women, aged 21 and 25, who live in the south of England (hope they move north) – are being allowed to keep the child temporarily under local authority supervision. One of the pair has a history of mental illness and drug addiction, while the other has been convicted of assault. Obviously this is the perfect basis for a stable environment. Just what any eight-month-old girl needs, in fact. The case will come before the high court again on 15th September. Luckily, if the little girl is taken away and placed with a well-balanced family, i.e. a woman and a man, mummy and daddy, at eight months old she is still young enough not to get too attached.

The 'Man from Lamont' has just announced that recovery will take up to three years. Well, at least we can plan for the future – a bit like Graham Taylor really. England 1, Sweden 2, was a score that did not please too many people. As my father says, footballers are paid far too much. Judging from the lamentable performances of the majority of the team, he is right. A goal up after 4 minutes – our first of the competition, remember, you would have thought we had a chance. Then again, we *were* playing some of the crème de la crème, as Miss Jean Brodie said in her prime. Graham Taylor's comments after the game took some beating. What I liked was when he said that it was a shame there had to be a half time as that was when the game began to turn for us. Again, the fans also let us down. There only had to be a Swede within five miles for our lot to sniff him out and start a bloodbath. Restaurants, shops, town squares, you name it, we can smash it up. Soon, the scum of England will be given the freedom of Europe in which to fight. It will certainly add a new dimension to Churchill's famous speech. We will fight them in the streets, we will fight them on the beaches. Yup, nowhere will be safe. The Channel Tunnel trains will probably be out of action for weeks at a time, which in itself will be no bad thing. I just wish it was official closure.

To be fair to the opinion polls, one has to say that they are not wrong all of the time. A NOP just published concludes that Jeremy Beadle is the least-liked personality on television. He is closely followed by Anneka Rice, Terry Wogan, Loyd Grossman and Esther Rantzen. In fact, everybody's unfavourites.

That ill-informed and misguided gathering that march under the collective name of the National Union of Teachers have just issued guidelines in a subject-to-subject form to help schools maintain anti-racist and multicultural teachings. This imposition has been sent to all schools stating that all children are pupils of the world. I don't want my nine-year-old being spoken about in the same breath as someone from Dunstable, let alone Addis Ababa. Mind you, Stoke D'Abernon would be perfectly acceptable! This meddling waste of paper continues with the call to widen pupils' awareness of blacks and other non-Europeans with regard to culture and achievement. What do they want? We have had Nelson Mandela shoved down our throats for the past two years, not to mention his estranged (or is it strange) wife and her bloody football team. Apparently pupils should appreciate that white music and art are no better than that produced by other cultures. Are they really trying to tell me that reggae is of the same standard as that provided by the likes of Chris Rhea, Simply Red, Scott Walker and Peter Skellern – not to mention Kylie Minogue. History is not immune from change either. Schools are to be urged not to present only British or European perspectives of colonisation but also that of the indigenous people who were exploited. It does not say that the pupil should explore the fate of the native people of this country, in the face of a multicultural stand, forced on them by latter-day dictators masquerading as an elected government. English teachers are to be asked to ensure that they include work by black writers while young children should listen to black and Asian poets who can be invited to the school. How nice! On a serious note, this will only help to fuel the fires that segregate because like Europe, it is being forced upon us. Nowhere is there any reference to cultures from America or Canada. In fact, the only references are to black and Asian countries. What about South America, New Zealand, Australia... well, maybe not Australia!

The NUT would be better advised raising the standards of their membership's dress sense, diction and taking a less biased view. This would be a good start. Co-ordinating dates for 'teacher training courses' would be appreciated, so that children do not have to take every other Friday off. It seems more than a coincidence that these one-day jollys, for they surely cannot learn that much in a day, other than to make a note of the next day off, always cling to weekends. When William returns to school in September to start his new term, he is actually to commence the day after the official first day – because they are training. Six weeks' holiday and then they have off the first day back. Amazing!

What is happening to some people? Are they on drugs? I have just read that a 72-year-old was tipped out of his wheelchair close to his home in Fakenham, Norfolk, by three men. They tried to grab the change in his pockets. The pensioner, who suffers from brittle bone disease, hit his face on a wall when he fell. The three cowardly bastards escaped empty-handed. Now don't tell me that they are not a prime case for a public flogging.

It doesn't add up, does it? Islington Borough Council are hiring, at £300 a day, its former Race Equality Officer. This action takes place a few weeks after he took early retirement and a £34,000 pay-off. £300 per day is not bad at all. I wonder how the taxpayers of the borough feel about that.

The re-formed Aldershot Town Football Club have been invited to join the Diadora League, Division 3, along with Farnham and Camberley. Oh, how the lowly have fallen. The trouble is they do not appear to be too well endowed with players. Here we are, three weeks away from training and they have registered just one player. The farce continues. Talking of 'endowed', Maureen still exercises her cruel streak. This morning as she was getting dressed, and I lay in bed, I felt a 'hardening' from below the covers. Was it due to the cheese I ate last night, or the remains of my dream about Kylie Minogue in schoolgirl uniform, wishing to do rude things with my body? Anyway, back to the real world, I asked Maureen if she wanted to take a look at my willy. You know, in between her putting on her shoes and brushing her hair. She grimaced. 'A lot of women would jump at the chance,' I said, feeling hurt and rejected, whilst looking under the blanket to see if it was still there. 'What you mean is, a lot of women would jump,' she replied. I don't know, you try to keep your love life alive with little tit-bits and throw-aways, and never a word of thanks, let alone an inspection.

I always feel sorry for people who show a little imagination with the naming of their offspring, but are tied to a boring surname. It follows then that I obviously feel sorry for Lucinda, who used to be a Page-Ratcliff. She has given birth to a Holly Beatrice D'Arcy, but her married name is Anderson, which rather lets the side down. Then again, Lucinda Prior-Palmer became a 'Green' didn't she. Is that the matrimonial fate of all Lucindas, I wonder.

Here's another. A little girl called Fiona Genevieve has been born to Margaret and Graham Murphy. The surname is all right if you are a road digger or a bottle of stout but not if you are the parents of an F.G.

The Pritchards have been busy. Maryanne and Tony are celebrating the arrival of Jocelyn George Clowes – surely not related to... This little lad, who appears to show all the right credentials with this first name for automatic entrance to most good clubs is a half-brother to another two chaps, and a brother for another five children. So they won't fit into a bedsit in Camden, will they.

Someone's given birth to an Alvery. At first sight I thought it said an aviary. Another name of stature given to a newly-born yesterday was Rollo. There also appear to be a lot of Max's around. Not a name I like personally, although it would be appropriate for an alsatian on a Portsmouth council estate!

The huge losses made at Lloyds by 'names' is not going to arouse much sympathy with the public. I read a letter to the *Daily Telegraph* a little while ago and having suffered paragraph after paragraph of self-pity, it was with some annoyance that I noted the address of the man allegedly losing his fortune as Jersey, C.I. It is all a question of relativity. If you and I, as poor mortals, put £50 into a national savings account, we expect a known rate of return that will not set the world alight, but will not attract risk. If, however, we use our money to make a very fast and hefty buck, then the risk of losing is generally equal to that of winning. Nowhere can I remember reading of names feeling suitably contrite about their exceptional achievements when things have been going well. So they have the good times and now they suffer, like the rest of us. One 'name' was seen outside Lloyds with a Penny Farthing bike and a hat, asking for donations. He has apparently lost his wife and his Ferrari. If it was a send-up it wasn't very funny, if he is being serious, he ought to consider the plight of many made redundant and not a word of thanks or a bean over their legal dues.

A friend of mine has recently been made redundant after giving eighteen years of loyal service to a multinational British company. All he has to show for it is £4,000. As he said, if he had been a miner or with BT he would be okay, but this, after eighteen years.

There has been an earth-shattering development in the town twinning stakes in Rushmoor. The Twinning Committee (makes you laugh thinking about it) has voted an ex-mayor on board as their new chairman, and his new deputy is someone who once lived in the French town of Meudon. I will give you a few seconds to settle down and loosen your tie, or blouse – the top six buttons should be sufficient! Actually, while you are there, could I just try to tune into Radio Four, using your left 'nipple'?

You would have thought they would have got the message by now, wouldn't you? This is the French town whose mayor was in Canada, when he should have been over here. On they go, however, always optimistic that it will come good in the end. All this on a day when Cornish fishermen have had their nets cut by bolshy French coves. To have to get the Royal Navy involved in the form of a landing party from HMS Brecon is a step in the right direction. Now we need a worsening of relations with France, a tit-for-tat, sending home ambassadors and staff and a complete cutting-off of all diplomatic relations. No, I know we won't be that lucky, but if we were, Rushmoor would still be trying to get hold of the Mayor by phone and making excuses for his being 'unavoidably delayed'.

As we approach the end of this volume, the Sunday trading issue has swung towards those of us who want to see it limited. The sword of Damocles is hanging over the heads of local authorities concerned about the possibility of compensation for loss of profits that Greedy Bastards PLC would seek to claw back. The House of Lords have ruled that councils can now seek court orders to restrain shops from opening without the financial risk to their taxpayers.

Homebase, B & Q, Safeway, Tesco, etc. still consider themselves above the law, but just might respond if the European Court of Justice rules against them in the forthcoming test case between Stoke-on-Trent and Norwich Council and B & Q.

I have to tell you that we have witnessed a couple of classics in the Hatch, Match and Despatch column, again. Amongst the new arrivals is Bertie Broughton, a brother for Georgia and Freya. There is a Guy, brother for Sophie and Tarquin. In York Hospital we have Poppy Arabella Knocker (glad she's up north), while Francesca Rose has been born to Julia, a sister for India Kate (glad she's down south).

Strange, having never heard the name before, we have now got it twice in one column. Amanda has deposited a little bundle called Freya Anne, sister for Freddie, whilst in Wellington Hospital, Clare's offering is a son, Piers, brother for Iona and India – quality throughout! With names like these I would give them the freedom of Guildford.

Josephine and Jonathan Jump have named their lad Samuel, obviously missing out on Jeremy, Jo or Jasper, which is all to their credit, really.

What I was saying about uninspiring surnames holds true with our last offerings. To Elise, a daughter, Natasha, sister for Xandie – surname 'Trevor', and to Oriska, a son, Gresham Robert Essex – surname 'Smith'. Ah, well.

I thought you might like to read this little offering from William, and, yes, Dorking survived his visit a fortnight ago. It is his homework. As usual, he did not tell us he had been given any, and we did not find out about it until the following morning. Maureen was out and I was looking after him. I packed him off to bed at 9 pm and thought no more about it. Apparently, it took him over one-and-a-half hours to write the following. (It is, as before, printed as it was 'rit'.)

Dolphins
dolphins are an indeangerd spiecie. Pepple (people) cach tuner to much. so the dolphins get carurt (caught) up in the nets to much so pepple just put them back in the river to die. and when the dolphins was put back in the sea with no flippers ript of they will just die sink to the ground and starve and ie.
The end.

Dinosaurs
Tyranosaururs-Rex was the *King* dinasaur and he was a meat-eather and if he saur a nver (another) dinosaur he would eat it part from the tryseratops. because the tryseratop always had battle with the king and if the tryseratop saw tryranosarous Rex he comes trople (here comes trouble) then they would charch at tyranosarus-Rex and tryserotops wyth ther houns (horns) to bettle with tranosaurus-Rex.

Monkies
Monkes thirst (first) startid living by comeing out of the sea and when they came out of the sea the tumd into these monkies and the next they turnd into men but they still had the entellidence (intelligence) of a monkie but they then lemt about more thinghs on earth this is how we have bee creatied.

Dogs

dogs are pets they are lovely animals. I have got a dog called Lucy she is part of a mongral-terya she is nearly part of evry dog. her birthday on Thursday 19th June 1992. todays her birthday. The End.

Bairds

Bairds are the small things that fly they are called bairds. Some bairds are even smaller than your foot. like robins. Some are as big as your foot.
The End.
Sorry fell a sleep.

You can tell he was getting bored by the time he had got to 'bairds', sorry, 'birds'. The footnote was necessary because his teacher had asked everyone to write about nine different animals, and he said that if he put down that he had fallen asleep after only five, that it would be all right with her! We haven't heard from his teacher, but next week is Parent Teacher's Night, so the subject might come up then.

Let's carry on this period of levity with a joke I heard last week – you will like this. A Jewish woman visits a local paper's office and asked about inserting an announcement regarding the death of her husband. She enquired how much it would be, word for word. The assistant tells her that it is £1 per word. The woman looks at the note of the screed she has made which she wants published. 'This comes to £15,' she said, 'I am not paying that much.' The young assistant informed the woman that she did not make up the prices, and that it was the same for everyone. The customer paused, and then said, 'Okay, just announce Cohen's dead.' The assistant was taken aback. 'You cannot put that,' she said, 'it is unfeeling and anyway, there is a minimum of five words, one line.' The potential customer paused again. 'So I have to spend a minimum of £5?' she asked. 'Yes,' replied the girl. 'Okay,' said the woman, 'insert "Cohen's dead, Volvo for sale." '

Now there's a race who are past masters at self-deprecation. Not for the Jewish people the neurosis suffered by those who cannot come to terms with humour. Here's one that is not as sordid as it might initially sound, so read on. A young lad is in his father's garage while his father repairs the family car. The lad enquires about a helmet he has discovered lying around. 'What's this for, Dad?' he asks. 'Oh,' says his father, looking up. 'Do you remember when I had to weld the sills so that the car could pass its MOT? Well, that is the visor I used. It stops the sparks from flying into your face and eyes.' The boy nodded and asked if he could wear the visor to school. His father agreed and the lad walked out in his uniform, carrying his satchel and wearing the visor. As he walked along the road, a car stopped. A male driver wound down the window and asked if the lad would like a lift to school. The boy lifted the glass section of the visor and said 'Yes, please:' In he got, next to the driver. A little way along the road the driver asked the boy if he knew what fornication was. The lad lifted the glass and shook his head, and then allowed the glass to shut tight again. Further along, the man enquired as to whether he knew what masturbation was, again he lifted the glass and shook his head. The glass again fell. Into another street the car turned, and the man asked if he knew what perversion was. The boy looked across at the man, pulled up the visor and said 'I'm not really a welder, you know!'

There, you thought that was going to be morally unacceptable, didn't you? You ask my mother. She will tell you I was a clean-living boy!

Someone Maureen knows was talking to a newly-found friend who asked her if the jumper she was wearing was hand-knitted'. She replied that it was, and that she derived pleasure from being able to wear something she had knitted. The other woman replied, 'Oh, I thought you were knitting it yourself to save money. Anyway, I know you buy your dresses from the Oxfam shop, but being tall, you can get away with second-hand clothes.' She went on to say that her husband had once given her a knitting machine, but she had never been able to get the hang of it (we presume it was beneath her). One day she resurrected it from a cupboard and decided to sell it at a car boot sale. She was all for going until the reality of it struck her. No, she couldn't bring herself to stand behind a table, selling things, so she sent her husband instead. The local school asked her if she would not mind manning (or womaning) one of the Jumble stalls at its annual fête. She agreed, but was not 100% enthusiastic about her decision. Later that week she asked if she could be put on either Cream Teas or Handicrafts as she really didn't think she could bring herself to touch other people's cast-offs. I don't know the lady myself but she reminds me of Penny's mother in *Just Good Friends*.

Whilst I am waiting for Maureen to pour out the tea, I will just tell you about some new training which the police are about to receive. They are, wait for it, to be taught how to counsel male rape victims. There were 95 cases of unlawful sex acts with men in London last year, plus 348 cases of indecent assaults. There has been an increase in the number of sex attacks on men. They reckon the number of 'gay rapes' is far higher, but the victims do not come forward because they are ashamed. A police spokesman said that as well as shame, they feel emasculated – well, they have been! Frankly, it seems a complete waste of police time, when they could be receiving training by ex-members of West Midland Senior Crime Squad on much more important matters.

I think it was early on in the book I commented that in my view, many women are not able to cope with the responsibility that promotion has often given them. I just found a cut-out from a paper I saved – and subsequently lost down the side of the desk. This article dealt with the fact that more women are being caught drink-driving. I suppose it is on a par with giving alcohol to the American Indians. Research quoted by a Birmingham coroner stated that 'Women are now starting to drink more, are becoming professionals and are being given cars. They are tending to socialise more, and consequently drink more.' So, the more professional they become, the more irresponsible, also.

After the upset of the vote by the Danes over Europe, they decided to upset football pundits and win the European Cup. They deserved it for their sheer ability to compete, if nothing else. It makes a mockery of our over-fed, over-priced apologies, who, with very few exceptions, played as though it did not matter.

So, it is to be Baroness Thatcher of Kesteven, in the County of Lincoln. She will wear the shortened title of Lady Thatcher. The other two announcements concern Sir David Owen, who is to be known as Baron Owen of the City of Plymouth, and Sir Geoffrey Howe, who will be known as Baron Hard-up, sorry, Baron Howe, of Aberavon, of Tandridge in the County of Surrey. I can still see him being referred to as Geoffrey Who!

Not that it will harm his political future one iota, but I was a tad miffed to see Michael Heseltine looking so happy as he stuck his fizzogg out of the side window of the first Jaguar XJ 220 to roll off the assembly line. Three hundred and fifty of these beasts are to escape, even allowing for the fact that it is no longer a British company, but a subsidiary of the American conglomerate Ford. It should be an occasion to savour. How can you be impressed though when the car has a speed of over 200 mph and costs £400,000 a throw? Why on earth, other than the kudos of macho superiority, does any manufacturer wish to produce a car capable of this speed? It is obscene, unnecessary, and totally against all conservation and environmental considerations.

What price being a hostage, then? Terry Waite has been exempted from the traffic ban which has been introduced in Cambridge. As a university academic he and his 69 fellow commoners are still allowed to use their cars. Really, the lengths some people will go to, just to be able to drive around Cambridge. He is there writing his memoirs, apparently, no doubt they will be serialised, televised, available on video, Radio 4 will make a play out of them and David Puttnam will make a film out of them. They will all be starring Terry Waite as – Terry Waite. What a Man For All Seasons!

So, whilst our own police cannot carry guns, the French gendarmes on our side of the Tunnel entrance will be allowed to carry firearms. There has been a great deal of argument over this matter. At one stage, the French threatened not to let British police have access to their side of the Tunnel at all. Talk about being petty! Needless to say, however, talks between the two governments have 'paved the way'. Why are they not honest, why cannot they just say that once again, they have given in. The face-saver from the Home Office is that these pistol-packing Frogs, who will only number two at any one time, are purely going to be in Cheriton to protect their colleagues when in danger. A likely story. They are there for shooting sheep more like!

There is an absolute corker in today's paper. Deep in the wilds of densest Dagenham a woman, born in the Cameroons, has been told to demolish the mud hut which she has built in the back garden of her council home. The lady concerned has said that it is staying, so that little show of petulance should be quite interesting. She says that the hut is preferable to the maisonette she shares with her six (yes, six) children. Not unreasonably, the neighbours are not best pleased but will doubtless be branded as racist, a term used about anyone these days. You have only got to say that you do not like dark chocolate to be admonished as a troublemaker and paid-up member of the National Front! The only good thing about our Dagenham Girl Mud-Pie Maker is that she doesn't like our country, so with a bit of luck, the maisonette can be given to someone, anyone, more deserving and grateful, while seven one-way tickets are hopefully issued for the Cameroons, probably via Clapham Junction. I bet an evening return ticket still works out cheaper!

They are still buggering about with our coinage. A brand-new 50 pence piece is to be issued tomorrow. I have seen a cock-up (sorry, mock-up) of it, and it is every bit as tacky as its Euro predecessor. This little offering is to commemorate Britain's inauguration as president of the EC's Council of Ministers. What is even more galling is that the – I was going to say the winning design, but that smacks of being an overstatement, so I will just say the design chosen – was the best of a bad bunch from two hundred entries. Not restricted to Britain, the hopefuls came from all over the 'community', so the Euro world and its wife could now have a go at designing our coins. Why don't we ask Sainsbury's and Tesco's if they would like their logos to be used instead of the Queen's head. Sponsored coinage, it will come. I can hear the conversation now. 'Right, sir, that will be 3 B & Qs, a Toys R Us and a Comet, or for the 3-speed model you will need to part with a couple of Marks & Sparks and a Halfords as well!'

Carolynn and John Martin St Valery have just announced the arrival of a little heir called John Jackson de Vismes Martin St Valery. He will, of course, be known as 'Jack', a decision no doubt greeted with delight by everyone who will come into contact with him. With a name like that, I expect he is already down for Charterhouse, at least.

The Girl Guides are no more. The new terminology is Guides. Even the promise that 'I will do my best, to do my duty to God, to serve the Queen and help other people' could go. Also passing into memory is the uniform. Tomorrow's gals will be donning guiding wear, so that is another British institution which has been infiltrated by some ego-boosting trendy.

Hard on the heels of the cock-crowing story from North Devon comes the finale of a similar case, this time in Dorset. A chappie in Verwood has been told by an Appeal Judge that his cockerels, banished to an animal sanctuary whilst the case was being held, can now return home. In similar circumstances to the other cock case, the complainants were ex-townies, who tried to change the country code once they had moved to the Styx, although Verwood is more like a dormitory town to Bournemouth than the rural area it was just a few years ago. One of these gang of two is a 69-year-old retired customs official, so he will be used to being officious, whilst the other is a 61-year-old former housekeeper. Satisfying to see that they lost the case. It might make others from similar backgrounds think twice about complaining and wasting public money.

Now this makes me smile. The Church of England expect their offices to be swamped with members of the clergy who need counselling for their 'hurt feelings' caused by the possible aftermath of the ordination of women. No joke, the church are actually to set up a number of schemes across the country to 'soften the trauma'. Bishops will meet those clergy who feel they have lost their cause celebre and reassure them that they are still wanted by their partners (sorry, that should read by the church). Professional counsellors will also be on hand to soften the blow and no doubt give them a chance to meet new friends in the process – soppy sods! If they thought for one moment about the plight of Mr Frank Tempest and the horrific fourteen months he has endured they might consider their own problems to be slightly less severe. Doubtless there are many worthy candidates for bravest soul of the year, but there can be fewer distressing cases than that of this 55-year-old bakery worker, who was attacked by two pit-bull terriers as he walked home from work. They literally ripped off his nose, right ear and the lobe of his left ear. A hole was made in his forehead and the area around his eyes and his lips were badly torn as well. A picture of him taken shortly after the attack shows the severity of the surgery required. Thanks to a new technique that the Swedes have been working on, his face has been rebuilt and he is now able to walk in a public park with his family without attracting the attention of other members of the public. He is still undergoing psychological counselling, and no wonder. Doesn't a real case of distress put the petty, feeble, neurotic views of certain members of that money-grabbing business to shame?

Have you seen those signs indicating that pavements are about to end and you will have to walk along the road? The symbol shows what can either be interpreted as two adults holding hands, one of whom is a pygmy, or an adult clutching a child's hand. The child is leaning awkwardly, indicating that he either has one foot shorter than the other, or that he is about to be the victim of an abduction by a child molester – or even worse, someone from social services! I have just been having a little set-to with William (again). He was, as usual, being unreasonable while I was being totally reasonable, as all parents are. This, of course, is a complete reversal of the role I held as a child, but then, that comes from human nature and the fact that I am bigger than him. William started making excuses for not having cleared up his room in the three weeks since I had first mentioned it. 'That's bull,' I exclaimed, having suffered his pathetic and illogical attempts to once again lay the blame on us. 'You shouldn't swear,' he said, 'it's bad for children.' I told him not to be so clever and to listen to me. 'I said "bull",' I re-iterated. 'Yes,' he said, 'but you were going to put an "s" on the end of it.' I know his spelling would have been out, but at least his heart was in the wrong place! There is nothing like a know-all.

So, in conclusion, what have we to look forward to? Well, the Channel Tunnel is still being bored stiff, so that will give us rabies for a kick-off. I liked Euro Tunnel's name for the trains which will ply the inglorious French connection, 'Le Shuttle'. They actually paid £½ million pounds to Wolff Olin, described as Britain's most exclusive design agency. Two years they took to come up with this train name, which sounds more like something launched from Cape Canaveral. Wolff Olin, it will not be remembered, are responsible for such acts of lack of imagination as renaming British Telecom – BT. That obviously took some thought and money. They then went on to an even greater lack of distinction by removing the Trusthouse from Trusthouse Forte and marketing the company simply as Forte. Again, they received money for this little exercise. Anyway, with the train service due to commence next autumn, we will no doubt be reading of bomb attacks, rapes (male and female), assaults and robbery on our side, while the train itself will still be stuck under the sea, due to French farmers blocking the track with sheep, all the way to Paris.

Whilst this is being played down as a minor incident by our puppet government, Rushmoor's Twinning Committee will still be trying to get hold of Meudon's mayor, whilst scanning the globe in their quest to find some other groups of poor sods on whom they can inflict marauding yobs in exchange for some cheap wine. Guildford will continue its love affair with the role of mayor, whilst still trying to foist its unwanted gypsies on those living at the most westerly extremity of its borders.

After seeing 'Carrington's Heroes' fail for the umpteenth time to stop the Slavs from killing each other to the point of extinction, we will no doubt open our doors – and wallets – to hordes of refugees from Bosnia Hertz Rent a Car, or whatever it is, who will doubtless be afraid to go back once it is all over. We have seen it all before. Over Christmas I will no doubt be able to watch Terry Waite playing Baron Hard-up in panto, while John McCarthy and Jill Morrell will probably have their own chat show, and Brian Keenan will be seen back-packing across his native Ireland. Despite all the threats uttered by the kids I doubt if they will have left home, the lights will still be left on, the doors unlocked, the house keys lost and the records still out of their jackets. After reading a judge' s comment that handcuffs on prisoners attending court lack civility, humanity and respect, will there be mandatory soft music, pink walls to soothe the vicious brow and comfort blankets available? Will Morlands Brewery be able to fight off the predatory aspirations of Greene King? Will Freddie Mercury be reincarnated as the First Aids God? He must surely have enough disciples. Will Eddie Edwards be training for the 1996 Olympics? Will I be able to get back on my diet by conquering my penchant for sugar sandwiches? Who knows what Fate may bring, other than another honorary doctorate for Terry Waite and the complete failure by any Briton to become a champion at tennis.

The End